IQ

Grow Your Mind

This edition published in 2009 by Arcturus Publishing Limited
26/27 Bickels Yard, 151–153 Bermondsey Street,
London SE1 3HA

ISBN: 978-1-84837-057-9
AD000275EN

Printed in Singapore

Contents

Grow Your Mind

Gymnasts are able to improve their performance, and increase their chances of success, at whatever level they are competing, by means of punishing training schedules and refinement of technique. In the same way cerebral gymnastics, provided by puzzles and tests, give you the opportunity to maximize your brain potential.

The human brain is the most vital organ in the human body and our most valuable asset. It gives rise to our perceptions and memory, and it shapes our speech, skills, thoughts and feelings – yet it is perhaps the part of the body which we tend to neglect the most. Despite the enormous capacity of the human brain, on average we use only three per cent of our potential brainpower. This is the amount of information available to us consciously and the rest is locked within our subconscious mind.

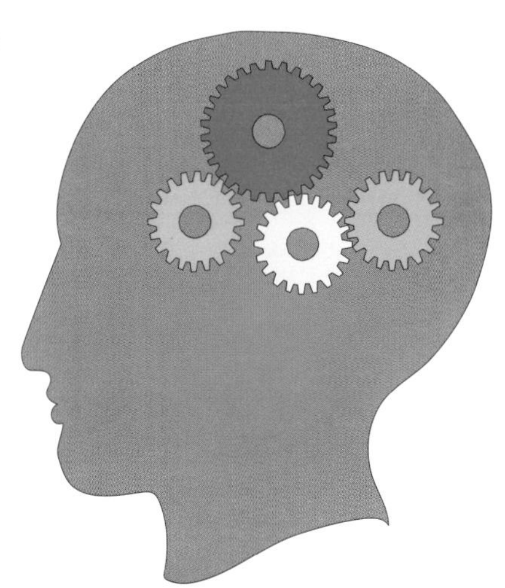

The belief that the brain we were born with can't be improved is widely held but erroneous. Brainpower can be considerably increased, just as brain potential can be utilized to a much greater degree. What you need in order to achieve these goals is a specially formulated programme of puzzles and tests and some expert guidance: all of which you will find in this book.

In addition to providing cerebral workouts in a fun and entertaining way, it enables you to explore different types of intelligence. These are verbal, numerical, visual, memory and personality (Emotional Quotient or EQ). In the first four sections, the puzzles get progressively harder and are divided into three levels: Quick Fire, More Challenging, and Difficult.

A performance rating is provided for a number of tests, enabling you to identify your strengths and weaknesses. In the final section, a total performance rating will allow you to discover your overall Brain Power (Brain Quotient or BQ), and an overall analysis of the results of the tests will provide invaluable feedback.

The brain is the most vital organ we possess. If we learn to get it in shape and keep it that way, it will enable us to tackle the real problems of life with renewed vigour and confidence.

Puzzles

People delight in playing with words – pulling words apart, reconstructing them in different guises, arranging them in clever patterns and finding hidden meanings within them.

Word puzzles have been used for recreational purposes for several hundreds of years; however, it was an event which occurred in the USA on 21 December 1913 that really led to an upsurge in the popularity of word puzzles, and of puzzles in general. It was on this day that the *New York World* newspaper introduced a new innovation, a diamond shaped word-cross puzzle, invented by Liverpool-born Arthur Wynne.

That puzzle, of which the exact design of grid is reproduced as Puzzle No 80 on page 21, had the word FUN already inserted at 2 Across, and no other word in the English language could be more appropriate.

Wynne's idea which, of course, was the forerunner of the modern crossword puzzle caught on immediately and the passion for crosswords swept America, with the Baltimore and Ohio railroads supplying all main-line trains with dictionaries for its addicts.

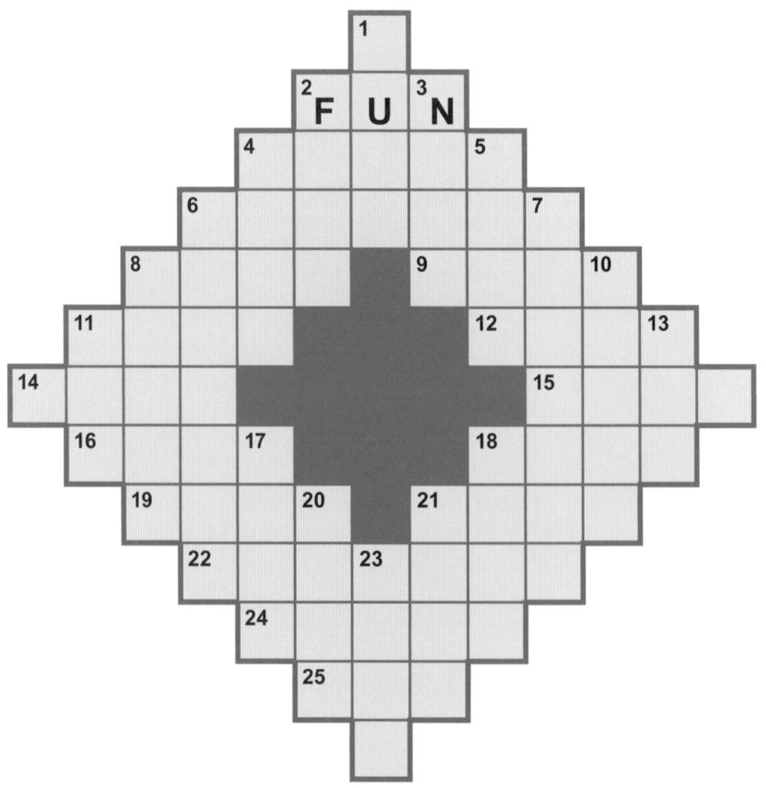

Eventually the idea reached Britain when the first British crossword, by C W Shepard, appeared in the *Sunday Express*, and the puzzle could be said to have finally arrived when *The Times* began its own up-market version in 1930. The first book of crosswords was published by the American publisher, Simon and Schuster, in 1924.

The popularity of crossword puzzles inevitably led to the creation of many spin-off puzzles and different types of word games, and there is no doubt that puzzles of this nature increase the vocabulary and word power of those who attempt them on a regular basis.

P	E	T	S
E	M	I	T
T	I	M	E
S	T	E	P

N	O	M	A	D
O	M	A	N	I
M	A	G	I	C
A	N	I	S	E
D	I	C	E	D

This section includes a varied selection of 185 newly-compiled word puzzles, each presenting its own challenge and with difficulty levels ranging from Quick Fire to Difficult.

Playing with words is a universal activity. Word puzzles are probably the most popular and widely published of all puzzles. We all have to understand and speak the language to communicate, and the challenge of solving a word puzzle is one which many people find irresistible.

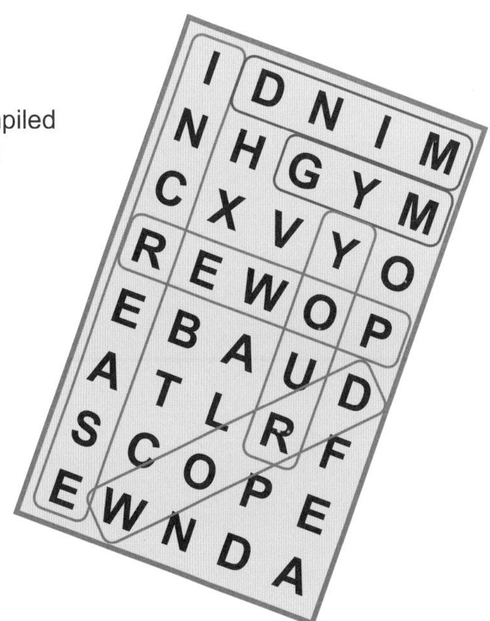

Quick Fire

1. Place a word in the brackets that has the same meaning as the definitions above and below the brackets.

Period of a year

(   )

Lend flavour to

2. Change one letter only in each of the words below to produce a familiar phrase.

THIS BED MINE

3. The termination of which nationality occurs with the eradication of one letter?

4. Find the starting point and track along the connecting lines visiting each circle once to spell out a 10-letter word.

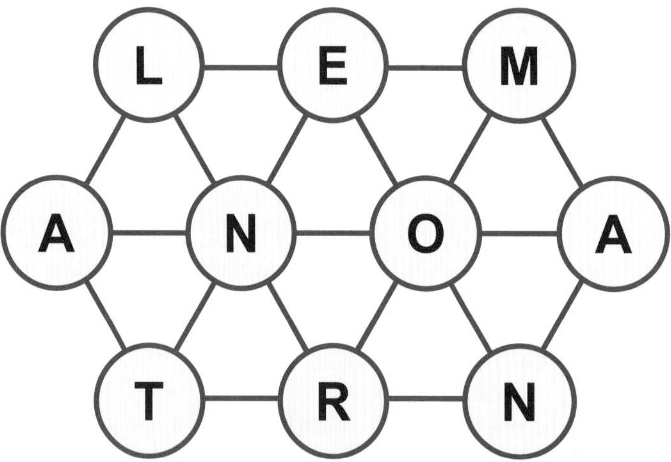

5. Find a pair of anagrams from the list of words below.

ELATEDLY	DESCRIBE	CORDELIA	ARTICLED
ESCRIBED	TAILORED	DETAILED	SEDATELY

Quick Fire

6. Change one letter only in each of the words below to produce a familiar phrase.

WISE LOU MERE HIRE

7. What word can be placed in the brackets so that it forms another word or phrase when tacked onto the end of the first word, and another word or phrase when placed in front of the second word?

DREAM ( ) CLASS

8. Start at one of the four corner letters and spiral clockwise around the perimeter, finishing at the central letter to spell out a nine-letter word. You must provide the missing letters.

C	I	
I		A
N	U	M

9. Which is the odd one out?

POTS PAST STOP TOPS

10. SEA EYE TEA WHY

What word is indicated above?

11. Which four groups of letters can be joined together to form two words that have opposite meanings?

ANT DID LOW CAN RCE SUB THY TLE PLI SCA

12. What word can be placed in the brackets so that it forms another word or phrase when tacked onto the end of the first word, and another word or phrase when placed in front of the second word?

CROSS ( ) ACCOUNT

Quick Fire

13. A totally wonderful phrase has been sliced up into six three-letter groups which are then arranged in random order. What is the phrase?

BUL	YFA	OLU
ABS	TEL	OUS

14. Change one letter only in each of the words below to produce a familiar phrase.

BLOT NOT ANY GOLD

15. Solve the cryptic clues below. Each clue leads to a one-word answer.

i. Ann Ziata arranges her destination (8)

ii. Olympic event to deliberate over, we hear (6)

iii. Biblical character arranges hard cash (8)

iv. Royal excavation unearths white fur (6)

v. Start off with a prank but then get the point, it's all rather flowery (8)

vi. Graceful mover disturbed one plate (8)

16. If 1 GTDA = one good turn deserves another, what does 2 STES equal?

17. Which two words are the closest in meaning?

FEASIBLE, FLIMSY, POSSIBLE, ABUNDANT, COMPREHENSIVE, EXTRAVAGANT

18. FIT TO TART is an anagram of which familiar phrase?

Clue: An equivalent return

19. Which two words are the most opposite in meaning?

ABOLISH, NUMB, SAFE, SENSITIVE, WHOLESOME, SHARP

Quick Fire

20.

The same four-letter word when inserted in front of the words listed will produce six well-known phrases. What is the word?

	PROGRESS
	BELIEVE
	HASTE
* * * *	CLEAR
	OVER
	SENSE

21.

Which of the following is not an anagram of a capital city?

LATE VAT
ROBINIA
IN CASIO
AIR TREE
LOCO MOB

22.

Which two words are the closest in meaning?

CONVINCED, SALUBRIOUS, CHEERFUL, HEALTHY, DEVOUT, DISPARAGING

23.

If 1 GTDA = one good turn deserves another, what does 2 HABTO equal?

24.

Now that you are getting 'warmed up' try the following quick-fire crossword:

Across
1 Divide into two (6)
6 Seep (4)
7 Skiing event (6)
9 Mysterious (9)
11 Attempting (6)
12 Cook in an oven (4)
13 Conventional (6)

Down
2 Away from the sea (6)
3 Educate (9)
4 Mark Twain character (3,6)
5 Allow (3)
8 Capital of Austria (6)
10 Japanese sash (3)

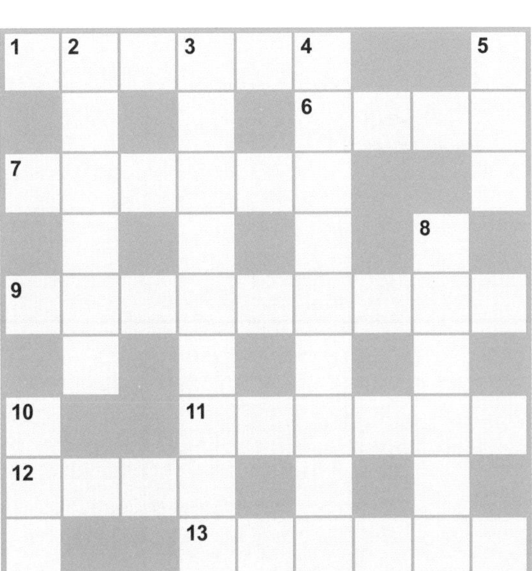

Quick Fire

25. DID TRUCE is an anagram of two 'this' and 'that' words: CUT DRIED (cut and dried).

WORLD ERA is an anagram of which two other 'this' and 'that' words?

26. Which four groups of letters can be joined together to produce two words that have similar meanings?

HOR	END	UNA	TRY
IRE	AUT	ANT	TER
DES	TIC	WRI	LAC

27. What word can be placed in front of date, kind and power to create three new words?

28. The clue 'evil spirited sailor' leads to which pair of rhyming words?

29. Solve the anagram in brackets to correctly complete the quotation by Ludwig Erhard.

"A (cop's memoir) is the art of dividing a cake in such a way that everyone believes he has the biggest piece."

30. Start at one of the four corner letters and spiral clockwise around the perimeter, finishing at the central letter to spell out a nine-letter word. You must provide the missing letters.

C	O	N
E		D
	R	A

31. The clue 'demented hysteria' leads to which pair of rhyming words?

32. If 9 L of a C = 9 lives of a cat, what does 4 M with TD equal?

33. Use every letter of the phrase CHEAPLY REAP PERCH once each only to spell out three types of fruit.

Quick Fire

34. What word can be placed in the brackets so that it forms another word or phrase when tacked onto the end of the first word, and another word or phrase when placed in front of the second word?

HAPPY ( ) SIZED

35. Which two words are the most opposite in meaning?

ARDENT, RESOLUTE, OPEN, DOUBTFUL, RESONANT, PUZZLED

36. Which two words are the closest in meaning?

INSINUATE, INVEIGLE, IMPUTE, INTRIGUE, IMPROVISE, IMBRICATE

37. Solve the anagram in brackets to correctly complete the quotation by Robert Frost.

"A liberal is a man too (dim and bored) to take his own side in a quarrel."

38. In order to explore other possible alternatives I am ensuring that the various choices which belong to me remain at my disposal. What am I doing?

39. Which four groups of letters can be joined together to produce two words that have opposite meanings?

TAP	ASE	OFF	URE	PLE
END	PAT	NAT	CAN	ATT

40. Find a pair of anagrams from the list of words below.

LEGATION	TIRESOME	ANTIPOLE
RELATION	MESOLITE	SEROTINE
LOCATION	ORIENTAL	ELATERIN

41. Which well-known phrase rhymes with the words GUN AND FLAMES (as in FIGHT AND PLAY / NIGHT AND DAY)?

Quick Fire

42. Solve the four anagrams below. All the answers are just one word and the number of letters in each word increases by one each time.

i. wet rep
ii. tame nag
iii. can pause
iv. irk and how

43. What word can be placed in the brackets so that it forms another word or phrase when tacked onto the end of the first word, and another word or phrase when placed in front of the second word?

GREASE ( ) BRUSH

44. *Western Video* is produced by which entertainer?

45. EARTH is to HEART as PEARS is to: SPARE, PARSE, SPEAR, REAPS, ASPER, PARES

46. Find a pair of anagrams from the list of words below.

DERELICT ARTICLED IDOLATRY
DIRECTLY LECTERNS ORDINATE
ADROITLY LEATRICE CERELITY

47. I am held in high esteem by a particular person due to my featured position in their desirable works of fiction. Where am I?

48. TEACH
HINGE
LURID
DAIRY

What word below is missing from the above list, and where should it be placed?

FINAL, PARTY, GRAND, ENROL, ELECT

49. What word can be placed in the brackets so that it forms another word or phrase when tacked onto the end of the first word, and another word or phrase when placed in front of the second word?

FOOD ( ) SAW

Quick Fire

50. Finally, to complete this section, another quick-fire crossword:

Across
1 Changeable (8)
5 Circuit (3)
6 Drink made from apples (5)
7 Afresh (4)
9 Barrier (4)
13 Brush (5)
14 Pole for rowing (3)
15 Retriever dog (8)
Down
1 Holiday home (5)
2 Indian currency unit (5)
3 Curved structure (4)
4 Build (5)
8 Support for a handrail (5)
10 Audibly (5)
11 Mistake (5)
12 Spiked wheel on a boot (4)

1		2		3			4	
5				6				
7	8				9	10		11
				12				
13						14		
	15							

More Challenging

51. If presented with the words MAR, AM and FAR and asked to find the shortest word in the English language from which all these three words can be produced you may be expected to come up with the word FARM.

Now here is a further list of words: SOLITARY POETRY REASON

What is the shortest word in the English language from which these three words can be produced?

More Challenging

52. RESULT CUBED is an anagram of which two words that are opposite in meaning?

53. In each circle, find the starting point and spell out an eight-letter word, one rotating clockwise round the top circle, and the other rotating anticlockwise around the bottom circle.

You must provide the missing letters.

The two words you are seeking are antonyms.

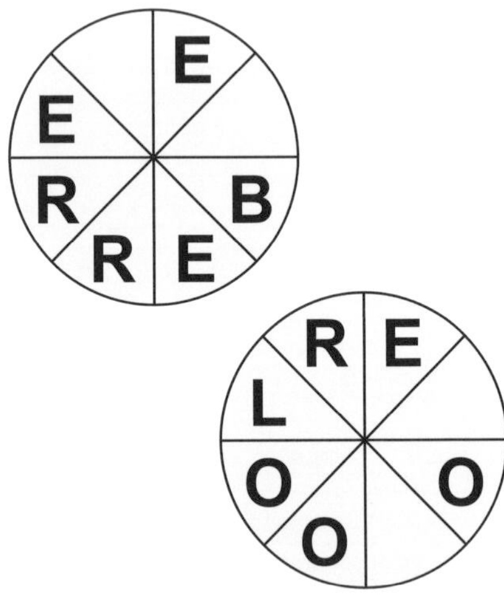

54. Each 3x3 block contains the letters of a nine-letter word. Find the two words that are antonyms.

55. Insert the name of a type of vehicle onto the bottom row so that seven three-letter words are produced reading down each column.

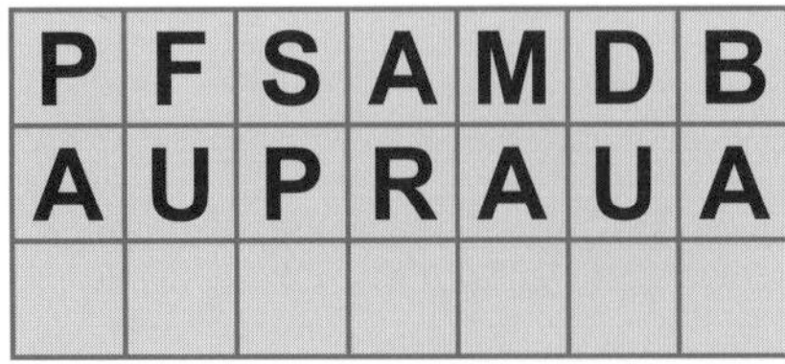

56. Select two words that are synonyms, plus an antonym of these two synonyms, from the list of words below.

CENSURE CONCENTRATE
CONDEMN EXPEDITE
CONDONE MOLLIFY REMIT

More Challenging

57. What is the longest word in the English language that can be produced from the 10 letters below? No letter may be used more than once.

M A F U R P L E G T

58. DID TRUCE is an anagram of two 'this' and 'that' words: CUT DRIED (cut and dried).

RAT CLAPPER is an anagram of which two other 'this' and 'that' words?

59. If meat in a river (3 in 6) is T(HAM)ES, find a circle in an outer boundary (4 in 6).

60. If 9 L of a C = 9 lives of a cat, what does 16 P on a C B equal?

61. Insert the name of a sport onto the bottom row so that eight three-letter words are produced reading down each column.

R	S	W	S	T	B	N	P
I	E	A	U	A	O	I	A

62. Find the starting point and spell out two words that are antonyms reading clockwise. Each word starts in a different circle and all letters in a word are consecutive.

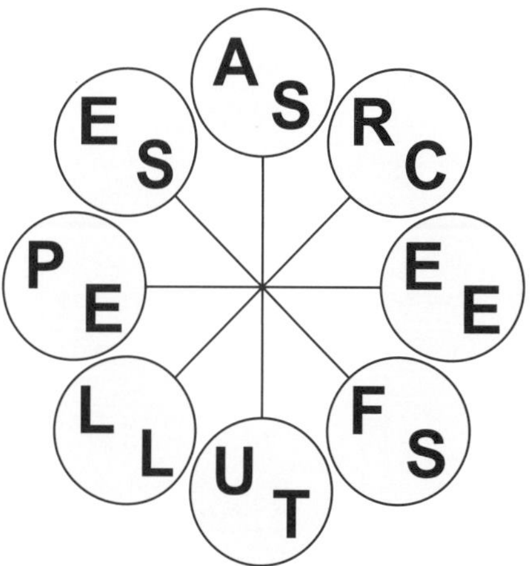

63. What word can be placed in the brackets so that it forms another word or phrase when tacked onto the end of the first word, and another word or phrase when placed in front of the second word?

WIND (   ) VISION

More Challenging

64. If meat in a river (3 in 6) is T(HAM)ES, find a swine in a closet (4 in 8).

65. If presented with the words MAR, AM and FAR and asked to find the shortest word in the English language from which all these three words can be produced you may be expected to come up with the word FARM.

Now here is a further list of words:
VULGAR FOULER BORING

What is the shortest word in the English language from which these three words can be produced?

66. Find the starting point and spell out a two-word phrase (8,6) working from circle to circle along the connecting lines.

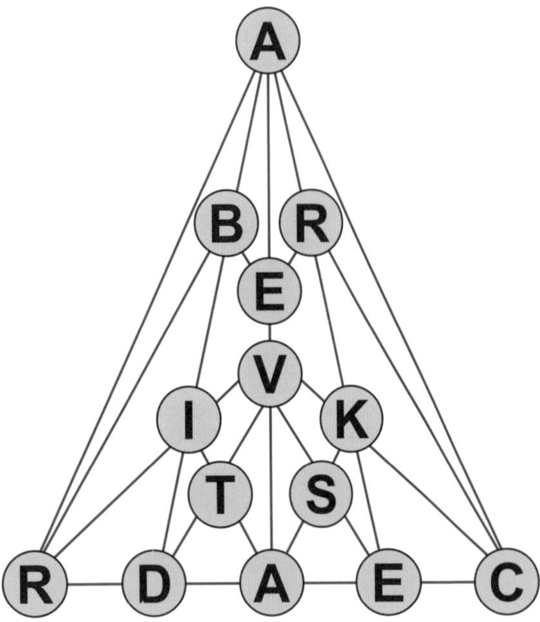

67. Each 3x3 block contains the letters of a nine-letter word. Find the two words that are synonyms.

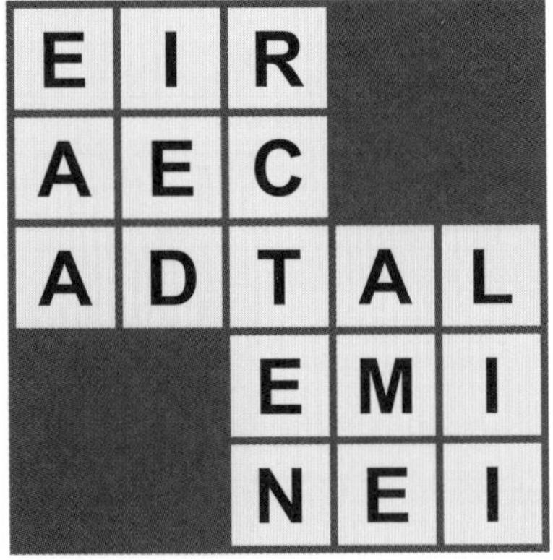

68. PLAINER SUITS is an anagram of which two words that are opposite in meaning?

69. Which well-known phrase rhymes with the words VAST AND LUXURIOUS (as in FIGHT AND PLAY / NIGHT AND DAY)?

70. PASTA is to TPASA as ALERT is to: RATEL, ALTER, LATER, ARTEL, TALER

More Challenging

71. The clue 'summerhouse manservant' leads to which pair of rhyming words?

72. Find the starting point and spell out a 14-letter word working from circle to circle along the connecting lines.

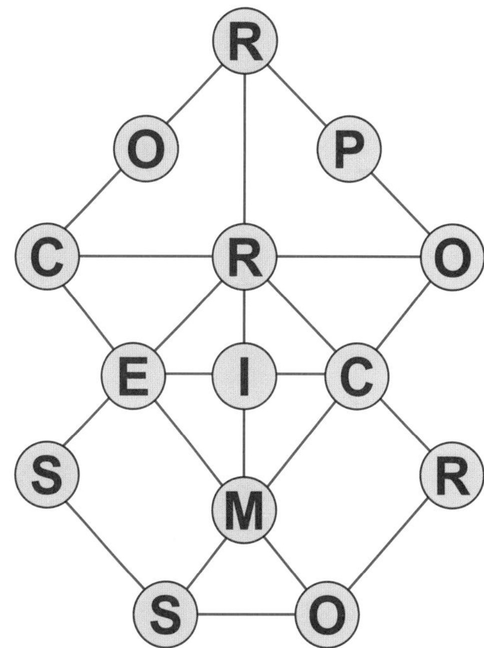

73. Mysterious and beautiful, the Phoenix was in early artistic representations with a plumage of five colours.

One word has been removed from the passage above. Select that word from the choice below and reinstate it into its correct place in the passage.

A resembled B sacred
C signified D strangely
E depicted F never

74. What word can be placed in front of able, king and lance to create three new words?

75. If 9 L of a C = 9 lives of a cat, what does 2 WDM a R equal?

76. Only one group of five letters below can be rearranged to spell out a five-letter word in the English language. Identify the word.

BYOPL TNLAK
ENTHO PALNI
GUIBL RAPOM

77.

G4 A6 E1 C9
I3 T7 I8 M5

What word/letter combination is missing?

More Challenging

78. Find the starting point and spell out a two-word phrase (8,8) working from circle to circle along the connecting lines.

Clue: Plasticine amenities.

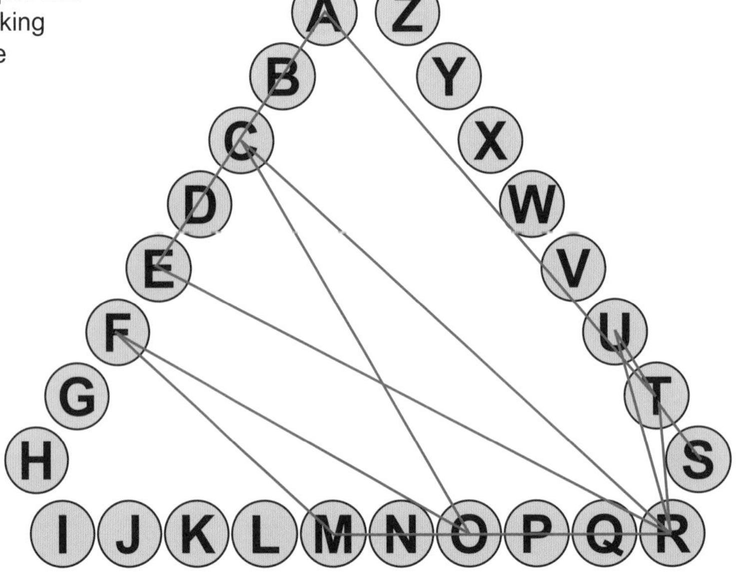

79. Four eight-letter words all on the theme of nautical terms have been jumbled. Solve the four anagrams and enter the answers next to each anagram, reading from left to right or top to bottom.

Next transfer the letters in the yellow squares to the keyword box below to find a fifth eight-letter word on the same theme.

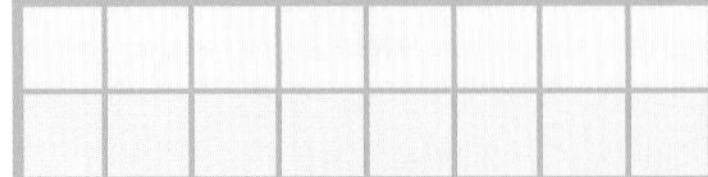

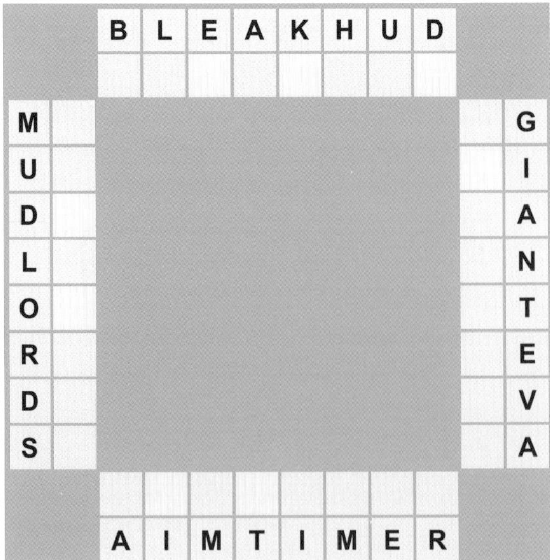

More Challenging

80. Wordcross Puzzle

Across
- 2 Unit of electrical current (3)
- 4 Cry of a sheep (5)
- 6 Wind or turn (7)
- 8 Leguminous vegetables (4)
- 9 Slender (4)
- 11 Bellow (4)
- 12 Mass of baked bread (4)
- 14 Muddle (4)
- 15 Layer (4)
- 16 Dispute (4)
- 18 Daydream (4)
- 19 Tie (4)
- 21 Type of freshwater fish (4)
- 22 Issuing or flowing forth (7)
- 24 Sheet of metal (5)
- 25 Prevarication (3)

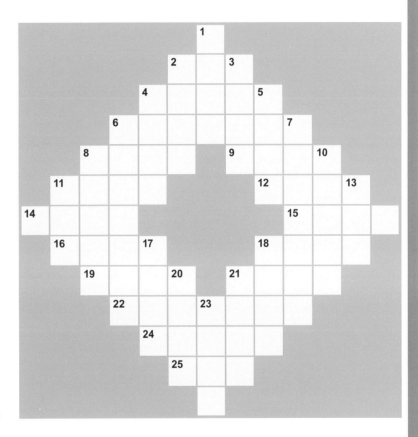

Down
- 1 Presage (4)
- 2 Unfortunately (4)
- 3 Stuffs, with soft material for example (4)
- 4 Ursine creature (4)
- 5 Relate (4)
- 6 Standard of dimension (7)
- 7 Vigorous reprimand when read (4,3)
- 8 Modelled (5)
- 10 Cereal grass (5)
- 11 Umpire (abbr) (3)
- 13 Charge (3)
- 17 Moist (4)
- 18 Narrow road (4)
- 20 Vertical smooth rock face (4)
- 21 Type of fruit (4)
- 23 Fastener (4)

More Challenging

81. Solve the anagram in brackets to correctly complete the quotation by Christopher Morley.

"Life is a foreign language, all men (numeric snoop) it."

82. Select two words that are synonyms, plus an antonym of these two synonyms, from the list of words below.

SPARSE MATURE
HEAVY MELLOW UNRIPE
SENTIMENTAL TANGIBLE

83. Using all nine letters of the word ANTEATERS once each only find three words that when placed in the grid will form a magic word square in which the same three words can be read both across and down.

Next find a further solution by altering the position of the letters in the grid to produce three different words which also produce a magic word square using the same nine letters.

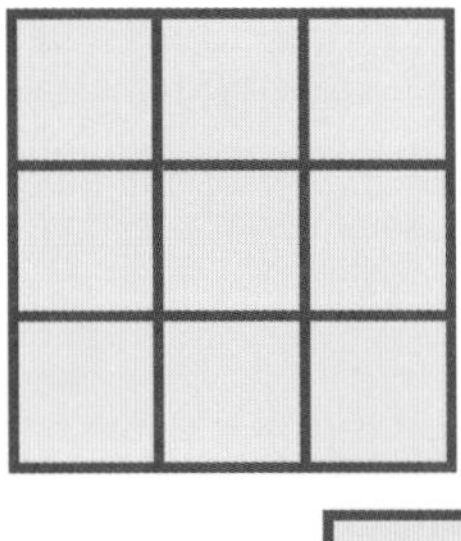

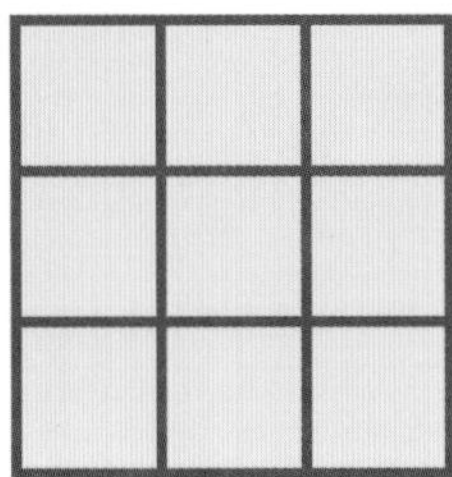

84. The 20th century has seen an increasing degree of state intervention to promote benefits.

One word has been removed from the passage above. Select that word from the choice below and reinstate it into its correct place in the passage.

A capitalist B social
C monopoly D male
E money F low

85. If presented with the words MAR, AM and FAR and asked to find the shortest word in the English language from which all these three words can be produced you may be expected to come up with the word FARM.

Now here is a further list of words:
MAESTRO PRIME CHAOS

What is the shortest word in the English language from which these three words can be produced?

More Challenging

86.

The answers to the clues are all five-letter words which, when placed correctly into the grid, will form a magic word square where the same five words can be read both horizontally and vertically. The clues are in no particular order:

- make amends
- expression of greeting
- gastropod mollusc
- strict
- monarchical

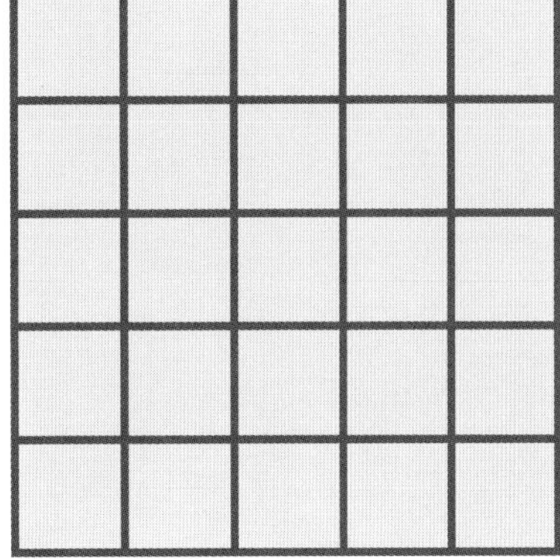

87.

Across
1 Tool for lifting (5)
6 Sex appeal (coll) (5)
7 Ring of bells (5)
8 Not restrained (5)
9 Native American race (5)
12 Maverick (5)
13 Italian seaport (5)
14 Give way (5)

Down
1 Body of water (4)
2 Place to survey (9)
3 Axial motion (4)
4 Not able to be shifted (9)
5 Item of footwear (4)
9 Sound made by breathing audibly (4)
10 Electromagnetic radiation (1-3)
11 Cheerful (4)

More Challenging

88. INSERTED MANURE is an anagram of which two words that mean the same?

89. Find the starting point and work from letter to adjacent letter horizontally and vertically to spell out a 12-letter word. You must provide the missing letters.

R	E		I
O	R	R	R
T	A	E	

90. RAGE SACK GASH AREA

What single letter can be added to each of the above words to form four new words without altering the order of the letters?

91. Select two words that are synonyms, plus an antonym of these two synonyms, from the list of words below.

AVOW IMPERMEABLE REPLETE EMPTY CONTRITE OBSCURE SATIATED

92. Place the remaining letters into the grid to produce three related words with the aid of the clue: In the eye of the beholder.

S P V L D U I U Y N T S L

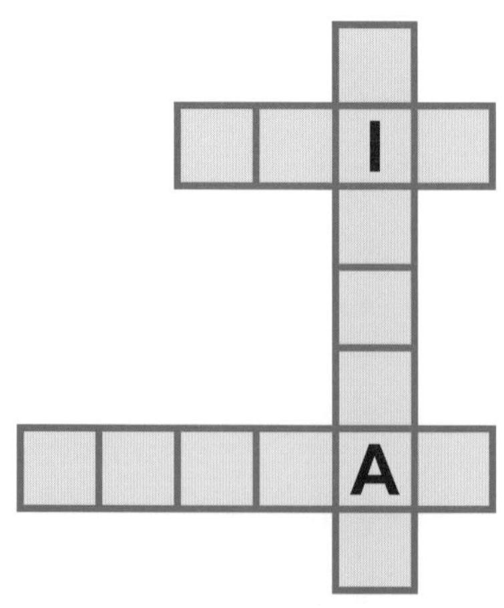

93. VANISHED FORT is an anagram of which familiar phrase (4,4,4)?

Clue: At a tremendous rate

94. The 10-letter word ANTHRACITE is an anagram of which two five-letter words that are similar in meaning?

More Challenging

95. What do all these words have in common?

MOTION ASTRONOMICALLY
INDICATE REASONABLE
EVOLUTION LEANER

96. Using every letter of the phrase HATE A CHEESY CHEAT once each find four words that when placed in the grid will form a magic word square in which the same four words can be read both across and down.

97. A phrase has had its initial letters and word spaces removed. What is the phrase?

NULLRY

98. FFTB are the initial letters of the phrase fortune favours the brave.

What phrase has the initial letters UWSDWF ?

99. Four eight-letter words all terms used in mathematics have been jumbled. Solve the four anagrams and enter the answers next to each anagram, reading from left to right or top to bottom.

Next transfer the letters in the yellow squares to the keyword box below to find a fifth word (of nine letters) on the same theme.

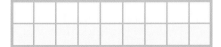

T R I A N G L E

R E A D I T E M

P A T H O G E N

G I V E N T E A

More Challenging

100. Place the remaining letters into the grid to produce two related words with the aid of the clue: Professional refurbisher.

C N I T T R I D O O O E E R A

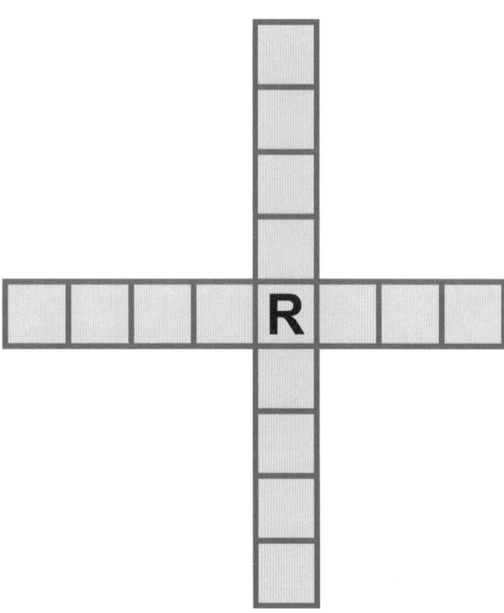

101.

Across
1 Wanderer (5)
6 Loosen (5)
7 Titled peer (5)
8 Type of glazed earthenware (5)
9 French impressionist painter, Claude ___ (5)
12 Employment (5)
13 South African grassland (5)
14 Overturn (5)

Down
1 Skating arena (4)
2 Spiritedly (9)
3 Regretted (4)
4 Impasse (9)
5 Sash (4)
9 Displace (4)
10 Ballet skirt (4)
11 Tear violently (4)

1		2		3		4		5
				6				
7								
				8				
9				10				11
				12				
13								
				14				

102. Use the letters in each quarter to create four words with the addition of the letters END, ie all four words end in E-N-D.

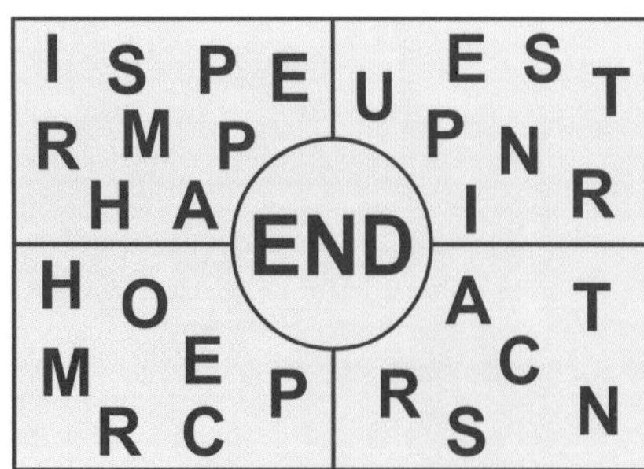

More Challenging

103. Solve the cryptogram below in which each letter of the alphabet has been substituted by another.

ZBUP COZ CAYBKQ FLH YBMYBYCH, CAH TBYXHLQH FBS ATRFB QCTWYSYCP, FBS Y'R BZC QTLH FVZTC CAH MZLRHL.

FUVHLC HYBQCHYB

105. The answers to the clues are all five-letter words which, when placed correctly into the grid, will form a magic word square where the same five words can be read both horizontally and vertically. The clues are in no particular order:

- Cardinal compass point
- Bright attractive girl (slang)
- Colourless highly flammable liquid
- Approximately
- Terpsichorean movement

104. Find the starting point and work from letter to adjacent letter horizontally and vertically to spell out a 12-letter word. You must provide the missing letter.

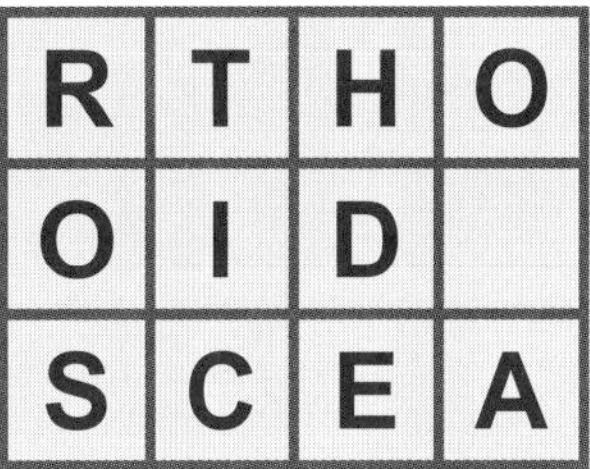

106. The thesis of determinism is regarded as a methodological principle or rule of thumb, rather than a true or false statement.

One word has been removed from the passage above. Select that word from the choice below and reinstate it into its correct place in the passage.

A freely B scientifically
C theory D choice
E predictable F often

107. Use each letter of MONKEY ORATOR WEPT once each only to spell out three cities which in the 20th century all hosted the Summer Olympic Games.

More Challenging

108. What is the longest word that can be produced from the ten letters below? No letter may be used more than once.

T M E G C I Y N W A

109. Only one group of six letters below can be rearranged to spell out a six-letter word in the English language. Identify the word.

BEIHGC	MIRPLA
HAONDE	FINBAK
AITHLM	JEROPD

110. HATE WALLY is an anagram of which phrase (3,3,3)?

Clue: Right to the end

111. In order not to be overly curious or inquisitive I am attending to none other than the personal activity belonging to me. What am I doing?

112. How many times, if any, does the word BANANA appear in the grid? It must appear in a straight line, vertically, horizontally or diagonally, backwards or forwards.

A	N	A	N	A	A	B	B	Q	Q
N	J	K	B	F	Z	L	A	H	W
A	P	H	Z	Y	D	I	Z	I	B
N	N	S	V	V	O	V	Y	H	D
N	N	A	R	I	S	N	V	M	I
A	E	W	N	L	B	F	A	X	F
B	A	N	A	A	N	A	B	N	A
A	L	M	A	W	B	Y	W	H	Y
N	M	B	V	Q	W	R	N	L	A
A	B	U	F	I	K	S	W	R	G

113. Identify two pairs of anagrams from the list of words below:

RESIDENTS	AMORTISED
PARAISON	ORDINATES
ORINASAL	TRAINEES
ERASTIAN	SENORITA
MEDIATORS	ARTESIAN

More Challenging

114. A phrase has had its initial letters and word spaces removed. What is the phrase?

PNRMS

115. SCORE TRUE CROONER is an anagram of which two words that are opposite in meaning?

116. Identify the Seven Sins with the aid of the clues. Each answer has the word SIN embedded in it in the positions shown.

SIN ******	quality of being open and truthful
*SIN*****	form of mica
SIN**	destroy micro organisms by cleansing
SIN	with humour
****SIN**	fortunes to be counted
*****SIN*	encouraging
******SIN	the US Badger State

117. Across

1 Treadle (5)
6 Reproductive structure (5)
7 South American animal (5)
8 Loud (5)
9 Canoe (5)
12 Small, water-surrounded area of land (5)
13 Create a work of art (5)
14 Terrestrial planet (5)

Down

1 Inner surface of the hand (4)
2 Envy or lust, for example (6,3)
3 Lend (4)
4 Mountain railway (9)
5 Refuse to accept (4)
9 Retained (4)
10 Type of hawk (4)
11 Skin infection (4)

1		2		3		4		5
				6				
7								
				8				
9				10				11
				12				
13								
				14				

More Challenging

118. What is the longest word that can be produced from the ten letters below? No letter may be used more than once.

N I D H L O P A C T

119. A phrase which may lead to a pleasant vocation has been sliced up into seven three-letter bits which are then arranged in random order. What is the phrase?

RKI UCA EWO
NGE NIC FYO TIT

120. Find the starting point and spell out two words that are antonyms reading clockwise. Each word starts in a different circle and all letters in a word are consecutive.

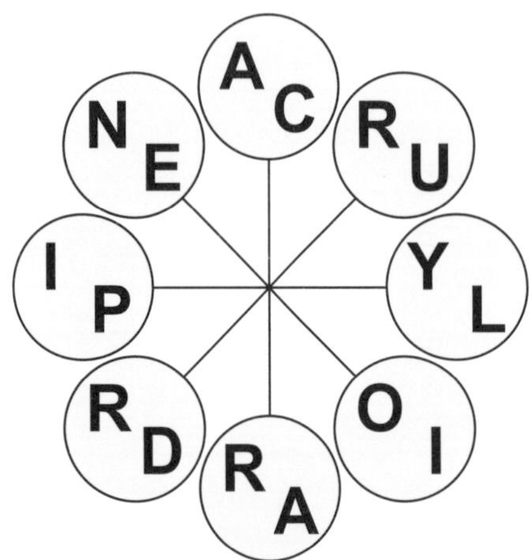

Difficult

121. Complete the six words below in such a way that the last two letters of the first word are the same as the first two letters of the second word, and so on. To complete the cycle, the last two letters of the sixth word are the same as the first two letters of the first word.

_ _ L I _ _   _ _ R I _ _   _ _ R T _ _   _ _ O D _ _   _ _ A B _ _   _ _ S S _ _

Difficult

122. Solve the multi-word anagrams in brackets to complete the quotation by Victor Borge.

(_ _ _ _ _ _ _ _ _ _) the (_ _ _ _ _ _ _ _ _ _ _ _ _ _ _ _ _)
(share guilt) (hardiest contests)

(_ _ _ _ _ _ _ _ _ _ _ _ _ _ _ _)
(weep wet noble poet)

123. The answers to the clues are all five-letter words which, when placed correctly into the grid, will form a magic word square where the same five words can be read both horizontally and vertically.
The clues are in no particular order:

- any of various willows the twigs of which are used in basketry
- approaches closely
- delete
- citrus fruit
- obsessional enthusiasm

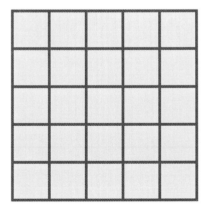

124. Which word below is in the wrong column?

WAY	KEY
FIVE	JUMP
CHAIR	DOWN
NOON	SLUNG
TAIL	

125. Use the letters of UNKEMPT BIBLE CHARMERS once each only to spell out three jobs or professions.

Difficult

126. _ _ _ _ _ _ _ _ _ _ _ _ _ _ _ _ _ _ can

_ _ _ _ _ _ _ _ _ _ _ _ _ _ _ _ _ _ a

_ _ _ _ _ _ _ _ _ and it is in this

_ _ _ _ _ _ _ _ _ that the _ _ _ _ _ _ _ _ _

_ _ _ _ _ _ _ _ _ of the _ _ _ _ _ _ _ _ _

_ _ _ _ _ _ _ _ _ through _ _ _ _ _ _ _ _ _ .

The eleven words below have been removed from the above passage. Restore them to their correct position.

heat, infrared, through, form, travels, radiant, travel, sun, radiation, space, vacuum.

127. Insert the letters provided into their respective segments so that two related eight-letter words can be read, one going one way round the outer circle and the other going the opposite way round the inner circle.

NE: MAIN **SE:** ASCA
SW: LICS **NW:** LYEH

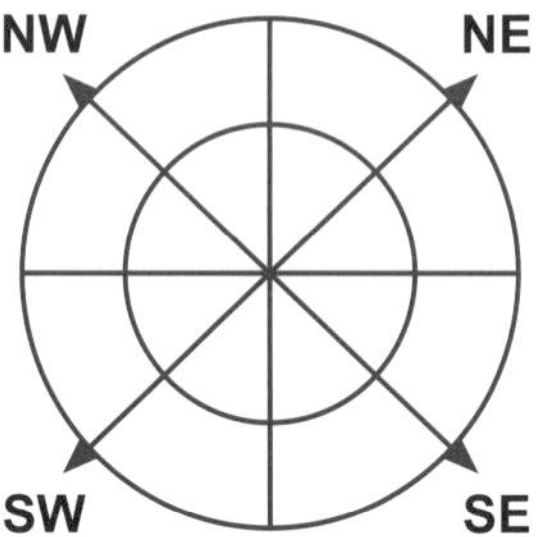

128. Which of the following is not an anagram of a form of transportation?

CHEER PILOT
OIL ME ABOUT
BETA ATOMS
MOTHER APES
MET COOL CRY

129. GULF INDEX PATH
EAT GOBLIN

Find the link between the words above, then choose from the following what word comes next:

RUN POD KEY DIP LID

130. Only one group of seven letters below can be rearranged to spell out a seven-letter word in the English language. Identify the word.

LODHYTA GICNITA LYENMAP DALCOGI NIORLDA HUENICK RCANIFL

Difficult

131. CART SPLIT LINE AGE MINIMUM PROFIT STONE CAST

Which word above right shares a common feature with the words above left?

132. A fall in the _ _ _ _ _ _ _ _ _ of the _ _ _ _ _ _ _ _ _, known as the _ _ _ _ _ _ _ _ _ _ _ _ _ _ _ _ _ _, accompanies _ _ _ _ _ _ _ _ _ because as the _ through the _ _ _ _ _ _ _ _ _ the mean _ _ _ _ _ _ _ _ _ of the _ _ _ _ _ _ _ _ _ _ _ _ _ _ _ _ _ _ falls.

The 12 words below have been removed from the above passage. Restore them to their correct position.

energy, temperature, faster, surface, evaporation, liquid, molecules, cooling, molecules, escape, remaining, effect.

133. Insert a pair of letters into each set of brackets so they form one word when tacked onto the letters on the left, and another word when placed in front of the letters on the right.

When read downward in pairs, they must spell out an eight-letter word.

MO (_ _) AL

TU (_ _) IL

LA (_ _) ND

LI (_ _) RE

134. If meat in a river (3 in 6) is T(HAM)ES, find a swine in a wood (3 in 8).

135. What is the longest word that can be produced from the nine letters below? No letter may be used more than once in the same word.

E R D O L J A K T

Difficult

136. R E V O D N E ?

What letter is missing?

137. What do all the following words have in common?

COW	DOE	ARK	TEN
CANE	RAKE	INCH	HERO
SNIP	SIFT		

138. If 9 L of a C = 9 lives of a cat, what does 2 L in the HB equal?

139. What do the following all have in common?

Elastic bands
Deutschemarks
The Red Cross
Punctuation marks
The garden of Eden
The Ballets Russes
That Monday morning feeling
Sponge cakes

140.

CAVE	HEAP	ONCE
OPAL	SEND	EAST
OVER	NEXT	?

Which tile should replace the question mark?

ECHO	PUMA
1	2
ARCH	**LAMB**
3	4

141. Which two words are the odd ones out?

HEARD
EXPATRIATE
DEMUR
DRAIN
ABORIGINAL
IRATE
PLAGIARIST
ALIGN
KETTLEDRUM
LOGGERHEAD

Difficult

142. In each of the following groups of three words your task is to find two of the three that can be paired to form an anagram of another word, which is a synonym of the word remaining. For example, LEG – MEEK – NET. The words LEG and NET are an anagram of GENTLE, which is a synonym of the remaining word MEEK.

LANE – MALE – MUSIC
BALD – ROAR – LEFT
IN – SIGN – DIATONIC
BOUNCER – BULGE – TAPER
VIOLENT – GREEN – MANNER
EXTRA – TENSE – PLUMP
LOST – SIDE – CLAMP
MOLE – GRAIN – CLUE
ATTAIN – SCORN – DEAL
SON – TERM – EXPIRES

143. Find the starting point and spell out two words that are synonyms reading clockwise. Each word starts in a different circle and all letters in a word are consecutive.

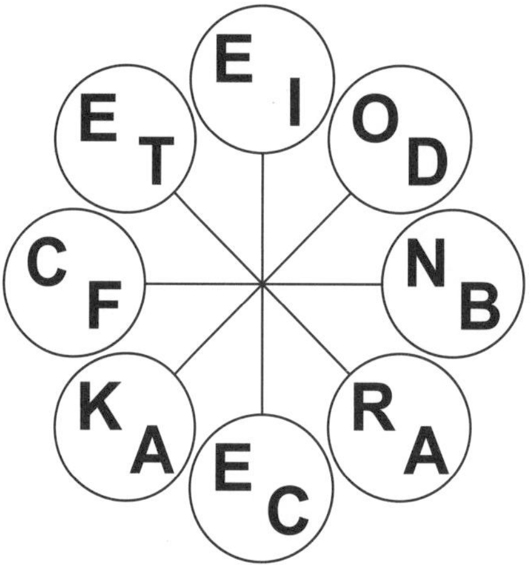

144. What do the following names from Shakespeare all have in common?

Pomgarnet Antipholus Telamonius Florentius Vaudemont Placentio Philarmonus

145. Complete the six words below in such a way that the last two letters of the first word are the same as the first two letters of the second word, and so on. To complete the cycle, the last two letters of the sixth word are the same as the first two letters of the first word.

_ _ M O _ _ _ _ A R _ _ _ _ A P _ _ _ _ A T _ _ _ _ I B _ _ _ _ T H _ _

Difficult

146. Alphabet Crossword

Complete the crossword with good English words by inserting each of the 26 letters of the alphabet once only into the empty squares.

A B C D E F G
H I J K L M N
O P Q R S T U
V W X Y Z

147.

_________ chimpanzees can _________ to _________ with _________ with the aid of _________ or _________ _________, but are _________ _________ from _________ speech by the _________ of the _________.

The twelve words below have been removed from the above passage. Restore them to their correct position.

probably, humans, trained, human, machines, communicate, voice-box, precluded, learn, sign, position, language.

148.

What is the longest word that can be spelled out by moving from letter to adjacent letter, horizontally, vertically and diagonally, using no letter more than once?

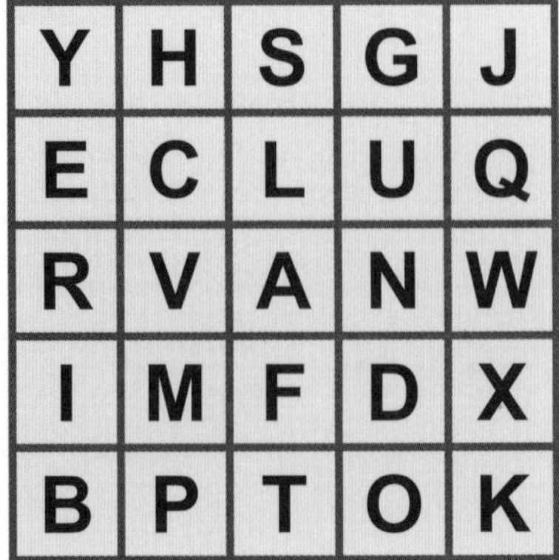

Y	H	S	G	J
E	C	L	U	Q
R	V	A	N	W
I	M	F	D	X
B	P	T	O	K

Difficult

149.

Insert the names of two types of food onto the top and bottom rows so that eight four-letter words are produced reading down each column.

O	W	A	R	E	N	O	C
O	A	S	A	A	C	V	E

150.

Insert a pair of letters into each set of brackets so they form a word when tacked onto the letters on the left, and another word when placed in front of the letters on the right.

The five pairs of letters, when read downward in pairs, must spell out a 10-letter word.

SO ( ) AT
MU ( ) IN
ME ( ) ON
CH ( ) ON
SE ( ) TO

151.

Four 11-letter words, all terms used in astronomy, have been jumbled. Solve the four anagrams and enter the answers next to each anagram, reading from left to right or top to bottom.

Next transfer the letters in the yellow squares to the keyword box below to find a fifth word (of nine letters) on the same theme.

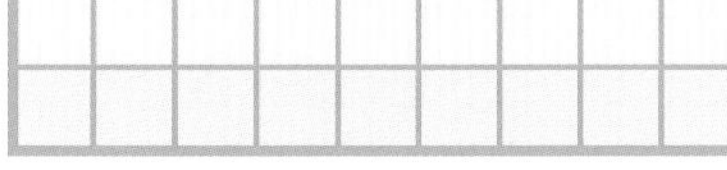

Top: P U R I T A N M E A L

Left: B R A V O O Y S T E R

Right: A S G U I T A R I S T

Bottom: A N C I E N T I D O L

Difficult

152. LAD RAS

The same letter can be added to both sets of letters to produce a phrase meaning finery. What is the phrase?

153. What four letters come next?

KLOP TFAT DROF ????

154. Place the tiles into the correct position in the grid so that two related words appear reading clockwise around the outer edge, and every two inner adjacent pairs of letters spells out a two-letter word.

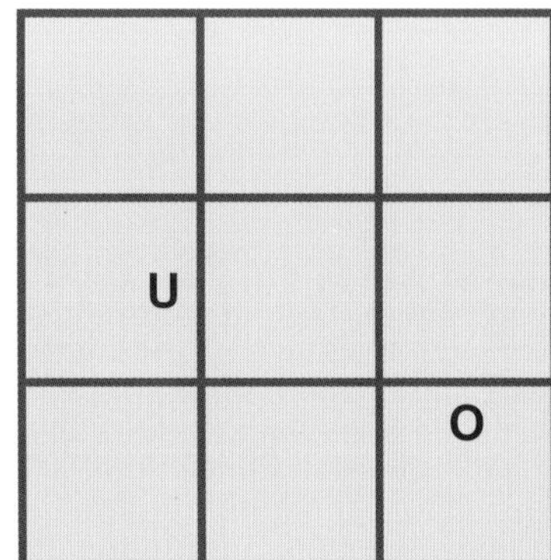

F E F G	Y O O M	T C U W
O R R A	U S M N	E I U T
R Y E I	O P D E	O P H B

155. Which of the following is not an anagram of a word beginning with ANT ?

TINIEST ASH
GAVE TAX RANT
TO DETAIN
CAPTAIN TIE
DECENT NEAT

156. SCARAB ORCHID SHERIF ?

Which comes next?

SECOND
URBANE
EIGHTH
KIRSCH
NUTMEG

Difficult

157. Insert the names of two seagoing vessels onto the top and bottom rows so that seven four-letter words are produced reading down each column.

O	O	R	C	O	A	E
R	A	G	E	N	S	A

158. CHANCIEST TORTURER is an anagram of which two words that are similar in meaning?

159. What links the following words?

ALIMONY INTERPLANETARY CONTRAPTION APPLICABLE

160. Four 11-letter words, all weather terms, have been jumbled. Solve the four anagrams and enter the answers next to each anagram, reading from left to right or top to bottom.

Next transfer the letters in the yellow squares to the keyword box below to find a fifth word (of nine letters) on the same theme.

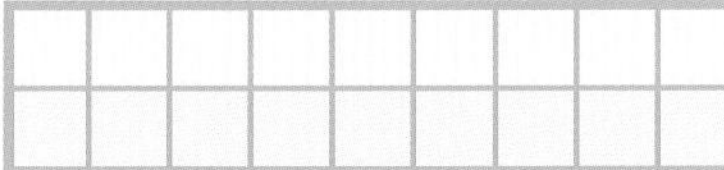

G E O M E T R Y L O O

D E P A R T L U N C H

C Y N I C A L T O N E

M E E T P U R E R A T

Difficult

161. Insert the letters provided into their respective segments so that two related eight-letter words can be read, one going one way round the outer circle and the other going the opposite way round the inner circle.

NE: LAIC **SE:** PETH
SW: BOAN **NW:** PETH

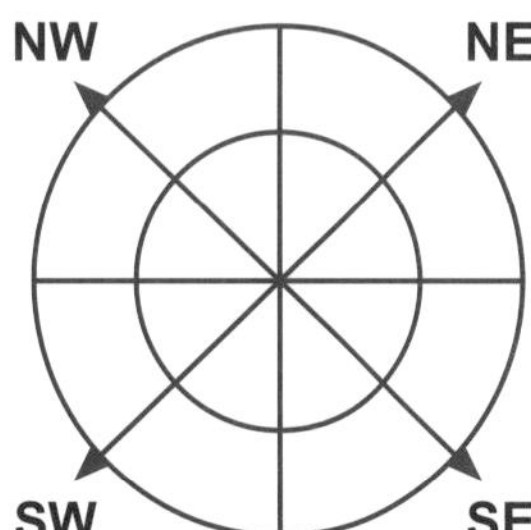

162. If meat in a river (3 in 6) is T(HAM)ES, find a valiant man in a cigar (4 in 7).

163. Using the letters of the phrase WEIRD, INDELICATE SUPER SAINT once each only find five words that when placed in the grid will form a magic word square in which the same five words can be read both across and down.

164. Complete the ten words below in such a way that, reading across, the last two letters of the first word are the same as the first two letters of the second word, and so on. To complete the cycle, the last two letters of the tenth word are the same as the first two letters of the first word.

_ _ R O _ _   _ _ L O _ _
_ _ N A _ _   _ _ N K _ _
_ _ E L _ _   _ _ I O _ _
_ _ M B _ _   _ _ L E _ _
_ _ I S _ _   _ _ U N _ _

165. Rod and Bob play a pivotal role in which household artefact?

166. Which is the odd one out?

CHEAPEN
REPLICATE
SPIGOT
MAGNUM
ANKLET
ACCURATE

Difficult

167. Find the starting point and find a phrase (4,4,4,4) reading clockwise.

Only alternate letters have been provided.

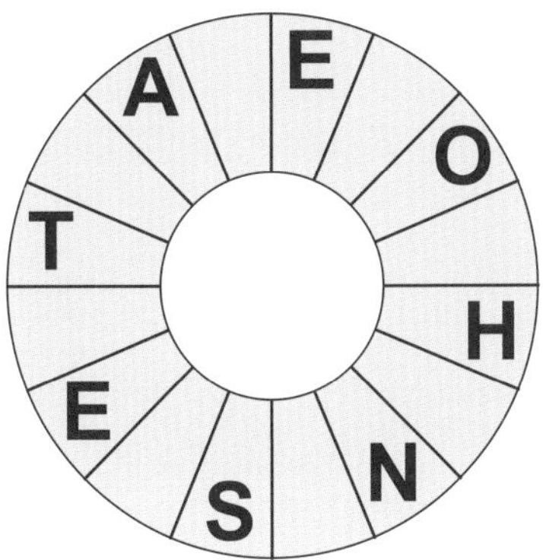

168. Find the starting point and spell out three words that are synonyms reading clockwise. Each word starts in a different circle and all letters in a word are consecutive.

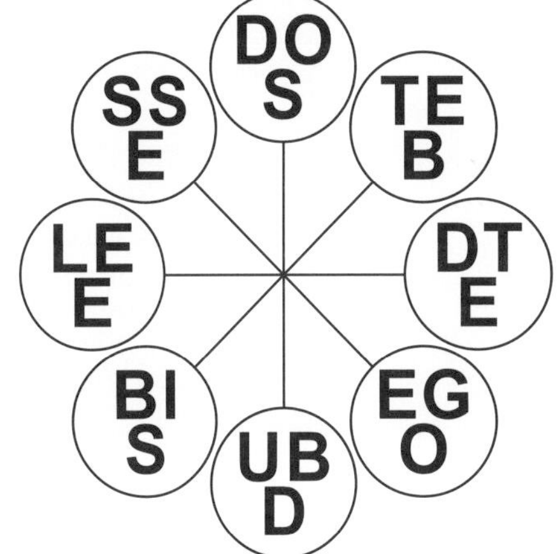

169. Find the starting point and work from letter to letter along the connecting lines across and around the circumference to spell out a three-word geographical area with the aid of the clue provided. Beware of one double letter (which is visited just once).

Clue: The place to keep a royal hale and hearty?

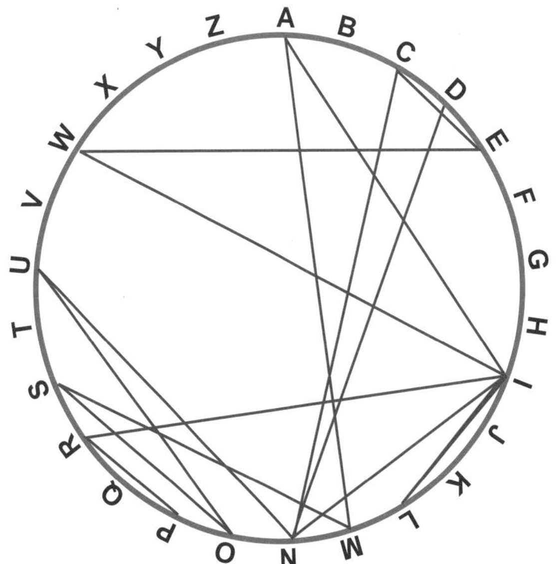

Difficult

170. Four 11-letter words, all on the subject of buildings and architecture, have been jumbled. Solve the four anagrams and enter the answers next to each anagram, reading from left to right or top to bottom.

Next transfer the letters in the yellow squares to the keyword box below to find a fifth word (of nine letters) on the same theme.

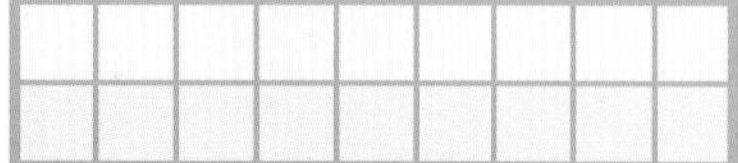

T E N C R O O N E R S

U N T R E A T A B L E

R E N A M E B A T C H

S C O F F I N G L A D

171. If 9 L of a C is Nine Lives of a Cat, what is represented by 60 D in EA of an ET?

172. In order to continue progressing actively I am causing the liquid in a metallic household vessel to remain in a state of ebullition. What am I doing?

173. INSPIRED = INDIGNATION
SPRYNESS = EAVESDROP
EXECUTIVE = ABBREVIATE
NAUSEATE = ?

What word should replace the question mark?

PROTECT FUNCTION EMBELLISH CHARGE DISPLAY

174. PLANET SPIGOT PULSAR TENDRIL ?

What comes next?

CROCUS BEGONIA LILY DAHLIA CYCLAMEN

Difficult

175. What is the longest word that can be spelled out by moving from letter to adjacent letter, horizontally, vertically and diagonally, using no letter more than once?

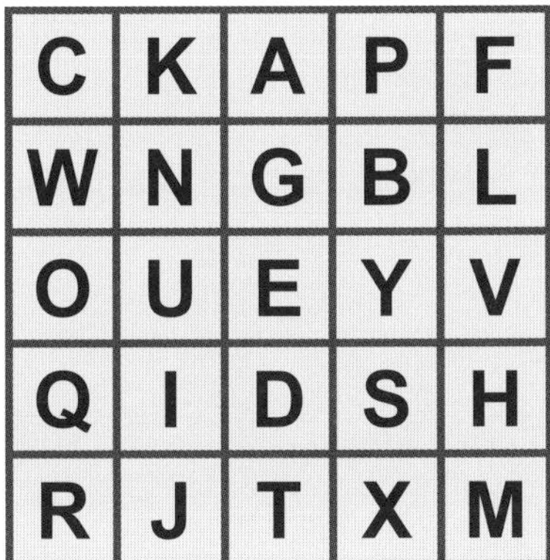

176. The clue 'past enigma' leads to what pair of rhyming words?

177. CROSS BLOSSOM RIBBON FINGERS ?

What comes next?

SUN MOON COMET ASTEROID PLUTO

178. The word STAGNATION is an anagram of which other 10-letter word?

179. Place the tiles into the correct position in the grid so that two related words appear reading clockwise around the outer edge, and every two inner adjacent pairs of letters spells out a two-letter word.

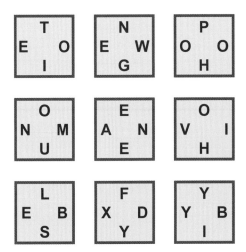

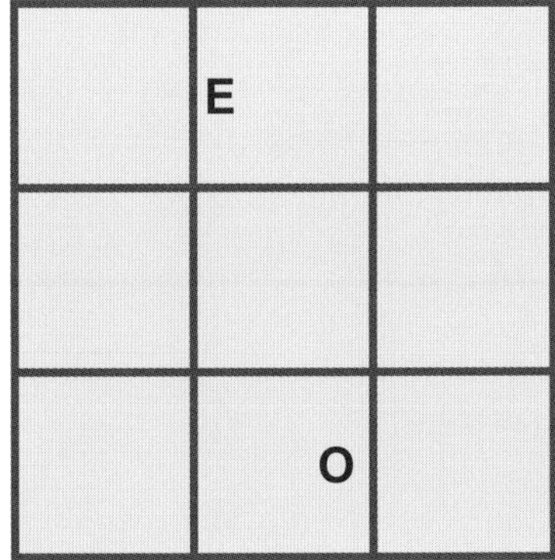

T E O I	N E W G	P O O H
O N M U	E A N E	O V I H
L E B S	F X D Y	Y Y B I

Difficult

180. Place a pair of letters in each set of brackets so that they form a word when tacked onto the two letters on the left, and another word when placed in front of the two letters on the right. The five pairs of letters, when read downwards in pairs must spell out a 10-letter word.

SA (_ _) LT
BI (_ _) HY
FO (_ _) GE
SL (_ _) ET
MA (_ _) SS

181. An example of a _ is that the _ _ _ _ _ _ _ _ _ appears _ _ _ _ _ _ _ _ _ when on the _ _ _ _ _ _ _ _ _ than when it is _ _ _ _ _ _ _ _ _ in the _ _ _ _ _ _ _ _ _ , due to the _ _ _ _ _ _ _ _ _ of _ _ _ _ _ _ _ _ _ rays by the _ _ _ _ _ _ _ _ _ _ _ _ _ _ _ _ _ _ .

The 12 words below have been removed from the above passage. Place the words into their correct position in the passage.

Moon, Earth's, optical, bigger, high, refraction, natural, sky, atmosphere, illusion, horizon, light

182. Solve the anagrams below. All are one-word answers and the number of letters in each word increases by one each time.

PERMIT SIGN
VIOLENT SQUIRT
MAP ENFORCER
LABORIOUS PATCH
PLAIN EXTREME
SOPRANO FLIMSIES

183. Solve the multi-word anagrams in brackets to complete the quotation by Desmond Morris.

The (_ _ _ _ _ _ _ _ _) a (_ _ _ _ _ _ _ _ _ _ _) it is a (_ _ _ _ _ _ _ _)
(itsy tonic) (glam June Hun) (Oz on a hum)

Difficult

184.

Insert the five-letter words into the crossword grid.

ANGEL	FLUTE	PSALM
BASIC	FRESH	REBUS
ECLAT	HORSE	REEVE
EDICT	HOTEL	ROTOR
EDUCE	HYENA	SABLE
ELEGY	INERT	SCRUB
EMEER	ISSUE	SEINE
ENSUE	KNOWN	SNEER
ENTER	LOSER	SWEEP
ESTOP	MACAW	TABLE
EXERT	OUSEL	UNITE
EXTRA	PICKY	XENON

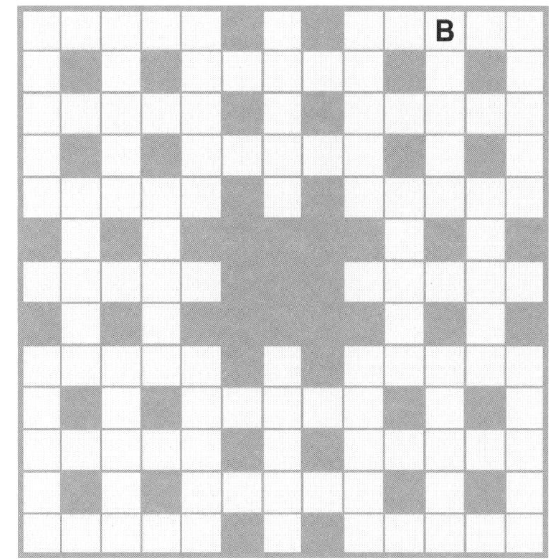

185.

Four 11-letter words, all on the subject of music, have been jumbled. Solve the four anagrams and enter the answers next to each anagram, reading from left to right or top to bottom.

Next transfer the letters in the yellow squares to the keyword box below to find a fifth word (of nine letters) on the same theme.

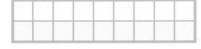

A S I X T H S P O O N

T H E C R E A T O R S

G R E A T M A N N E R

S H A R P O R C H I D

Solutions – Quick Fire

1. Season.
2. Thin red line.
3. Finnish = finish.
4. Ornamental.
5. Describe and escribed.
6. Wish you were here.
7. World.
8. Municipal.
9. Past: the rest are all anagrams.
10. City: each letter has the same sound as the letters C I T Y in turn.
11. Candid and subtle.
12. Current.
13. Absolutely fabulous.
14. Blow hot and cold.
15. i. Tanzania, ii. Discus, iii. Shadrach, iv. Ermine, v. Larkspur, vi. Antelope.
16. Two sides to every story.
17. Feasible and possible.
18. Tit for tat.
19. Numb and sensitive.
20. Make.
21. AIR TREE = Eritrea (a country). The capital cities are Valetta (LATE VAT), Nairobi (ROBINIA), Nicosia (IN CASIO) and Colombo (LOCO MOB).
22. Salubrious and healthy.
23. Two heads are better than one.
24. Across: 1 Bisect, 6 Ooze, 7 Slalom, 9 Enigmatic, 11 Trying, 12 Bake, 13 Normal.
    Down: 2 Inland, 3 Enlighten, 4 Tom Sawyer, 5 Let, 8 Vienna, 10 Obi.
25. Law and order.

Solutions – Quick Fire

26. Writer and author.

27. Man.

28. Demon seaman.

29. Compromise.

30. Secondary.

31. Manic panic.

32. 4 months with 30 days.

33. Apple, cherry and peach.

34. Medium.

35. Resolute and doubtful.

36. Insinuate and impute.

37. Broad-minded.

38. Keeping my options open.

39. Please and offend.

40. Relation and oriental.

41. Fun and games.

42. i. Pewter, ii. Magenta, iii. Saucepan, iv. Handiwork.

43. Paint.

44. Stevie Wonder (anagram: Western Video).

45. Spear: the S moves from last to first as with the letter H in earth/heart.

46. Idolatry and Adroitly.

47. In someone's good books.

48. ENROL: each word commences with the last letter of the previous word. ENROL is missing from the list and should be placed between HINGE and LURID.

49. Chain.

50. Across: 1 Variable, 5 Lap, 6 Cider, 7 Anew, 9 Gate, 13 Sweep, 14 Oar, 15 Labrador.
Down: 1 Villa, 2 Rupee, 3 Arch, 4 Erect, 8 Newel, 10 Aloud, 11 Error, 12 Spur.

Solutions – More Challenging

51. Personality.
52. Crude and subtle.
53. Remember and overlook.
54. Nefarious and admirable.
55. Tractor: pat, fur, spa, arc, mat, duo, bar.
56. Synonyms: Censure and condemn; Antonym: Condone.
57. Grateful.
58. Part and parcel.
59. F(RING)E.
60. Sixteen pawns on a chess board.
61. Baseball: rib, sea, was, sue, tab, boa, nil, pal.
62. Peaceful and restless.
63. Tunnel.
64. CUP(BOAR)D.
65. Unforgivable.
66. Backseat driver.
67. Eradicate and eliminate.
68. Insult and praise.
69. Fast and furious.
70. RATEL: the letters move positions from 1,2,3,4,5 to 4,1,5,3,2.
71. Chalet and valet.
72. Microprocessor.
73. E – depicted (between the words ‘was’ and ‘in’).
74. Par.
75. Two wrongs don’t make a right.
76. PALNI = plain (or lapin).
77. N2. The letters rearranged in numerical order as shown spell out Enigmatic.
78. Creature Comforts.
79. Bulkhead, doldrums, navigate and maritime. Key anagram: Halliard.
80. Across: 2 Amp, 4 Bleat, 6 Meander, 8 Peas, 9 Slim, 11 Roar, 12 Loaf, 14 Mess, 15 Tier, 16 Feud, 18 Laze, 19 Draw, 21 Dace, 22 Emanant, 24 Plate, 25 Lie.
Down: 1 Omen, 2 Alas, 3 Pads, 4 Bear, 5 Tell, 6 Measure, 7 Riot act, 8 Posed, 10 Maize, 11 Ref, 13 Fee, 17 Damp, 18 Lane, 20 Wall, 21 Date, 23 Nail.
81. Mispronounce.
82. Synonyms: Mature and mellow; Antonym: Unripe.
83. Reading from the top, the words are: SAT, ARE, TEN and SET, ERA, TAN.
84. B – social (between the words ‘promote’ and ‘benefits’).
85. Atmospheric.
86. Reading from the top, the words are: HARSH, ATONE, ROYAL, SNAIL, HELLO.

Solutions – More Challenging

87. Across: 1 Lever, 6 Oomph, 7 Knell, 8 Loose, 9 Sioux, 12 Rebel, 13 Genoa, 14 Yield.
Down: 1 Lake, 2 Viewpoint, 3 Roll, 4 Immovable, 5 Shoe, 9 Sigh, 10 X-ray, 11 Glad.
88. Remnant and residue.
89. Refrigerator.
90. N = Range, Snack, Gnash and Arena.
91. Synonyms: Replete and satiated, Antonym: Empty.
92. Across: Unit and Visual. Down: Display.
93. Hand over fist.
94. Teach and train.
95. They all can be converted into a new word with the addition of one letter at the front: Emotion, gastronomically, vindicate, treasonable, devolution or revolution, cleaner.
96. Reading from the top, the words are: SEAT, EACH, ACHE and THEY.
97. In full cry.
98. United we stand, divided we fall
99. Integral, diameter, heptagon and negative. Keyword: Logarithm.
100. Across: Interior. Down: Decorator.
101. Across: 1 Rover, 6 Untie, 7 Noble, 8 Delft, 9 Monet, 12 Usage, 13 Veldt, 14 Upend.
Down: 1 Rink, 2 Vibrantly, 3 Rued, 4 Stalemate, 5 Belt, 9 Move, 10 Tutu, 11 Rend.
102. Misapprehend, comprehend, superintend and transcend.
103. Only two things are infinite, the universe and human stupidity, and I'm not sure about the former. Albert Einstein.
104. Orthopaedics.
105. From the top, the words read: Dance, About, North, Cutie and Ether.
106. F – often (between the words 'is' and 'regarded').
107. Antwerp, Rome and Tokyo.
108. Magnetic.
109. MIRPLA = primal.
110. All the way.
111. Minding my own business.
112. Once (from the centre of the third row from the bottom, read upwards and backwards).
113. Amortised and Mediators, Artesian and Erastian.
114. Up in arms.
115. Erroneous and correct.
116. Sincerity, Isinglass, Disinfect, Amusingly, Blessings, Promising and Wisconsin.
117. Across: 1 Pedal, 6 Ovule, 7 Llama, 8 Noisy, 9 Kayak, 12 Islet, 13 Paint, 14 Earth.
Down: 1 Palm, 2 Deadly sin, 3 Loan, 4 Funicular, 5 Deny, 9 Kept, 10 Kite, 11 Itch.
118. Platonic.
119. Nice work if you can get it.
120. Ordinary and peculiar.

Solutions – Difficult

121. Enlist, Strive, Vertex, Exodus, Usable, Lessen.

122. Laughter is the shortest distance between two people.

123. Reading from the top, the words are: LEMON, ERASE, MANIA, OSIER, NEARS.

124. Jump: all the words in the left column can be prefixed with 'high' and all those in the right column can be prefixed with 'low'.

125. Chemist, banker and plumber.

126. Infrared radiation can travel through a vacuum and it is in this form that the radiant heat of the sun travels through space.

127. Chemical analysis.

128. MOTHER APES = atmosphere. The forms of transportation are (in order): helicopter, automobile, steamboat, motorcycle.

129. KEY: GUL(F IND)EX PA(TH E)AT GOB(LIN K)EY.

130. NIORLDA = Ordinal (or nailrod).

131. Stone: All words can be prefixed with a type of fruit: applecart, banana split, date-line, plumage, limestone.

132. A fall in the temperature of the liquid, known as the cooling effect, accompanies evaporation because as the faster molecules escape through the surface the mean energy of the remaining molecules falls.

133. Ornately: moor/oral, tuna/nail, late/tend, lily/lyre.

134. MA(HOG)ANY.

135. Leotard.

136. B – to spell bend over backwards.

137. They can all be converted to birds with the addition of one letter: crow, dove, lark, tern, crane, drake, finch, heron, snipe, swift.

138. 2 lungs in the human body.

139. They all contain three successive letters of the alphabet in reverse: Elastic bands, Deutschemarks, The Red Cross, Punctuation marks, The garden of Eden, The Ballets Russes, That Monday morning feeling, Sponge cakes.

140. 1. ECHO: read the initial letters of each word line by line to reveal the command: CHOOSE ONE.

Solutions – Difficult

141. Plagiarist and Drain: The rest can be paired so that each five-letter word is an anagram of the last five letters of a 10-letter word: Align/Aboriginal, Demur/Kettledrum, Heard/Loggerhead, Irate/Expatriate.

142. Male-Masculine, Left-Larboard, Sign-Indication, Bulge-Protuberance, Green-Environmental, Extra-Supplement, Lost-Misplaced, Grain-Molecule, Deal-Transaction, Term-Expression.

143. Reaction and Feedback.

144. No name has a repeated letter.

145. Almost, Starch, Chapel, Elated, Edible, Lethal.

146.

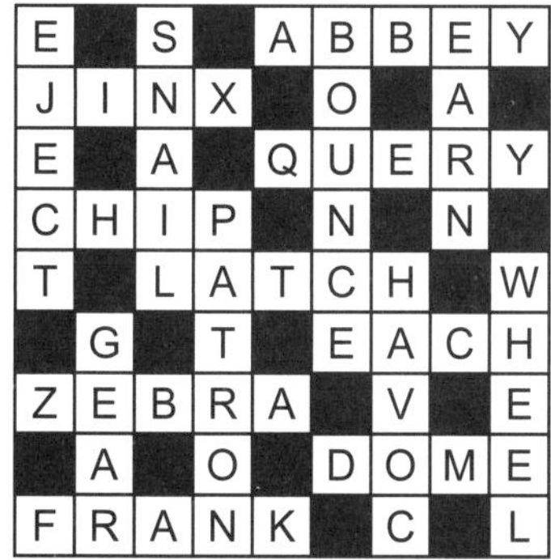

147. Trained chimpanzees can learn to communicate with humans with the aid of machines or sign language, but are probably precluded from human speech by the position of the voice-box.

148. Manuscript.

149. Macaroni and Ryebread: moor, away, case, Arab, rear, once, nova, iced.

150. Mechanical: some/meat, much/chin, mean/anon, chic/icon, seal/alto.

151. Planetarium, Observatory, Sagittarius, Declination. Keyword: Supernova.

152. Glad rags.

153. HSUB: it is a list of US Presidents with surnames of four letters, spelled in reverse.

154. The words Picture and Frame appear around the outer edge.

155. GAVE TAX RANT (Extravagant). The ANT words are Antithesis (tiniest ash), Antidote (to detain), Anticipate (captain tie) and Antecedent (decent neat).

156. EIGHTH: the third and sixth letters of each word are in the sequence AB, CD, EF and GH.

Solutions – Difficult

157. Cruiser and Dredger: cord, roar, urge, iced, song, ease, rear.

158. Teacher and instructor.

159. They all contain forms of transport: A(limo)ny, Inter(plane)tary, Con(trap)tion, Appli(cab)le.

160. Meteorology, Thunderclap, Anticyclone, Temperature. Keyword: Hurricane.

161. Phonetic and Alphabet.

162. C(HERO)OT.

163. Reading from the top, the words are: PAINS, AUDIT, IDLER, NIECE and STREW.

164. Chrome, Melody, Dynamo, Monkey, Eyelid, Idiocy, Cymbal, Allege, Geisha, Haunch.

165. A pendulum clock. It has a weight (bob) suspended at the end of a rod.

166. Anklet: it contains the name of an animal (elk) spelled backwards. The rest all contain the name of an animal (ape, cat, pig, gnu and rat) spelled forwards.

167. Make both ends meet.

168. Besotted, Beguiled and Obsessed.

169. Prince William Sound.

170. Cornerstone, Entablature, Antechamber, Scaffolding. Keyword: Cathedral.

171. Sixty degrees in each angle of an equilateral triangle.

172. Keeping the pot boiling.

173. FUNCTION: each word contains an internal synonym of the word it is equal to, so that insp<u>ire</u>d = indignation, s<u>pry</u>ness = eavesdrop, exe<u>cut</u>ive = abbreviate and na<u>use</u>ate = function.

174. CROCUS: the vowels AEIOU are being repeated.

175. Questionably.

176. History mystery.

177. MOON: all words can be prefixed with consecutive colours of the rainbow: Red Cross, orange blossom, yellow ribbon, green fingers, blue moon.

178. Antagonist.

179. The words Heavenly and Body appear around the outer edge.

180. MEASURABLE: same/melt, bias/ashy, four/urge, slab/abet, male/less.

Solutions – Difficult

181. An example of a natural optical illusion is that the Moon appears bigger when on the horizon than when it is high in the sky, due to the refraction of light rays by the Earth's atmosphere.

182. Springtime, Performance, Experimental, Ventriloquist, Claustrophobia, Professionalism.

183. The city is not a human jungle it is a human zoo.

184.

H	O	R	S	E		S		S	A	B	L	E
O		E		M	A	C	A	W		A		L
T	A	B	L	E		R		E	N	S	U	E
E		U		E	D	U	C	E		I		G
L	O	S	E	R		B		P	I	C	K	Y
	U		C						S		N	
P	S	A	L	M				E	S	T	O	P
	E		A						U		W	
F	L	U	T	E		A		S	E	I	N	E
R		N		X	E	N	O	N		N		N
E	D	I	C	T		G		E	X	E	R	T
S		T		R	E	E	V	E		R		E
H	Y	E	N	A		L		R	O	T	O	R

185. Saxophonist, Orchestrate, Arrangement, Harpsichord. Keyword: Harmonica.

Brain Fact

In vertebrates the brain is the portion of the central nervous system within the skull. Often referred to as *grey matter* it is, in humans, a mass of pink-grey tissue and weighs approximately 1.3 kg (3 lb).

Tests

Word Power Part 2 consists of two separate tests of verbal aptitude. Each test comprises 25 questions. Both tests are set at the same difficulty level.

Verbal reasoning tests are designed to measure the ability to understand and use words and typically include synonyms, antonyms, analogy, odd one out and verbal comprehension.

Because mastery of words is regarded by many as having in one's possession the ability to produce order out of chaos, it is argued that command of vocabulary is seen as a true measure of intelligence with the result that verbal tests are widely used in IQ (Intelligence Quotient) testing.

The following is a brief explanation of some of the more common types of question and terminology used in the formation of verbal IQ tests.

Synonym:
A synonym is a word having the same meaning as another word in the same language.
Examples of synonyms are chase/pursue, apt/relevant and pull/tug.

Question:
Which word in brackets is the closest in meaning to the word in capitals?
SENSIBLE (clever, rational, steady, lavish, open)
Answer:
Rational is the word closest in meaning to the keyword SENSIBLE.

Antonym:
An antonym is a word having the opposite meaning to another word in the same language.
Examples of antonyms are big/small, careless/heedful and happy/sad.

Question:
Which two words are the most opposite in meaning?
SLOW CALM UNSAFE AGITATED LONELY STRICT
Answer:
Calm and agitated are the most opposite in meaning.

Analogy:
An analogy is a comparison in which it is necessary to find a similar relationship in two parallel cases.

Question:
WRITE is to PEN as PAINT is to (INK, PAPER, CANVAS, BRUSH, WALL)
Answer:
Brush has the same relationship to paint as pen has to write because one writes with a pen and paints with a brush.

For each of the two 25-question tests that follow, a time limit of 30 minutes per test is allowed.

Before attempting the two tests you may like to work through the four practice questions below, the answers to which are to be found at the foot of this page.

1.
CHAPTER is to BOOK as ACT is to: STAGE, THESPIAN, PLAY, AUDIENCE, PRETEND

2.
Which word in brackets is the closest in meaning to the word in capitals?
SURPLUS (outcome, mole, glut, robe, cure)

3.
What letter can be added to the words HARE and TAKE to produce two words which have the same meaning?

4.
Which word in brackets is the most opposite in meaning to the word in capitals?
DEFLATE (elucidate, enjoy, sidetrack, expand, chaste)

Answers:
1. Play (a chapter is a division of a book and an act is a division of a play), 2. Glut, 3. The letter S; to produce share and stake, 4. Expand.

Test 1

1. Identify two words (one from each set of brackets) that form a connection (analogy), thereby relating to the words in capitals in the same way.

MOON (satellite, orbit, lunar)
SUN (heat, solar, aureole)

2. Find two words from the clues provided that differ only by the omission of a single letter.

Clue: Locality
Clue: Velocity

3. Which two words are the closest in meaning?

IMPETUOUS RAVENOUS
EXPANSIVE INSATIABLE
ENRAPTURED ACQUIESCENT

4. Which word in brackets is most opposite in meaning to the word in capitals?

CONTEMPORARY (unthinking, unattractive, antique, rare, intangible)

5. Which word in brackets is the closest in meaning to the word in capitals?

CELEBRANT (dignitary, rival, priest, tutor, praise)

6. Which two words are the most opposite in meaning?

PROLIX PITHY COMICAL
CARING SPRITE CLEAR

7. Change the position of four words only in the paragraph below in order for it to make complete sense literally and grammatically.

Shamrocks have been considered by the Irish has good-luck symbols since modern times, and this superstition as persisted in earliest times among people of many nationalities.

8. What is an ACOLYTE?

A. a small segment of meat on a skewer

B. an administrative officer

C. a bulb of the snowdrop family

D. a follower or disciple

E. synthetic resin

Test 1

9. Identify two words (one from each set of brackets) that form a connection (analogy), thereby relating to the words in capitals in the same way.

RATION (amount, limit, size)
TEMPER (moderate, regret, confine)

10. Which two words are the most opposite in meaning?

TIMID SPIRITUAL UNCANNY PHYSICAL MORIBUND ISOLATED

11. Which two words are the closest in meaning?

APPEAR ATOLL SEAM MARK POINT JOINT

12. Place a word in the brackets that has the same meaning as the definitions either side of the brackets.

GUIDE ( ) OUTSPOKEN

13. Select two words that are synonyms, plus an antonym of these two synonyms, from the list of words below.

ENGAGING LISTLESS ENERVATED INTREPID INSIDIOUS ENERGETIC SMART

14. Change one letter only in each of the words below to produce a familiar phrase.

FIVE SHE GAVE SWAY

15. Change the position of four words only in the paragraph below in order for it to make complete sense literally and grammatically.

The portal is usually surmounted by rose spires, and the twin window set above the central façade provides a focus for the whole west front.

16. Select two words that are synonyms, plus an antonym of these two synonyms, from the list of words below.

SINCERE CREDULOUS ANALYTICAL DISHONEST CYNICAL GULLIBLE HOPEFUL

Test 1

17. CONCEPT is to NOTION as PREOCCUPATION is to : IDEA, WHIM, VAGARY, FIXATION, PREMISE

18. Which word in brackets is the closest in meaning to the word in capitals?

CAVIL (leap, call, dispute, gap, grade)

19. Identify two words (one from each set of brackets) that form a connection (analogy), thereby relating to the words in capitals in the same way.

CONNIVE (hinder, scheme, support)
FACILITATE (expedite, comfort, enlist)

20. Put the following words in alphabetical order:

ABSORBENCY, ABSOLUTION, ABSOLUTIST, ABSORPTIVE, ABSOLUTELY, ABSORPTION, ABSOLUTISM

21. Which is the odd one out?

INVOLUNTARY DISINCLINED RETICENT COMPLIANT TACITURN

22. Which word in brackets is the most opposite in meaning to the word in capitals?

PLAUSIBLE (tenable, frivolous, repulsive, authentic, unlikely)

23. Identify two words (one from each set of brackets) that form a connection (analogy), thereby relating to the words in capitals in the same way.

HIPPOPHOBIA (horses, monkeys, cattle)
ENTOMOPHOBIA (sharks, insects, fish)

24. Which word in brackets is the closest in meaning to the word in capitals?

OBSTRUCTIVE (obvious, restrictive, annoying, unfair, restive)

25. Which word in brackets is the most opposite in meaning to the word in capitals?

NEGATE (appreciate, ratify, prove, join, supply)

Test 2

1. Identify two words (one from each set of brackets) that form a connection (analogy), thereby relating to the words in capitals in the same way.

EPIGRAPH (stone, wording, monument)
EFFIGY (person, plinth, inscription)

2. Which two words are the most opposite in meaning?

WORKABLE POTENT SWEET WEAK HEAVY UNSOUND

3. Which two words are the closest in meaning?

CONDESCEND INVEST VOUCHSAFE ASSUME CHANGE INTERDICT

4. Which word in brackets is the closest in meaning to the word in capitals?

ASCERTAIN (emphasize, determine, originate, regulate, attribute)

5. Select two words that are synonyms, plus an antonym of these two synonyms, from the list of words below.

OCEANIC TERRITORIAL PACIFIC VIOLENT GRANDIOSE MANIFEST SERENE

6. Which well known phrase rhymes with the words REVEALING AND PEELING (as in FIGHT AND PLAY / NIGHT AND DAY)?

7. Identify two words (one from each set of brackets) that form a connection (analogy), thereby relating to the words in capitals in the same way.

MILITARY (weapons, protect, martial)
ORGANIZE (marshal, troops, clarify)

8. Change the position of four words in the passage below in order for it to make complete sense.

Continuing to write in a fashionable, eccentric vein, he frequented fanciful salons and dressed in an romantic manner.

Test 2

9. WHERE is to PARIS as WHEN is to: TRAIN, SOON, HOW, MAYBE, WHERE

10. Which word in brackets is the most opposite in meaning to the word in capitals?

ROUTINE (devious, irregular, illogical, volatile, corporeal)

11. Select two words that are synonyms, plus an antonym of these two synonyms, from the list of words below.

UNREALISTIC FINE FORWARD
ACCURATE PRECOCIOUS
UNRESPONSIVE SARCASTIC

12. Put the following words in alphabetical order.

ABSORBED, ABSENTLY,
ABSCISSA, ABSTRUSE,
ABSENTEE, ABSINTHE,
ABSTRACT, ABSOLUTE

13. Which is the odd one out?

BOFFIN NEOPHYTE GOURMET
AUTHORITY PUNDIT

14. Which two words are the most opposite in meaning?

WIDESPREAD RAPID
NARROW TUMULTUOUS
FIERCE SPORADIC

15. Identify two words (one from each set of brackets) that form a connection (analogy), thereby relating to the words in capitals in the same way.

KINETICS (pressure, motion, mechanics)
DYNAMICS (force, physics, strain)

16. Which word in brackets is closest in meaning to the word in capitals?

FINESSE (semblance, acerbity, beauty, panache, spirit)

17. Which word in brackets is most opposite in meaning to the word in capitals?

COMPLEMENTARY (incongruous, reciprocal, disparaging, intricate, uneasy)

Test 2

18. What word can be placed in the brackets so that it forms another word or phrase when tacked onto the end of the first word, and another word or phrase when placed in front of the second word?

BATTLE ( ) FLUSH

19. Which two words are the most opposite in meaning?

RETIRING ASSIDUOUS
SWEET NEGLIGENT
HOMOGENEOUS BANAL

20. Which two words are the closest in meaning?

EXTEMPORIZE IMPUGN
INSULT CRITICIZE
SQUANDER INVEST

21. Find two words from the clues provided that differ only by the omission of a single letter.

Clue: Human being
Clue: Ethical

22. Which two words are the closest in meaning?

SUNDRY FISCAL ANNULAR
MONASTIC MONETARY
PRUDENT

23. TIMELY is to OPPORTUNE as APPOSITE is to: VALID, PERTINENT, INAPPROPRIATE, CONTRARY, RELIABLE

24. Change the position of four words in the paragraph below in order for it to make complete sense.

Pressure is measured equally in all techniques in air and may be transmitted using a variety of directions.

25. What is the meaning of COMESTIBLE?

A. ignitable
B. edible
C. argumentative
D. pleasurable
E. lying along the same line

Solutions Test 1

1. Lunar and solar.
2. Place and pace.
3. Ravenous and insatiable.
4. Antique.
5. Priest.
6. Prolix and pithy.
7. Shamrocks have been considered by the Irish AS good-luck symbols since EARLIEST times, and this superstition HAS persisted in MODERN times among people of many nationalities.
8. D – a follower or disciple.
9. Limit and moderate.
10. Spiritual and physical.
11. Seam and joint.
12. Direct.
13. Synonyms: Listless and enervated; Antonym: Energetic.
14. Give the game away.
15. The FAÇADE is usually surmounted by TWIN spires, and the ROSE window set above the central PORTAL provides a focus for the whole west front.
16. Synonyms: Credulous and gullible; Antonym: Cynical.
17. Fixation.
18. Dispute.
19. Scheme and expedite.
20. Absolutely, absolution, absolutism, absolutist, absorbency, absorption, absorptive.
21. Compliant: it is a willing word, the rest are unwilling words.
22. Unlikely.
23. Horses and insects.
24. Restrictive.
25. Ratify.

Performance Rating

Score 1 point for each correct answer

Total Score	Rating	Percentage of Population
20 / 25	Genius level	Top 5%
18 / 21	High Expert	Top 10%
15 / 17	Expert	Top 30%
13 / 14	High Average	Top 40%
11 / 12	Middle Average	Top 60%
9 / 10	Low Average	Bottom 40%
7 / 8	Borderline Low	Bottom 30%
5 / 6	Low	Bottom 10%
0 / 4	Very Low	Bottom 5%

Transfer your score to the chart in the Assessment Section on page 302.

Brain Fact

The two hemispheres of the brain are highly specialized and serve opposite sides of the body. A touch on the right side of the body, for example, is perceived by the left somatosensory area and to move the right arm, neurons in the left motor cortex have to be activated. For most people the left side of the brain is the more dominant, which explains why most people are right-handed.

Solutions Test 2

1. Wording and person.
2. Potent and weak.
3. Condescend and vouchsafe.
4. Determine.
5. Synonyms: Pacific and serene; Antonym: Violent.
6. Wheeling and dealing.
7. Martial and marshal.
8. Continuing to write in a FANCIFUL, ROMANTIC vein, he frequented FASHIONABLE salons and dressed in an ECCENTRIC manner.
9. Soon.
10. Irregular.
11. Synonyms: Precocious and forward; Antonym: Unresponsive.
12. Abscissa, absentee, absently, absinthe, absolute, absorbed, abstract, abstruse.
13. Neophyte: it is a novice; the rest are experts.
14. Widespread and sporadic.
15. Motion and force.
16. Panache.
17. Incongruous.
18. Royal.
19. Assiduous and negligent.
20. Impugn and criticize.
21. Mortal and moral.
22. Fiscal and monetary.
23. Pertinent.
24. Pressure is TRANSMITTED equally in all DIRECTIONS in air and may be MEASURED using a variety of TECHNIQUES.
25. B – edible.

Performance Rating

Score 1 point for each correct answer

Total Score	Rating	Percentage of Population
20 / 25	Genius level	Top 5%
18 / 21	High Expert	Top 10%
15 / 17	Expert	Top 30%
13 / 14	High Average	Top 40%
11 / 12	Middle Average	Top 60%
9 / 10	Low Average	Bottom 40%
7 / 8	Borderline Low	Bottom 30%
5 / 6	Low	Bottom 10%
0 / 4	Very Low	Bottom 5%

Transfer your score to the chart in the Assessment Section on page 302.

Brain Fact

The brain relies on the five senses for the bulk of its information on the world outside its domain. Because of the importance of this role, human perception is extremely acute. Scientific research has revealed that the nose can detect one molecule of gas, while a cell in the retina of the eye is sensitive to one photon of light.

Puzzles

The philosopher and mathematician Bertrand Russell once said: "Mathematics may be defined as the subject in which we never know what we are talking about, nor whether what we are saying is true."

> eXpeCt the DeVIL
>
> X + C + D + V + I + L = 666

Mathematics is an exact science, and there is but one solution to a correctly set calculation or puzzle. There may, however, be different ways at arriving at a solution, some more laborious than others. The subject of mathematics can be challenging, fascinating, confusing and at times frustrating, but once you have developed an interest in the science of numbers a whole new world is opened up as you discover their many characteristics and patterns.

> The square of the hypotenuse of a right-angled triangle is equal to the sum of the squares on the other two sides.
>
> Pythagoras' Theorem

For many adults whose school days were plagued by an intense case of maths phobia, mathematics remains a dreaded subject. But there is no need for this to be the case, especially if fear factor is replaced by fun factor, as anything that becomes fun is then an enjoyable experience.

We all require some mathematical skills in our lives, whether it is to calculate our shopping bill on a visit to the supermarket or to budget how to use our monthly income, but for many people mathematics is a subject they regard as being too difficult when confronted by what are considered to be its higher branches. When broken down and analysed, and explained in layman's terms, however, many of these aspects can be readily understood by those with only a rudimentary grasp of the subject.

> If mathematically you end up with the incorrect answer, try multiplying by the page number.
>
> Murphy's Ninth Law

There is little doubt that proficiency with numbers can increase dramatically with constant practise. Think about the top darts players we see on television; the players and referees have the ability to calculate scores instantaneously. At the moment the last of the three darts thuds into the board, the referee announces the score for the three darts and deducts this from the previous total just as quickly. A player has to finish on a double to win a particular round. When he comes to the oche wanting a score of 174, for example, a player knows he cannot finish on a double. However, he calculates immediately that if he hits treble 20, treble 19 and 25 with his three darts, he will leave himself on double 16 and in with a very good chance of success with one dart on his next visit to the oche.

142857 x 1 = 142857

142857 x 2 = 285714

142857 x 3 = 428571

142857 x 4 = 571428

142857 x 5 = 714285

142857 x 6 = 857142

142857 x 7 = 999999

The reason why players possess these apparently astonishing powers of calculation is, of course, very simple. During their career they have performed similar calculations many thousands of times and can thus do the computations faster than if they were using a hand-held calculating machine.

The puzzles in this section are all designed to encourage readers to Think Numerically and to increase confidence when working with numbers. Many of the puzzles are challenging, but deliberately so, as the more you practise on this type of puzzle, the more you will come to understand the methodology and thought processes necessary to solve them, develop the power to identify relationships between numbers, and think logically and laterally when necessary.

4	9	8	47	48	49	10
38	19	20	17	34	35	12
39	37	26	27	22	13	11
43	36	21	25	29	14	7
6	18	28	23	24	32	44
5	15	30	33	16	31	45
40	41	42	3	2	1	46

I'm very well acquainted too with matters mathematical,
I understand equations both the simple and quadratical.

W S Gilbert

Quick Fire

1. 4 8 2 9 6 3 8 1 7 4 2 9 8 7 6

What is the sum (total) of all the odd numbers that are immediately preceded by an even number in the list above?

2.

3	1	4
2	5	1
3	2	?

What number should replace the question mark?

3. 3 6 9 2 1 5 8 7 3 5 8

Strike out all the odd numbers in the above list and multiply the remaining numbers together.

Now take this total and repeat the process, striking out the odd number(s) and multiplying the remaining numbers together.

What number remains?

4. 100 96 88 72 40 ?

What number should replace the question mark in order to continue the sequence?

5. What is double one half of 9826?

6. 10 10 11 13 16 ?

What number should replace the question mark in order to continue the sequence?

7. Three coins are tossed in the air at the same time. What are the chances that at least two of the coins will finish heads up?

8. How many cases do you need if you have to pack 148 pairs of shoes into cases that each hold 37 shoes?

9. Divide 120 by a quarter and add 15. What is the result?

Quick Fire

10.

7	3	6	4	1
2	6	9	7	4
9	4	?	6	9
6	7	3	3	4
1	4	3	2	3

What number should replace the question mark?

11. Bill and Jill had 105 between them; however, Jill had one and a half times as many as Bill. How many had each?

12. Looking at straight lines of numbers either horizontally, vertically or diagonally, what number is three places away from itself plus 5, two places away from itself minus 4, two places away from itself minus 3 and two places away from itself divided by 2?

5	12	4	16
6	3	15	14
8	1	2	13
7	9	10	21

13. At 11.00am today my watch was showing the correct time, after which it began to lose 14 minutes per hour until three hours ago when it stopped completely.

It is now wrongly showing the time as 2.50pm. What is the correct time now?

14. Harry, Barry and Larry wish to share out a certain sum of money between them. Harry gets 2/5, Barry gets 0.45 and Larry gets £840.00. How much is the original amount of money?

Quick Fire

15. 1 2 5 14 41 ?

What number should replace the question mark?

16. 9 2 6 3 5 1 7 8 6 2 9 3

What is the sum (total) of all the numbers in the above list that are immediately followed by an even number?

17.

49	12	25	11
3	8	64	9
81	24	6	4
36	5	16	14

What is the difference between the square of the lowest cube number and the cube of the lowest square number in the array of numbers above?

18.

78	(52)	3
75	(30)	5
96	(?)	8

What number should replace the question mark?

19. Gordon buys £600.00 worth of wallpaper and Alistair buys £120.00 worth of paint for their new adjoining offices. If they decide to split the cost evenly how much does Alistair owe Gordon?

20. In my fruit bowl all but nine fruit are oranges, all but nine are apples, all but nine are grapefruit and all but nine are pears.

How many pieces of fruit do I have in my fruit bowl?

21. What number gives the same total when added to 3 as when multiplied by 3?

22. In 45 minutes it will be twice as many minutes past 9.00am as it is minutes before 9.00am now. What time is it now?

23. What is the weight of a bag of potatoes if it weighs 50 kg divided by half its own weight?

Quick Fire

24. What number should replace the question mark?

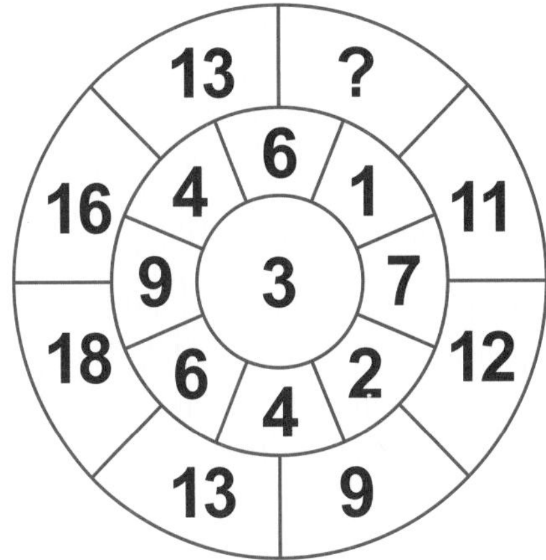

25.

3	4	6	9
		9	12
8	9		14
9	10	12	

Which is the missing section?

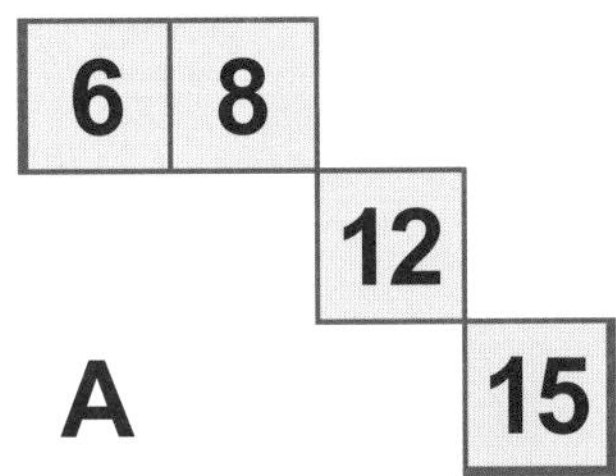

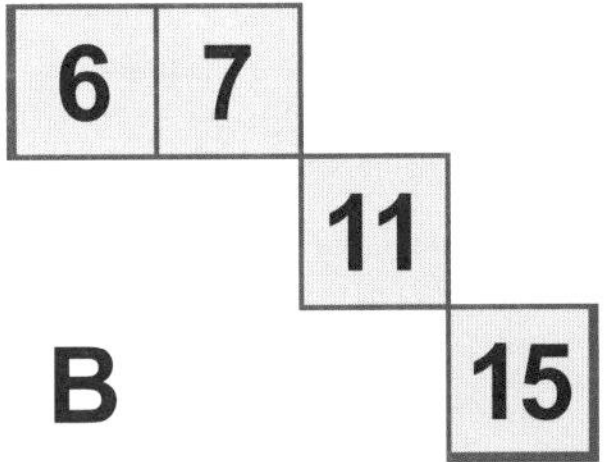

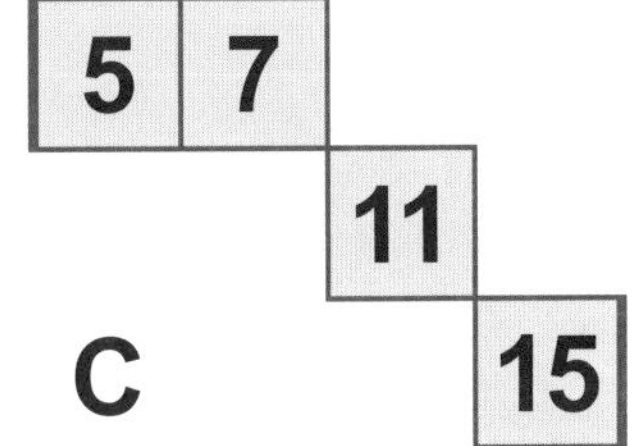

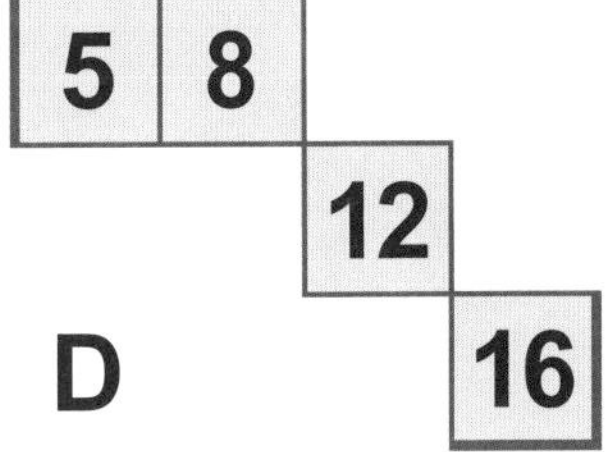

Quick Fire

26. I am four times as old as my son. In 20 years from now I will be twice as old as my son. How old are we today?

27. 100 99 96 91 84 ? 64

What number should replace the question mark?

28.

The five rings of the Olympic Flag are Blue, Black, Red, Yellow and Green in that order. In how many different ways could the five rings have been arranged in addition to the order shown above?

29.

4	7	3
5	?	4
9	?	7

Which are the two missing numbers?

A	B	C	D
8	9	8	9
15	16	16	15

30. What is the only number that is twice the sum of its digits (for example the number 48 is four times the sum of its digits 4 + 8 = 12 and 12 x 4 = 48)?

31. 0.65 0.65 ? 1.95 2.6 3.25

What number should replace the question mark?

32. 7 6 1 3 5 4 1 7 4 2 4

What is the difference between the average of all the numbers above and the average of all the even numbers in the list?

33. The combined age of Harry and Sally is 25. Two years ago, Harry was twice as old as Sally. How old will Harry be when Sally is 10?

Quick Fire

34. Two golfers were discussing what might have been after they had played a par 5.

"If I had taken one shot less and you had taken one shot more, we would have shared the hole," remarked Ernie.

"Yes," replied Colin, "and if I had taken one shot less and you had taken one shot more you would have taken twice as many shots as me."

How many shots did each take?

35. A ball is dropped to the ground from a height of 12 feet. It then bounces up half the original height, then falls to the ground again. It repeats this, always bouncing back half its previous height. How far does it travel (round up the answer to the nearest foot)?

36. The clock tower at Birmingham University, known as Old Joe, or Chamberlain's Clock Tower, stands 164 feet high plus half its own height. How high is Old Joe?

37. At a car boot sale I purchased 12 CDs for exactly £12.00. Some were £0.50 each, some were £1.50 each and some were £2 each. How many CDs at each price did I buy?

38. A company offers a wage increase providing it increases production by 2.5% per week. If the company works a five and a half day week, by how much per day on average must the workforce increase production to achieve the desired target?

39. Find five consecutive numbers which total 21 from those in the list below.

7 5 2 9 6 1 4 2 7 9 4 2 1 3 6 8 3 2 3 4 8 5

40.

	684927	is to	864279
and	315928	is to	821359
as	694253	is to	?

41. A market trader took delivery of a box of eggs and was disgruntled to find that 56 were cracked, which was eight per cent of the total quantity of eggs in the box. How many eggs were in the box?

42. 99 97 93 ? 79 69 57

What number should replace the question mark?

Quick Fire

43.

What number should replace the question mark to correctly complete the equation?

4	5	6	7	9
A	B	C	D	E

44.

On which target below has 155 been scored according to the score indicator to the left?

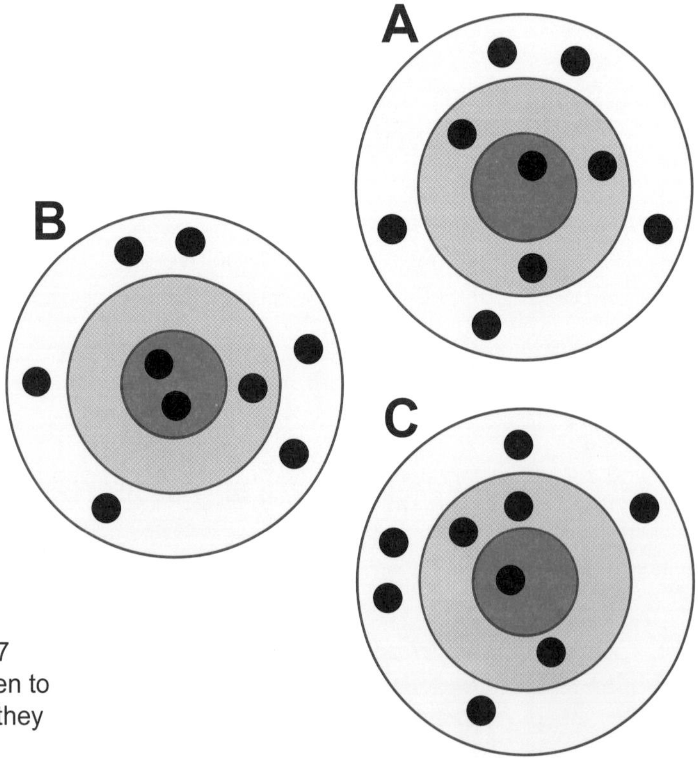

A

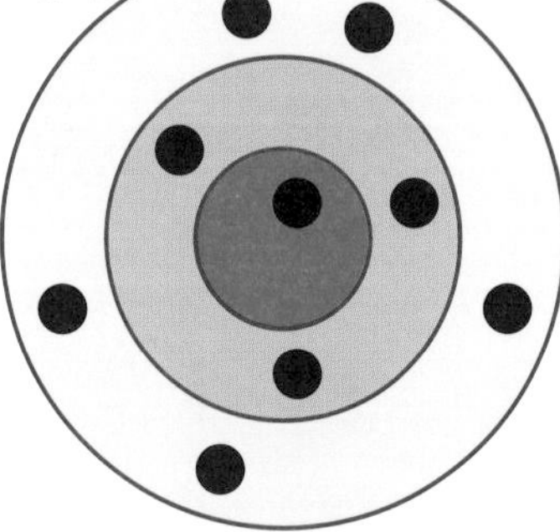

B

C

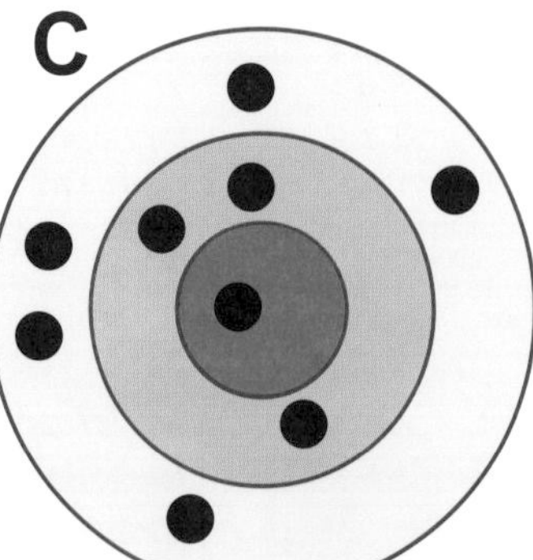

45. If five men can build a house in 27 days, how long will it take nine men to build the same house, assuming they all work at the same rate?

Quick Fire

46. What number is 35 less than when multiplied by eight times itself?

47. A photograph measuring 9.5 cm by 7.5 cm is to be enlarged. If the enlargement of the longest side is 11.4 cm, what is the length of the smallest side?

48.

2	5	1	3	6	2		5	3	6	2	4	2
3	7	4	7	11	8		?	?	?	?	?	?

The top set of six numbers has a relationship to the set of six numbers below. The two sets of six boxes on the left have the same relationship as the two sets of six boxes on the right.

Which set of numbers should, therefore, replace the question marks?

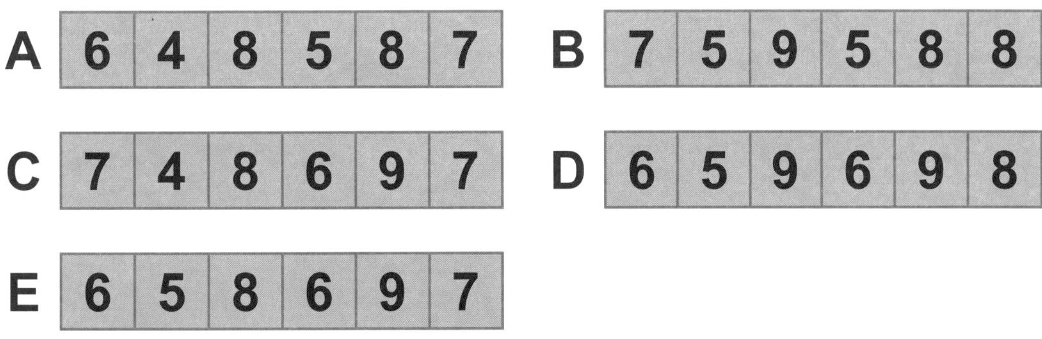

A	6	4	8	5	8	7
B	7	5	9	5	8	8
C	7	4	8	6	9	7
D	6	5	9	6	9	8
E	6	5	8	6	9	7

49. Identify the only two numbers between 50 and 100 which meet the following criteria:
- both are divisible by three;
- both are odd numbers;
- when the digits of either number are added together the total is between 10 and 15;
- when the digits of either number are multiplied together the total is between 30 and 40.

50. Two years ago I was one and a half times as old as my brother. Five years from now I will be one and a third times as old. In how many years from now will I be one and a quarter times as old as my brother?

More Challenging

51.

6	2	7		5	3	7
5	2	6		7	2	8
8	1	8		6	8	?

Each set of nine numbers relates to each other in a certain way. Work out the logic behind the numbers in the left-hand box in order to determine which number is missing from the right-hand box.

52.

$$\frac{\sqrt{49} \times (4 + 2)}{?} = \frac{264 - 168}{3^3 - \sqrt{121}}$$

Complete the equation by correctly identifying the missing part of the calculation from the list of options below.

A $2^3 - 2$ **B** $2 + 2^3$ **C** $\sqrt{36} + \sqrt{4}$ **D** $27 - 2^4$ **E** $23 - 2^4$

53. In a game of eight players lasting for 55 minutes, three reserves alternate equally with each player. This means that all players, including the reserves are on the field of play for exactly the same length of time. For how long?

54. In the two numerical sequences below, one number that appears in the top sequence should appear in the bottom sequence and vice versa. Which two numbers should be changed round?

18 33 48 62 75 87

17 35 51 66 80 93

55. At the end of the day one market stall has 9 cabbages and 6 cauliflowers left. Another market stall has 4 cabbages and 12 cauliflowers left.

What is the difference between the percentages of cabbages left in each market stall?

56. 1 4 18 87 431 ?

What number should replace the question mark to continue the sequence?

More Challenging

57.

In this puzzle, the assumption is made that trains arrive at their destination precisely on time. The puzzle, therefore, can only work in theory!

My wife usually leaves work at 5.00pm calls at the supermarket, then catches the 5.30pm train which arrives at our local station at 18.00 hours. I leave home each day, drive to the station and pick up my wife at 6.00pm, just as she gets off the train.

One day last week my wife was able to finish five minutes earlier than usual, decided to go straight to the station and managed to catch the 5.00pm train, which arrived at our local station at 5.30pm. Because I was not there to pick her up she began to walk home. I left home at the usual time, saw my wife walking, turned round and picked her up and drove home arriving there 10 minutes earlier than usual.

For how long did my wife walk before I picked her up?

58.

5	4	7	8	6	3		7	9	8	2	5	3
10	2	14	4	3	6		?	?	?	?	?	?

The top set of six numbers has a relationship to the set of six numbers below. The two sets of six boxes on the left have the same relationship as the two sets of six boxes on the right. Which set of numbers should, therefore, replace the question marks?

A	21	18	24	4	15	6
B	14	18	16	4	10	6
C	14	18	4	1	10	6
D	16	20	4	1	14	8
E	16	20	16	6	12	8

More Challenging

59. The average of three numbers is 26.

The average of two of these numbers is 31.

What is the third number?

60. Change the position of four numbers only to create a magic number square in which each horizontal row, vertical column and corner to corner line totals 34.

1	12	14	13
15	2	10	3
8	7	11	6
4	9	5	16

61. A man has 35 socks in his drawer, 12 identically blue, 9 identically grey and 14 identically black.

The lights have fused leaving him completely in the dark.

How many socks must he take out of the drawer to be 100% certain that he has a pair of each colour?

62. Which two numbers should replace the question marks?

?	
25	17
76	35
229	?
688	143

63. 3 6 11 ? ? 54 59 118

Which two numbers should replace the question marks?

64. Calculate the value of:

$$\left(\frac{481}{962}\right)^2 \times 468$$

65. 87963 63978 78936 36987 ?

What comes next?

More Challenging

66.

12	27	32	81	94	16		42	86	17	25	63	45
3	9	5	9	13	7		?	?	?	?	?	?

The top set of six numbers has a relationship to the set of six numbers below. The two sets of six boxes on the left have the same relationship as the two sets of six boxes on the right.

Which set of numbers should, therefore, replace the question marks?

A 6 14 8 7 9 9

B 8 48 7 10 18 20

C 6 14 8 9 7 9

D 8 16 8 9 7 9

E 6 14 8 9 7 7

67. If at each stage the black dot moves three segments clockwise and the white dot moves four places anticlockwise, after how many stages will both dots be in the same segment?

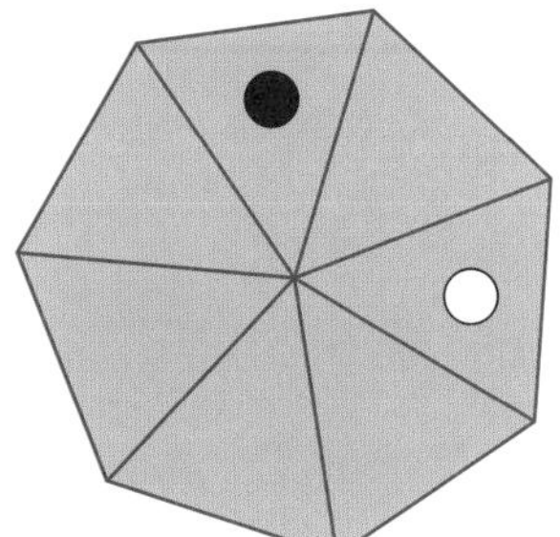

68. What number should replace the question mark?

2	1	1	2
3	1	2	2
1	3	2	4
4	1	2	?

More Challenging

69.

1	3	6	8	11
4	6		11	14
6	8	11		16
9	11		16	19
11		16		21

Which is the missing section?

A

	10	
		13
	14	
14		18

B

	9	
		13
	14	
13		18

C

	10	
		14
	13	
14		17

D

	9	
		14
	13	
13		17

70.

62 (3) 49
92 (4) 98
17 (?) 87

What number should replace the question mark?

71. What is

$3\frac{3}{4} \div 3\frac{5}{8}$

72. What is the length of the shortest side of a right-angled triangle if its two longest sides are 63 cm and 65 cm respectively?

73. How many minutes is it before midnight if eight minutes ago it was three times as many minutes after 9.00pm?

74. 2.5 25 7.9 ? ? 16 18.7 11.5

What two numbers should replace the question marks?

75. 2 6 9 3 8 6 4 7 6 9 1 7 3 5 ?

What number should replace the question mark?

More Challenging

76. 7 15 31 63 127 ?

What number should replace the question mark?

77. Which number is the odd one out?

4688 1342 5786 7639
4955 7892 4672

78. What number should replace the question mark?

	5	
4	6	7

	13	
8	4	9

	8	
7	11	?

79. In 12 years' time the combined age of my four cousins will be 72. What will be the combined age of my four cousins in seven years' time?

80. 72 (84) 36 27 (36) 54

45 (?) 81

What number should replace the question mark?

81. In the two numerical sequences below, one number that appears in the left sequence should appear in the right sequence and vice versa. Which two numbers should be changed round?

12 19 32 54 82 117 14 20 33 50 74 104

82.

$$\frac{102 \div 1.5}{4} = \frac{76.5}{?}$$

Complete the equation by correctly identifying the missing part of the calculation from the list of options below.

A 6.7 – 2.3 **B** 2.1^2 **C** 5.5 **D** 0.5 x $\sqrt{81}$ **E** 0.75 x $\sqrt{64}$

More Challenging

83.

4	5	3	4	2
7	8	6		5
5			5	
	9	7	8	6
6	7	5	6	4

Which is the missing section?

A

			8	
	6	7		3
7				

B

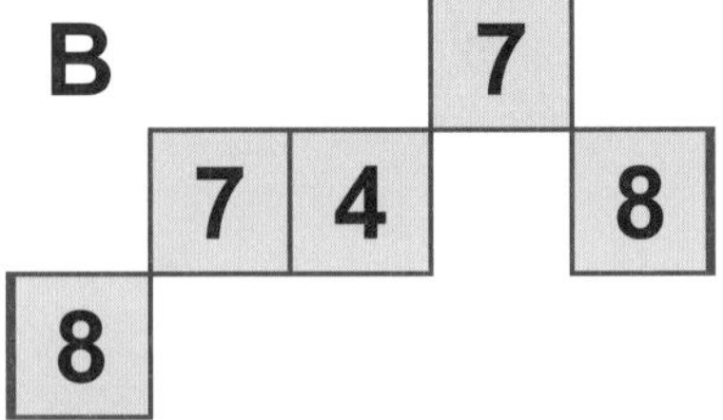

C

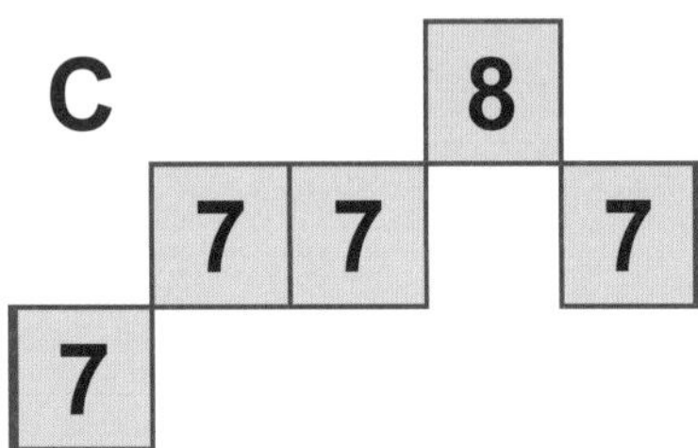

D

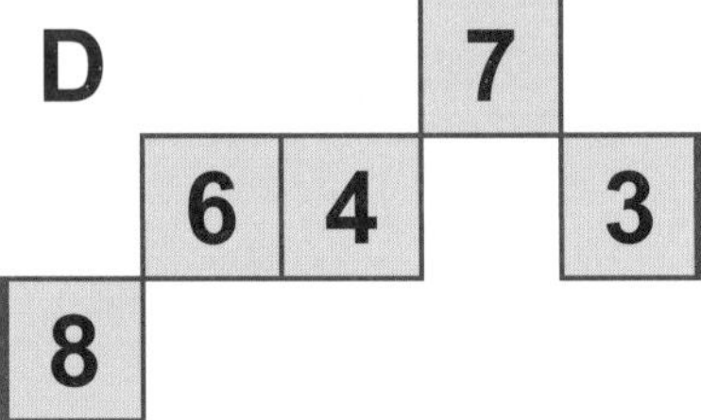

84. Find the smallest two-digit number which is one less than twice its reverse (for example, 21 is three less than twice its reverse, ie 12 x 2 = 24).

85. Which is the largest fraction?

$\frac{6}{9}$ $\frac{12}{27}$ $\frac{11}{18}$

86. A car travels a motorway journey at an average speed of 60 miles per hour and returns on exactly the same route at an average speed of 40 miles per hour. What is the average speed of the car for the whole journey?

More Challenging

87. 469257 296412 ? 9645 699

What number is missing?

88. Looking in straight lines horizontally, vertically or diagonally, what number is two places away from itself multiplied by 3, three places away from itself plus 4 and two places away from itself less 2?

2	16	13	15	22
28	20	11	1	33
4	5	21	12	9
10	18	17	6	14
8	3	7	19	27

89. What is the length of the hypotenuse of a right-angled triangle the two shortest sides of which are 15 cm and 36 cm respectively?

90. In the two numerical sequences below, one number that appears in the top sequence should appear in the bottom sequence and vice versa. Which two numbers should be changed round?

10 14 22 38 50 70

11 17 26 34 53 71

91. What number should replace the question mark?

7

? 8

92. What number should replace the question mark?

5	8	2	3
2	7	6	5
9	1	7	1
4	2	5	?

More Challenging

93. 1 1 5 3 10 6 16 10 ? ? Which two numbers continue the sequence?

94. What is the value of:

$$\frac{5}{9} \div \frac{7}{18}$$

95. In my fish tank I have 15 measle fish. The male measle fish have 81 spots each and the female measle fish 27 spots each. If I take out two-thirds of the male fish how many spots in total will remain in my fish tank?

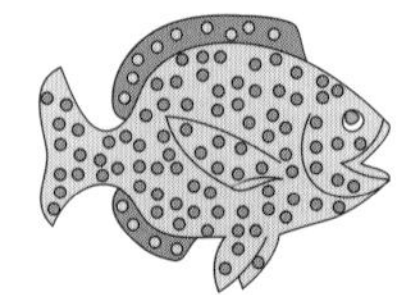

96.

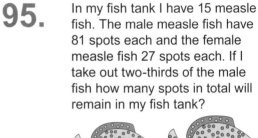

3		5	7	9
	6		9	11
7	8	9		13
8	9		12	14
9	10	11	13	15

Which is the missing section?

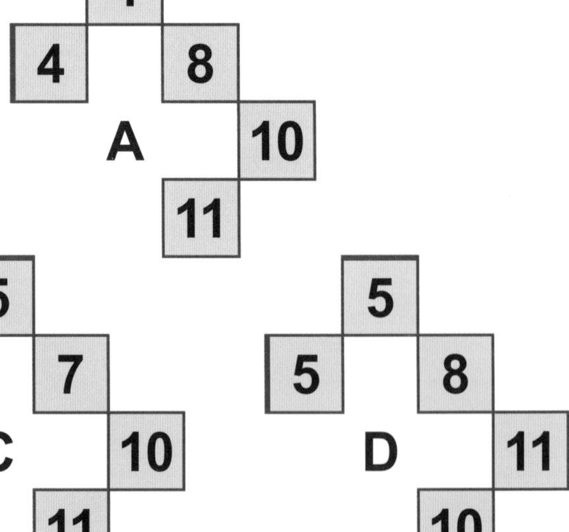

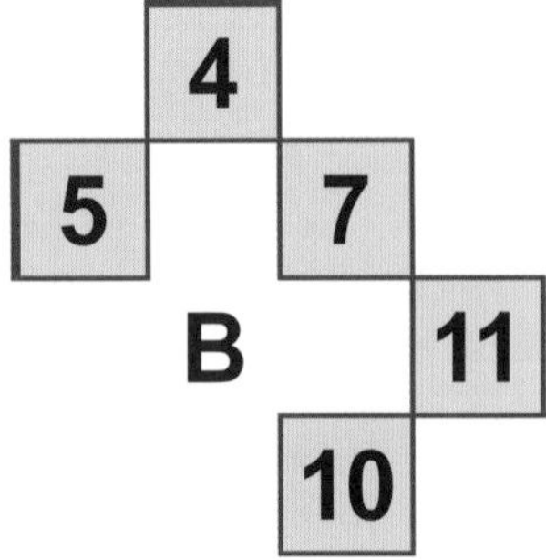

More Challenging

97. Complete the equation by correctly identifying the missing part of the calculation from the list of options below.

(36 + 42) + (?) = 144

A 7 x 9 **B** 55% x 120 **C** 45% x 160
D 8 x 7 **E** 22 x 3.5

98. What number should replace the question mark?

	5	
7		13

	9	
7		17

	5	
2		?

99.
346 : 18
971 : 64
827 : ?

What number should replace the question mark?

100.

18	24	9		42	?	21
12	3	27		28	7	?
6	21	15		14	?	35

Each set of nine numbers relates to each other in a certain way. Work out the logic behind the numbers in the left-hand box in order to determine which numbers are missing from the right-hand box.

Difficult

101. Out of 100 people surveyed leaving a supermarket, 87 had purchased bread, 75 had purchased butter, 60 had purchased fresh meat and 90 had purchased frozen food.

At least how many of the 100 people must have purchased all four items?

102. Insert single digit numbers into the remaining blank squares so that the sums in each row and column are correct.

	÷		x		=	6
+		–		–		–
	–		+	1	=	
÷		+		+		x
	x	2	–		=	
=		=		=		=
5	+		–		=	

103. 427 : 5684 : 374
535 : 7596 : 438
642 : ? : 833

What number should replace the question mark?

104. What number should replace the question mark?

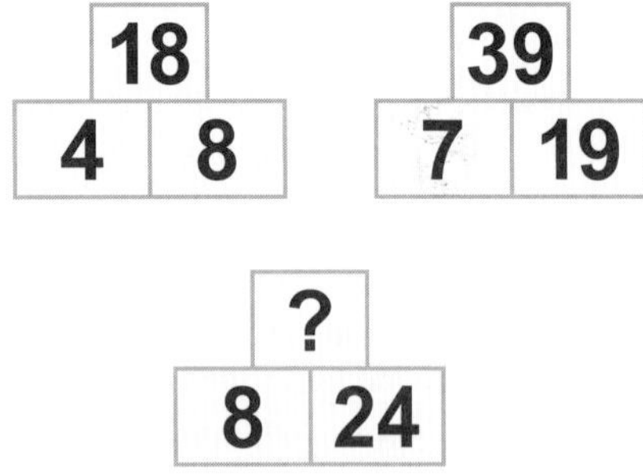

105. The link between the numbers in each row is the same. From the information already provided fill in the missing numbers.

5735	?	50
2864	?	?
4392	216	?

106. Find the smallest two-digit number that becomes a square number if the number produced by reversing its digits is taken from it (for example 32 – 23 = 9) and another square number if the number produced by reversing its digits is added to it.

Difficult

107. A train travelling at a speed of 40 miles per hour enters a tunnel that is 2¼ miles long. The length of the train is one quarter of a mile.

How long does it take for all of the train to pass through the tunnel, from the moment the front enters to the moment the rear emerges?

108. What number should replace the question mark?

6	3	15	30
8	4	9	32
5	3	15	?

109. In the addition sum below, only one decimal point is in the correct position. Alter the position of the decimal point in four of the numbers to make the sum correct.

```
 287.5
 365.9
 822.2
  135.69
8752.34
```

110. What number should replace the question mark?

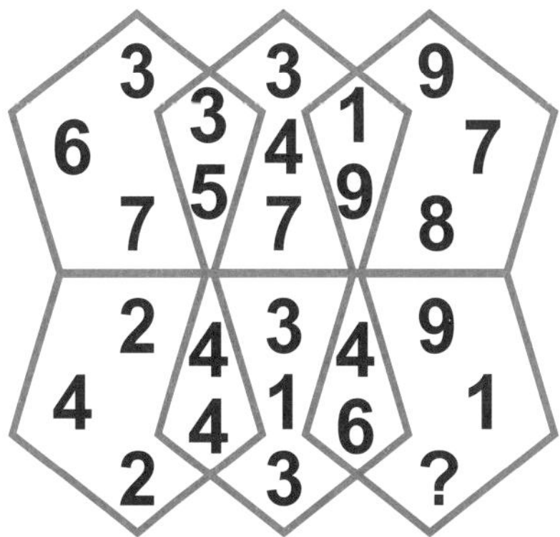

111. With a handbag full of money, Tessa visits four stores in a day-long shopping spree.

In the first store she spends £20.00 in the first half hour, half the money she had left in the second half hour and £20.00 in the third half hour.

She repeats this throughout all four stores and leaves the fourth store having spent all the money with which she started out.

With how much did she start out?

112. A sample of 12 gizmos is known to contain three defective gizmos. What is the probability of selecting the three defective gizmos in the first three selections?

Difficult

113. What number should replace the question mark?

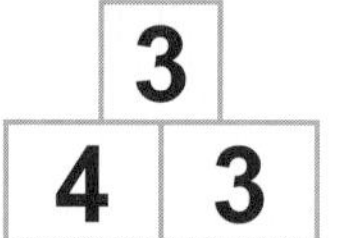

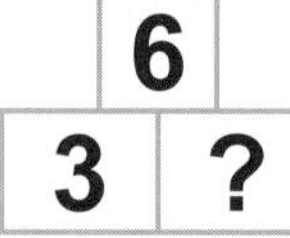

114. Insert the numbers listed into the circles so that for any particular circle the sum of the numbers in the circles connected to it equals the value corresponding to that circled number in the list. For example:

1 = 6 (4 + 2)
2 = 5 (1 + 4)
4 = 10 (1 + 2 + 7)
7 = 4

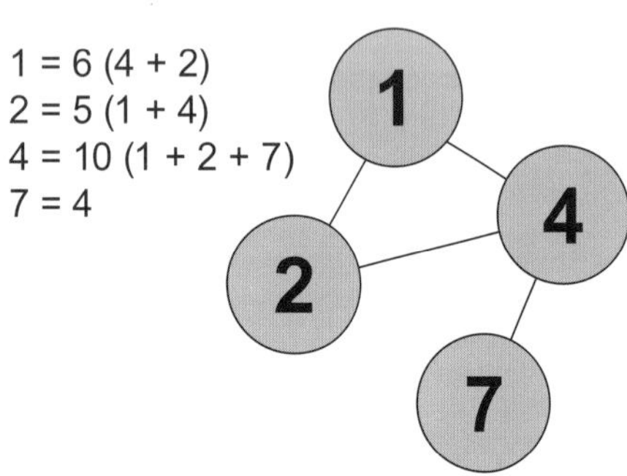

1 = 16
2 = 5
3 = 11
4 = 5
5 = 1
6 = 4

115. Insert the weights 1 kg, 2 kg, 3 kg and 4 kg into the empty pans to make the scales balance.

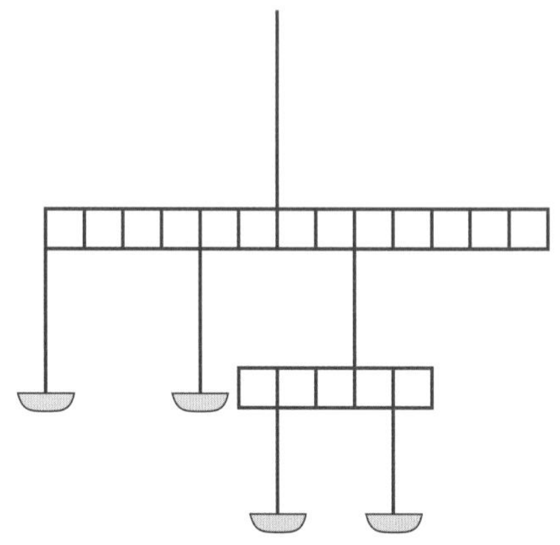

116. In the addition sum below, only one decimal point is in the correct position. Alter the position of the decimal point in four of the numbers to make the sum correct.

$$\begin{array}{r} 3.659 \\ 12.365 \\ 98.25 \\ \underline{17.3} \\ 1873.65 \end{array}$$

Difficult

117. What number should replace the question mark?

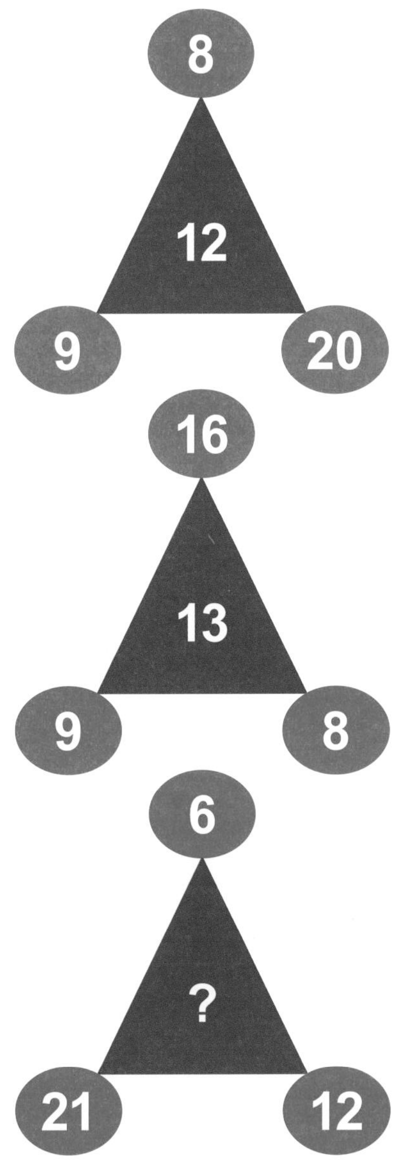

118. Find the largest number (it is lower than 50) that is the sum of the digits of its cube.

119. What number should replace the question mark?

3	9	2	7
6	7	4	2
5	3	1	?
4	8	3	2

120. 36842 : 149
28741 : 157
39413 : 137
18353 : ???

What number should replace the question mark?

121. 25 32 27 36 ?

What number should replace the question mark?

Difficult

122. What number should replace the question mark?

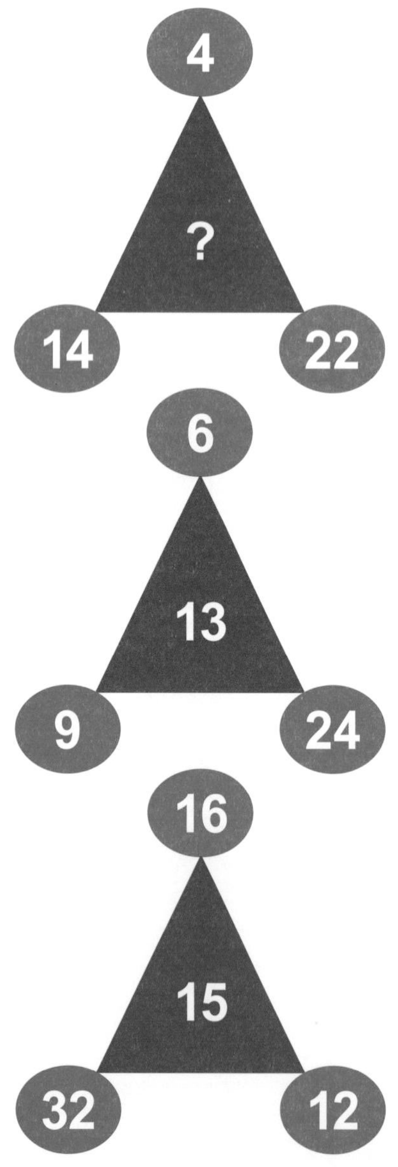

123. 38492 28473 36472
26453 ?

What number should replace the question mark?

124. At a recent by-election a total of 32,684 votes were cast for the four candidates, the winner exceeding his opponents by 593, 2,642 and 6,429 votes respectively.

How many votes were cast for each candidate?

125. Which number is the odd one out?

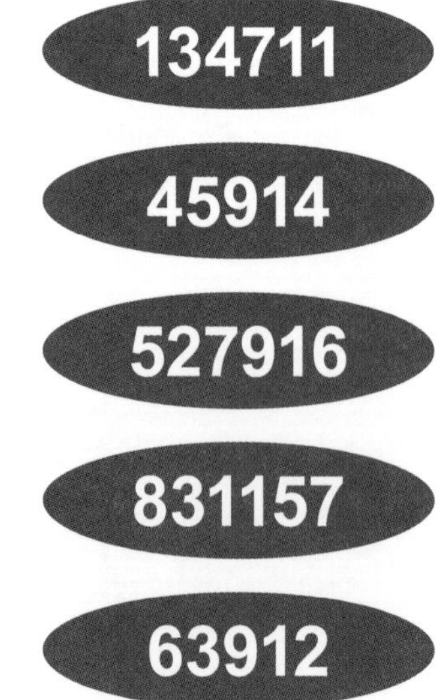

Difficult

126.

	12789	is to	28917
and	24567	is to	57624
as	12489	is to	?

127.

2	7		4	6		6	5
4	1		3	?		2	9

What number should replace the question mark?

128. What number should replace the question mark?

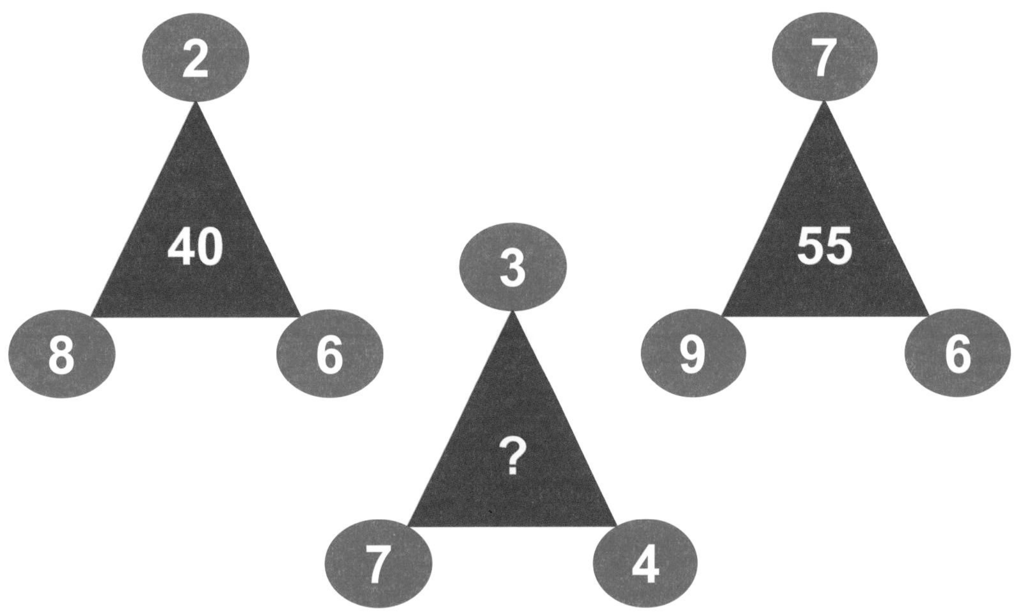

Difficult

129. Insert the numbers listed into the circles so that for any particular circle the sum of the numbers in the circles connected to it equals the value corresponding to that circled number in the list. For example:

1 = 11 (4 + 7)
3 = 4
4 = 11 (1 + 7 + 3)
7 = 5 (1 + 4)

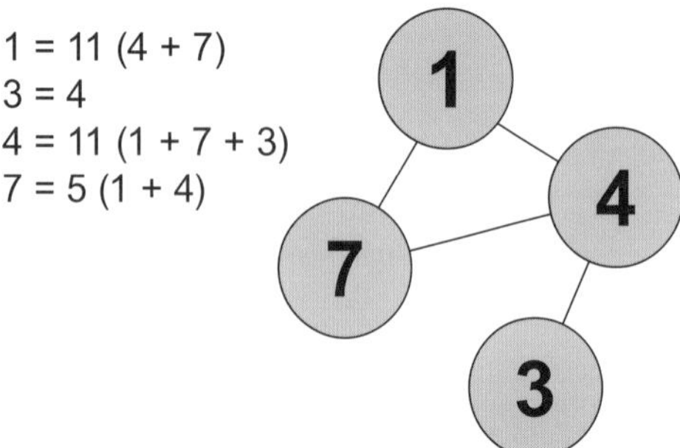

1 = 19
2 = 16
3 = 3
4 = 8
5 = 1
6 = 2
7 = 7

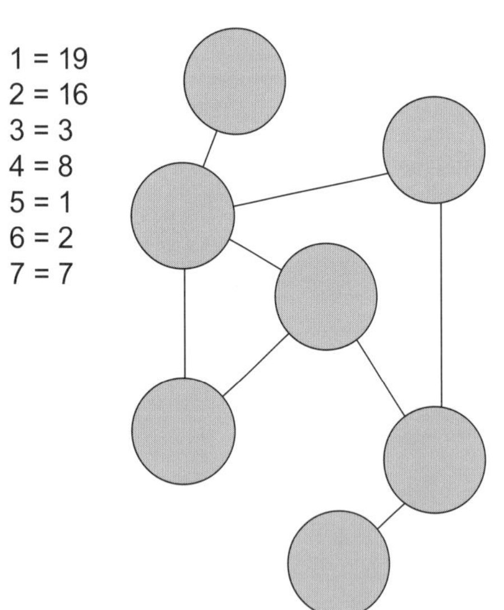

130. 768 (91012) 244
427 (7815) 368
281 (?) 964

What number should replace the question mark?

131. What number should replace the question mark?

4	6	6
8	28	56
8	42	?

132. 12689 : 1610
52734 : 615
98143 : 1213
68725 : ?

What number should replace the question mark?

133. 72549 65286 39168 31328 ? What number comes next?

Difficult

134. Insert the numbers listed into the circles so that for any particular circle the sum of the numbers in the circles connected to it equals the value corresponding to that circled number in the list. For example:

1 = 11 (4 + 7)
3 = 4
4 = 11 (1 + 7 + 3)
7 = 5 (1 + 4)

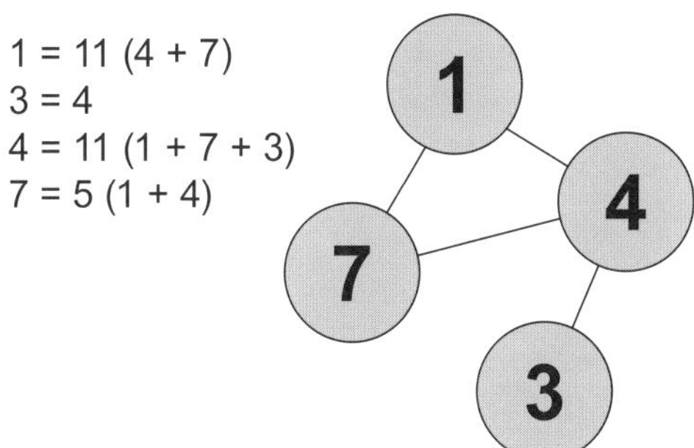

1 = 15
2 = 16
3 = 9
4 = 7
5 = 8
6 = 5
7 = 12

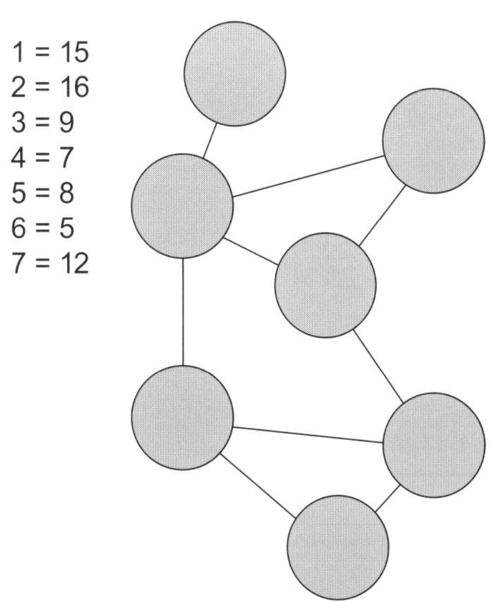

135.

1	3	5
4	1	4
7	2	5

3	2	1
3	7	5
3	9	?

Work out the logic behind the numbers in the two boxes in order to determine which number is missing from the bottom box.

136. What number should replace the question mark?

9	3	9	4
2	7	2	6
8	4	8	?

137. 364 827 ? 7106 13123 What number is missing?

Difficult

138. What numbers should replace the question marks?

2	7	6	3
1	4	5	?
9	7	5	5
8	3	6	?

139. Insert the remaining odd numbers between 1 and 25 inclusive into the yellow squares to produce a magic number square in which each vertical, horizontal and corner to corner line totals 65.

18	22		10	14
24				20
6				2
12	16		4	8

140. Divide the square into two identical sized and shaped halves so that the numbers in each total exactly the same.

43
26 20
81
14
74
28 15
10

141. What number should replace the question mark?

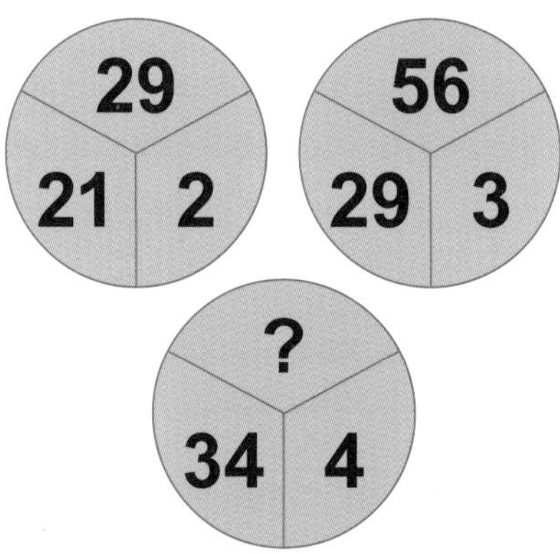

142. ?, ?, 147, 144, 12, 9, 3, 0

What are the first two numbers in this sequence?

Difficult

143. Which number is the odd one out?

144. 36529 : 41
25374 : 41
76243 : 56
82935 : ??

What number should replace the question mark?

145.

4	8	9		5	8	6
2	7	8		2	9	7
7	6	7		8	?	3

Each set of nine numbers relates to each other in a certain way. Work out the logic behind the numbers in the left-hand box in order to determine which number is missing from the right-hand box.

146. Find a four figure number that is exactly a quarter of its original value when its digits are reversed.

Difficult

147. What number should replace the question mark?

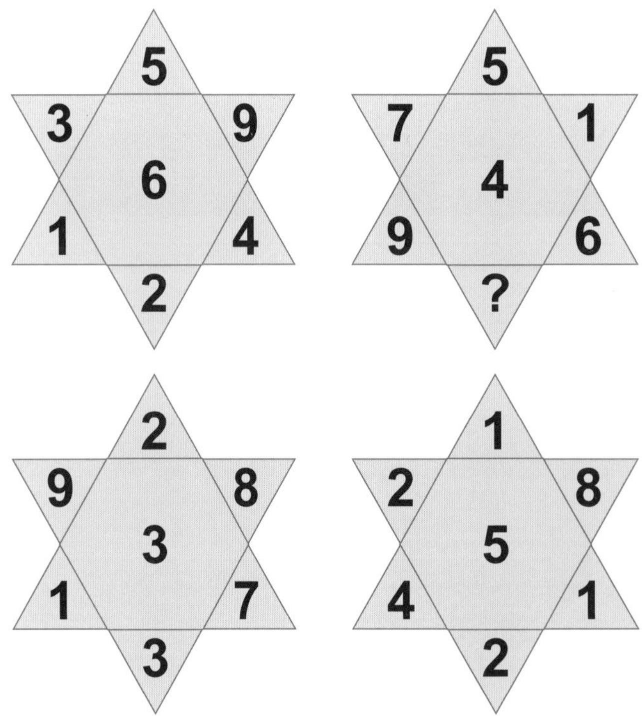

148. Which number is the odd one out?

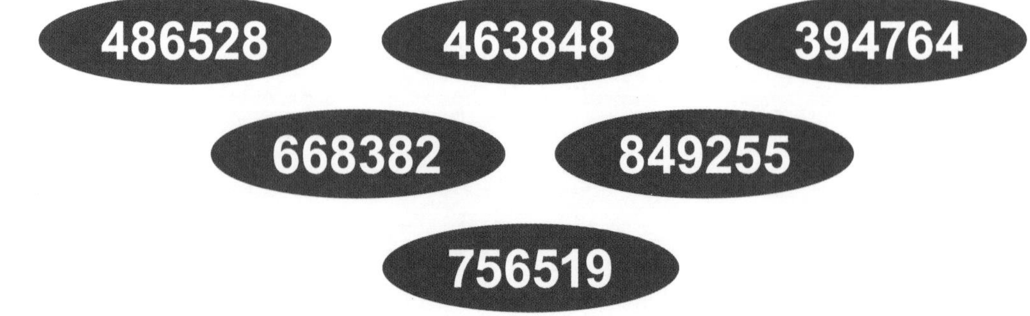

Difficult

149. Insert single digit numbers into the remaining blank squares so that the sums in each row and column are correct.

	+		÷		=	3
–		–		x		+
	+	1	x	2	=	
x		+		÷		–
2	x		÷		=	
=		=		=		=
	–	6	x		=	

150. What number should replace the question mark?

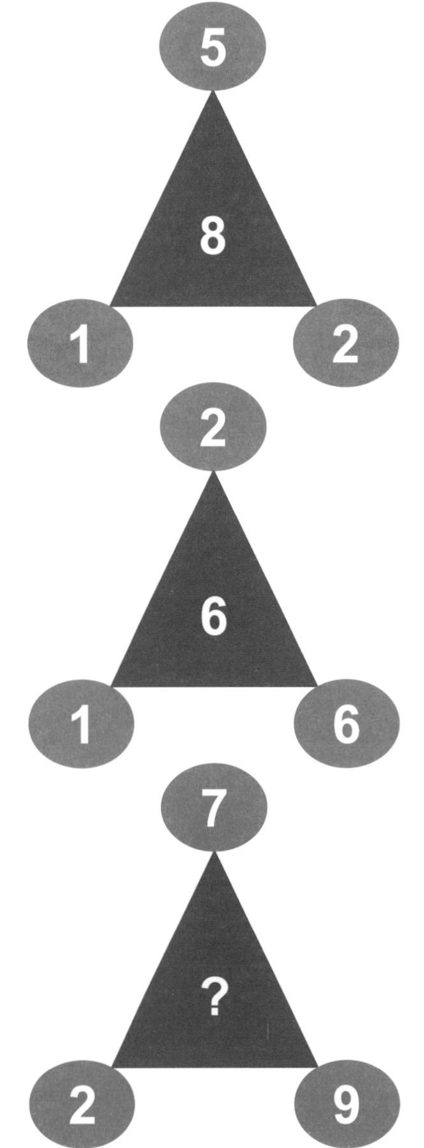

Brain Fact

The largest part of the human brain is the cerebrum which makes up approximately 85% of the brain's weight and has a large surface area called the cortex. It is an intricately developed part of the brain which accounts for the superior intelligence of humans, compared with other creatures. The cerebrum is divided by a fissure into identical right and left hemispheres.

Solutions – Quick Fire

1. 29 (9 + 3 + 1 + 9 + 7).
2. 3: The numbers in each row and column total eight.
3. 48.
4. –24: Deduct 4, 8, 16, 32, 64 (ie doubling the amount deducted each time).
5. 9826: Double one half of anything is always the same as the original number.
6. 20: Add 0, 1, 2, 3 and 4 in turn.
7. It is a 50/50 or 50% chance. It is a certainty that at least two coins will finish with the same side up. Thus it is just as likely that these two coins will be heads up as it is they will be tails up.
8. 8 cases: 148 pairs = 296 shoes and 296 ÷ 37 = 8.
9. 495: There are four quarters in one, therefore, there are 480 quarters in 120.
10. 2: The total of each column is 25, 24, 23, 22 and 21.
11. Bill 42 and Jill 63. 42 x 1.5 = 63.
12. 8.
13. 7.00pm: At 11.00am it was showing 11.00am, at 12 noon it showed 11.46am, at 1.00pm it showed 12.32pm, at 2.00pm it showed 1.18pm, at 3.00pm it showed 2.04pm and at 4.00pm it showed 2.50pm. Plus 3 hours means that the time is now 7.00pm.
14. £5,600: $0.45 = \frac{45}{100} = \frac{9}{20}$ $\quad \frac{2}{5} = \frac{8}{20}$ $\quad \frac{9}{20} + \frac{8}{20} = \frac{17}{20}$

    Therefore $\frac{3}{20}$ = £840 (Larry's share) and, therefore, $\frac{1}{20}$ = £280 20 x £280 = £5,600.
15. 122: Add 1, 3, 9, 27, 81 i.e. the amount added is multiplied by 3 at each stage.
16. 32: 9 + 2 + 7 + 8 + 6 (**9 2** 6 3 5 1 **7 8 6** 2 9 3).
17. 0: The lowest cube number is 8 (2x2x2). The square of 8 (8x8) = 64. The lowest square number is 4 (2x2). The cube of 4 (4x4x4) = 64.
18. 24: (96 ÷ 8) x 2.
19. £240.00: The total is £720.00 = £360.00 each. Therefore, Alistair owes Gordon £240.00.
20. 12: 3 oranges, 3 apples, 3 grapefruit and 3 pears.

Solutions – Quick Fire

21. 1.5.

22. 8.45am: 15 minutes before 9.00am. In 45 minutes it will be 30 minutes past 9.00am.

23. 10 kg: 50 kg ÷ 5 kg = 10 kg.

24. 10: Add the middle number (3) to the numbers in the adjoining middle section (6 and 1). Similarly, 3 + 1 + 7 = 11; 3 + 7 + 2 = 12, etc.

25. B: looking across lines progress +1, +2, +3. Looking down they progress +3, +2, +1.

26. I am 40 and he is 10. In twenty years I will be 60 and he will be 30.

27. 75: Deduct 1, 3, 5, 7, 9 and 11.

28. 119 different ways apart from the one shown above (the calculation is 5 x 4 x 3 x 2 x 1 = 120).

29. B: Looking across the middle number in each line is the total of the first and third numbers. Looking down, the first two numbers added together produce the third number.

30. 18.

31. 1.3: Multiply 0.65 by 1, 2, 3, 4 and 5.

32. 0: The total of all the numbers listed is 44 and as there are eleven numbers the average is 4 (44 ÷ 11). The total of all the even numbers is 20 (6 + 4 + 4 + 2 + 4) and as there are five such numbers the average is 4 (20 ÷ 5).

33. 17. Harry is now 16 and Sally is 9. Two years ago Harry was 14 and Sally 7, and in one year's time Harry will be 17 and Sally 10.

34. Ernie 7, Colin 5.

35. 36 feet: 12 + 6 + 6 + 3 + 3 + 1.5 + 1.5 + 0.75 + 0.75 + 0.375 + 0.375 + 0.1875 + 0.1875 + 0.09375 + 0.09375.

36. 328 feet.

37. Seven at £0.50, three at £1.50 and two at £2.

38. 2.5%. If the average daily increase over the week falls below 2.5%, the target will not be met.

39. 752961427942-**13683**-23485.

40. 642359. List the even numbers in descending order followed by the odd numbers in ascending order.

41. 700. (56 ÷ 8) x 100.

42. 87. Deduct 2, 4, 6, 8, 10 and 12.

Solutions – Quick Fire

43. C: 23 x 42=966.

44. B.

45. 15 days. 5 x 27 = 135 man days and 135 ÷ 9 = 15 man days.

46. 5.

47. 9 cm. (11.4 ÷ 9.5) x 7.5.

48. D: Add 1, 2, 3, 4, 5 and 6 respectively to the numbers on the top to obtain those on the bottom.

49. 57 and 75

50. 12 years. Now my brother is 16 and I am 23; two years ago I was 21 and he was 14 (14 x 1½ = 21); in five years I will be 28 and he will be 21 (21 x 1⅓ = 28); and in 12 years I will be 35 and he will be 28 (28 x 1¼ = 35).

Solutions – More Challenging

51. 13: Looking across each row of three numbers, add the first two numbers then deduct 1 to obtain the third number: (6 + 8) – 1 = 13.

52. E – 23 – 2^4.

53. 40 minutes. The total time for eight players = 440 minutes. However, as 11 people (8 + 3) are on the pitch an equal length of time, they are each on the pitch for 40 minutes (440 ÷ 11).

54. 18 and 17 should be interchanged: The top sequence progresses +16, +15, +14, +13, +12 and the bottom sequence progresses +17, +16, +15, +14, +13.

55. 1st stall: 9 out of 15 ie 9/15 or 3/5 = 60%, 2nd stall: 4 out of 16, ie 4/16 or 1/4 = 25%: The difference is 35% (60-25).

56. 2150: The sequence progresses x 5 – 1, x 5 – 2, x 5 – 3, x 5 – 4, x 5 – 5.

57. As I leave according to my usual schedule, we know it is before 6.00pm when I pick up my wife. Because we have saved 10 minutes, that must be the same time that it takes me to drive from the point I picked her up, to the station, and back again to the same point. Assuming it takes an equal five minutes each way I have, therefore, picked up my wife five minutes before I would normally do so. So my wife walked from 5.30pm to 5.55pm, or for 25 minutes.

Solutions – More Challenging

58. C – From top to bottom, multiply odd numbers by 2 and divide even numbers by 2.

59. 16. Three numbers total 78 and two numbers total 62, so the third number is 78 – 62 = 16.

60.

1	12	8	13
15	6	10	3
14	7	11	2
4	9	5	16

61. 28: If he takes out 26 socks, although very unlikely, they could be all the blue and black socks. To make 100% certain he also has a pair of grey socks he must take out two more.

62. 8 and 71. The numbers down the left side increase by x3 + 1 and the numbers down the right side increase by x2 +1.

63. 22 and 27: the sequence progresses x2, +5 repeated.

64. 117.

65. 87963: The last two digits of the previous number followed by its first three digits in reverse.

66. A – Add the digits of each number on the top row to obtain those on the bottom.

67. They never will be. In a heptagon three segments clockwise is the same as four anticlockwise. The dots will, therefore, always remain the same distance apart.

68. 5: Looking across the numbers in each row total 6, 8, 10 then 12 respectively.

69. B – Looking across numbers in each row progress +2, +3, +2, +3 and looking down, numbers in each column progress +3, +2, +3, +2.

70. 8: 6 x 2 = 12 and 4 x 9 = 36, thus 36 ÷ 12 = 3; 9 x 2 = 18 and 9 x 8 = 72, thus 72 ÷ 18 = 4; so 1 x 7 = 7 and 8 x 7 = 56, thus 56 ÷ 7 = 8.

71. 1 1/29. $3\frac{3}{4} \div 3\frac{5}{8} = \frac{15}{4} \div \frac{29}{8} = \frac{15}{4} \times \frac{8}{29} = \frac{15}{1} \times \frac{2}{29} = \frac{30}{29}$

72. 16 cm. Pythagoras' Theorem states that the square of the hypotenuse of a right-angled triangle is equal to the sum of the squares of the other two sides. 65 cm is the hypotenuse, 65 squared (4225) minus 63 squared (3969) = 256 and the square root of 256 = 16.

73. 43 minutes. 43 minutes before midnight = 11.17, 11.17 less 8 minutes = 11.09, 9.00pm plus 129 minutes (3 x 43) = 11.09.

74. 20.5 and 13.3: There are two alternate sequences. The first starts at 2.5 and progresses +5.4. The second starts at 25 and progresses –4.5.

Solutions – More Challenging

75. 9: Progressing from left to right, the numbers when read in sets of three total 17.
76. 255: The sequence progresses x2 +1 at each stage.
77. 7639: In all the others multiply the middle two digits to obtain the two-digit number formed by combining the first and last digits.
78. 12: (7 + 12) – 11 = 8. Similarly (4 + 7) – 6 = 5 and (8 + 9) – 4 = 13.
79. 52: Their combined age in 12 years' time = 72 and 4 x 12 = 48, thus their combined age now is 72 – 48 = 24. In seven years' time, their combined age = 24 + 28 (4 x 7) = 52.
80. 59: 45 ÷ 9 = 5 and 81 ÷ 9 = 9.
81. 32 and 33 should be interchanged. The left sequence progresses +7, +14, +21, +28, +35 and the right sequence progresses +6, +12, +18, +24, +30.
82. D.
83. D: Rows across progress +1, –2, +1, –2 and columns down progress +3, –2, +3, –2.
84. 73.
85. 6/9. Change the fractions to 54ths, ie 36, 24 and 33 54ths respectively.
86. 48 miles per hour. Say the journey was 60 miles each way, then at 60 miles per hour, the outward journey would take 60 minutes and the inward journey 90 minutes. This means that it takes 150 minutes to travel 120 miles or 60 minutes to travel 48 miles.
87. 46923: Reverse all but the last two digits of the previous number, then add the last two digits.
88. 5.
89. 39 cm. 15 squared = 225, 36 squared = 1296, and the square root of 1521 (225+1296) is 39.
90. 38 and 34 should be interchanged. The top sequence progresses +4, +8, +12, +16, +20 and the bottom sequence progresses +6, +9, +12, +15, +18.
91. 28: 7 x 8 = 56 and 56 ÷ 2 = 28.
92. 9: Looking across rows the total of the numbers in each row is 18, 20, 18, 20. Looking down columns the total is 20, 18, 20, 18.
93. 23 and 15. There are two interwoven sequences: starting at the first 1, the sequence progresses +4, +5, +6, +7 and starting at the second 1 the sequence progresses +2, +3, +4, +5.
94. 1 3/7. $\frac{5}{9} \div \frac{7}{18} = \frac{5}{9} \times \frac{18}{7} = \frac{10}{7}$
95. 405: Since 27 is one third of 81, each fish has the equivalent of 27 spots after two-thirds of the male fish have been removed.
96. B: Looking across rows progress +1, +1, +2, +2 and looking down, columns progress +2, +2, +1, +1.
97. B: 55% x 120.
98. 8: (5 + 2) +1. Similarly (5 + 7) +1 = 13 and (9 + 7) + 1 = 17.
99. 23: (8 x 2) + 7. Similarly (3 x 4) + 6 = 18 and (9 x 7) + 1 = 64.
100. Top row 56, middle row 63 and bottom row 49. The numbers are all multiples of the middle number, 7. They are in the same position as the equivalent multiples of the middle number 3 in the left-hand array.

Solutions – Difficult

101. 12: add the number of items together, which gives 87 + 75 + 60 + 90 = 312 among the 100 people surveyed. This gives three items to each and four items to 12 of these people. The fewest number of people to have purchased all four items, therefore, is 12.

102.

8	÷	4	x	3	=	6
+		–		–		–
7	–	3	+	1	=	5
÷		+		+		x
3	x	2	–	4	=	2
=		=		=		=
5	+	3	–	6	=	2

103. 4872. To obtain 4872, multiply together the digits on either side: 6 x 4 x 2 = 48 and 8 x 3 x 3 = 72.

104. 48: (8 + 24) x 1.5.

105. In each row multiply the digits to obtain the next number, eg 4 x 3 x 9 x 2 = 216; and 2 x 1 x 6 = 12. The missing numbers are 525, 384, 96 and 12.

106. 65: 65 – 56 = 9, which is 3 squared and 65 + 56 = 121, which is 11 squared.

107. 3 minutes 45 seconds, ie 2.5 x 60/40.

108. 25: Multiply the first three numbers in each row and then divide by nine to obtain the final number.

109. From the top, the numbers should read as follows: 2.875, 36.59, 822.2, 13.569, totalling 875.234.

110. 2: Add the numbers in each segment. In the larger segments the total of the numbers at the top is double the total of the numbers in the opposite bottom segment and in the smaller segments the total is the same.

111. £900.00: Start at the last store in which she spends her last £20.00 in the last half hour. She therefore had £60.00 when she entered, ie she spent £20.00 in the first half hour, half the money left in the second half hour (40/2) and £20.00 in the last half hour. Now work this back throughout all four stores:

Enters 4th store with £60.00	20	20	20	(60 less 60 = 0).
Enters 3rd store with £180.00	20	80	20	(180 less 120 = 60)
Enters 2nd store with £420.00	20	200	20	(420 less 240 = 180)
Enters 1st store with £900.00	20	440	20	(900 less 480 = 420)

Solutions – Difficult

112. 1 in 220: 3/12 x 2/11 x 1/10 = 6/1320 or 1 in 220.

113. 2: In each pyramid the three numbers when multiplied together total 36.

114.

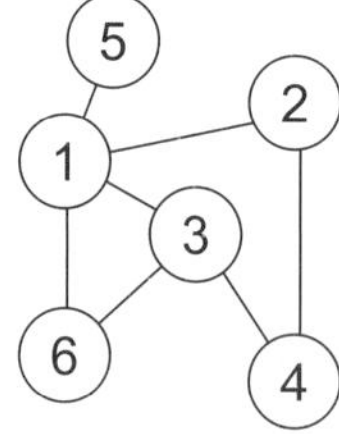

115. From left to right, the weights are 1kg, 3kg, 2kg and 4kg. On the left side of the scale: 1 x 6 = 6 and 2 x 3 = 6, giving a total of 12. On the right side of the scale: 2 x 6 (2 + 4) = 12. The right-hand sub-scale also balances 2 x 2 = 4 and 1 x 4 = 4.

116. From the top, the numbers should read as follows: 36.59, 123.65, 9.825, 17.3, totalling 187.365.

117. 13: In each set, divide the top number by two, the bottom left-hand number by three and the bottom right-hand number by four, then add the results to obtain the number in the middle.

118. 27: Cube = 27 x 27 x 27 = 19683 and 1 + 9 + 6 + 8 + 3 = 27

119. 5: In each row multiply the first two numbers to obtain the number formed by the third and fourth digits. So, 5 x 3 = 15, and similarly 3 x 9 = 27, etc.

120. 119: The sum total of the second and third digits is written before the sum total of the first, fourth and fifth digits.

121. 27: Add the digits of each number and then alternately add and deduct to obtain the next number. Thus, 2 + 7 = 9 and 27 + 9 = 36, then 3 + 6 = 9 and 36 – 9 = 27.

122. 20: Divide the numbers in the first set by 2 and add the results to obtain the number in the middle. In the second set divide by 3 and in the third set divide by 4.

123. 34452: Reverse each number and deduct 1 from the second and fourth digits.

124. The number of votes the winning candidate received was (32,684 + 593 + 2,642 + 6,429) ÷ 4 = 10,587, the second received 10,587 – 593 = 9,994, the third received 10,587 – 2,642 = 7,945, and the fourth received 10,587 – 6,429 = 4,158.

125. 831157: In the others keep adding digits to produce the final number, for example, 134711, where 1 + 3 = 4, 3 + 4 = 7 and 4 + 7 = 11.

126. 84129: Arrange the digits so that a square number is followed by its square root, ie $\sqrt{841} = 29$.

Solutions – Difficult

127. 5: The numbers in the middle section are arrived at by adding the two numbers in the same position in the left and right sections and dividing by 2. Thus 2 + 6 = 8 and 8 ÷ 2 = 4; similarly 7 + 5 = 12 and 12 ÷ 2 = 6 etc.

128. 35: (3 + 7 + 4) x 2.5 = 35.

129.

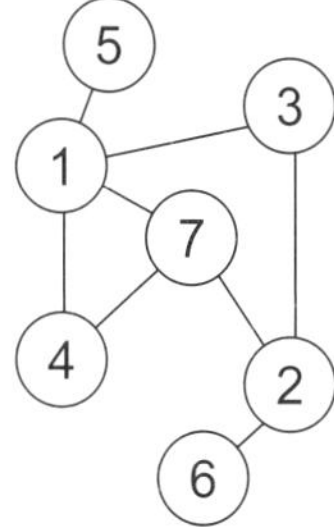

130. 11145: 2 + 9 = 11, 8 + 6 = 14, 1 + 4 = 5.

131. 84: Looking across and down, multiply the first two numbers together, then divide the result by four to obtain the number in the third square. So 8 x 42 = 336 and 6 x 56 = 336, thus 336 ÷ 4 = 84.

132. 1612: Add the even numbers in the first number and then add the odd numbers.

133. 25056: (3132 x 8).

134.

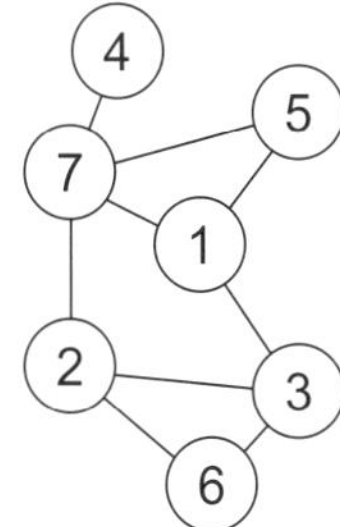

135. 7: The two numbers in identical positions in each box add up to 4, 5, 6, 7, 8, 9, 10, 11 and 12 in turn, ie 1 + 3 = 4, 3 + 2 = 5, 5 + 1 = 6, 4 + 3 = 7, etc.

136. 5: Each block of four numbers totals 21.

Solutions – Difficult

137. 1555: 827 plus its reverse, 728 = 1555.

138. There are four different sequences as indicated by the coloured squares.

2	7	6	3
1	4	5	8
9	7	5	5
8	3	6	7

139.

18	22	1	10	14
24	3	7	11	20
5	9	13	17	21
6	15	19	23	2
12	16	25	4	8

140.

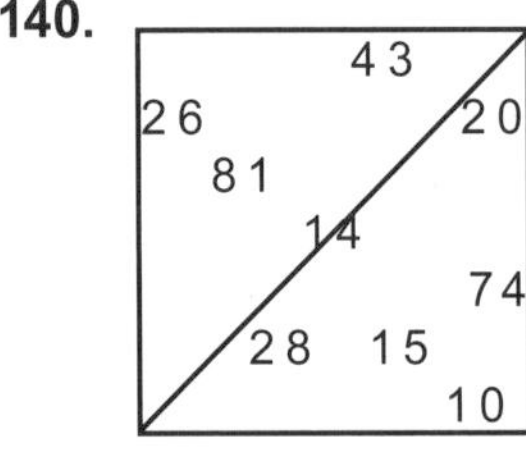

Each half totals 151.

141. 98: 98 – 34 = 64 and then take the cube root of 64 which is 4. Similarly 29 – 21 = 8 and the cube root of 8 = 2, and 56 – 29 = 27 and the cube root of 27 = 3.

142. 21612 and 21609: Deduct 3 and then take the square root alternately.

143. 526815: In all the others the two sides add up to 999, eg 746253 (746 + 253 = 999).

144. 40: (8 x 2) + 9 + (3 x 5).

145. 8: 489 + 278 = 767 and 586 + 297 = 883.

Solutions – Difficult

146. 8712.

147. 8: In each pair of stars the number in the middle of the left star is the average of the numbers around the outside of the right star and vice versa.

148. 463848: In all the others the first two digits total 12, the second two digits total 11 and the third two digits total 10: 463848 is the other way round.

149.

7	+	2	÷	3	=	3
–		–		x		+
3	+	1	x	2	=	8
x		+		÷		–
2	x	5	÷	2	=	5
=		=		=		=
8	–	6	x	3	=	6

150. 9: Take the cube root of the number formed by the digits going anti-clockwise around the outside, starting at the top. So, the cube root of 729 is 9, the cube root of 512 is 8 and the cube root of 216 is 6.

Brain Fact

Oxygen and glucose are supplied to the brain by two sets of cranial arteries known as the Vascular System. Below the neck, each of the common carotid arteries divides into an external branch to supply the forward portion of the brain. The rest of the brain is supplied by the two vertebral arteries and these join together with the two internal carotid arteries to form the Circle of Willis at the base of the brain. Of all the blood pumped by the heart, 25% is circulated within the brain tissue by a large network of cerebral arteries.

Tests

Numerical ability tests are designed to asses how well a person can reason with numbers.

In the case of numerical problem solving, the actual mathematical process involved may be quite basic; however, you are being assessed on your ability to apply your basic mathematical knowledge in order to correctly solve the problem as quickly as possible.

This section consists of three tests which are all timed and assessed.

You should keep strictly within the time limits otherwise your score will be invalidated.

The use of a calculating machine is not permitted in any of these tests; however, for Tests 1 and 3 written working out notes may be made.

On Test 2 written notes are not permitted as all workings out must be done in the head.

Test 1: Complete the Equation Test

This test consists of 20 questions in which you are given an incomplete equation and must find the missing part of the equation from the choices available. The time limit allowed for completing this test is 60 minutes.

Test 2: Mental Arithmetic Test

This test consists of 20 questions involving basic arithmetical calculations. The time limit allowed for completing this test is 30 minutes.

Test 3: Number Sequence Test

The time limit allowed for completing the 10 questions in this test is 30 minutes.

Test 1 – Quick Fire

1. What number should replace the question mark to correctly complete the equation?

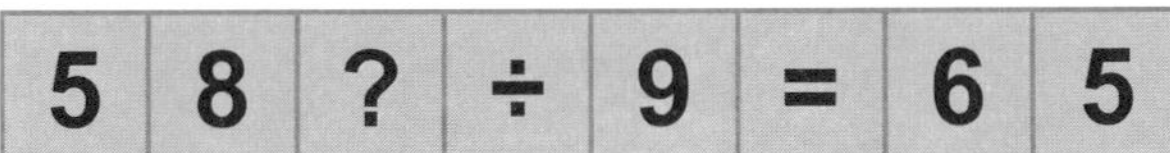

5	8	?	÷	9	=	6	5

3	5	6	7	9
A	B	C	D	E

2. What number should replace the question mark to correctly complete the equation?

3	?	8	+	8	4	=	4	6	2

4	5	6	7	9
A	B	C	D	E

3. What number should replace the question mark to correctly complete the equation?

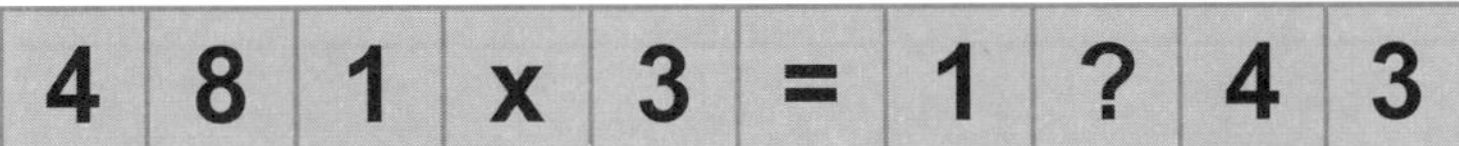

4	8	1	x	3	=	1	?	4	3

6	3	5	8	4
A	B	C	D	E

Test 1 – Quick Fire

4. What number should replace the question mark to correctly complete the equation?

7	2	9	3	8
A	B	C	D	E

5. What number should replace the question mark to correctly complete the equation?

0	2	3	4	6
A	B	C	D	E

6. What number should replace the question mark to correctly complete the equation?

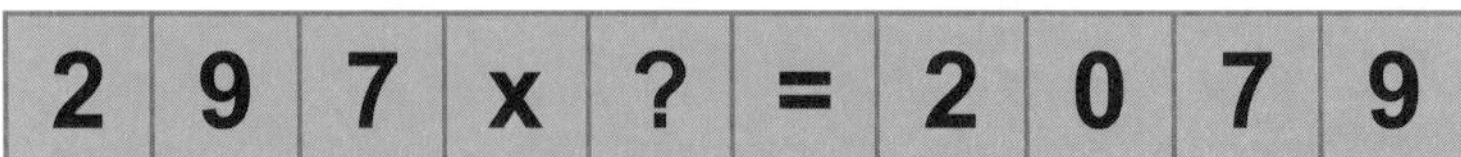

3	5	6	7	9
A	B	C	D	E

Test 1 – Quick Fire

7. What number should replace the question mark to correctly complete the equation?

1	2	0	x	2	.	5	=	3	?	0

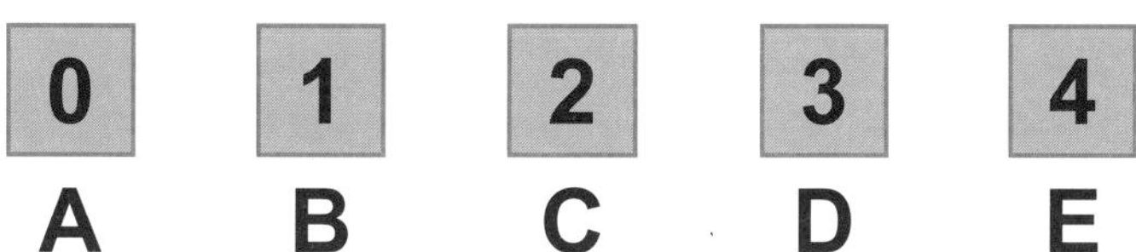

0	1	2	3	4
A	B	C	D	E

Test 1 – More Challenging

8. What number should replace the question mark to correctly complete the equation?

$3\frac{1}{2}$	x	?	=	1	5	.	7	5

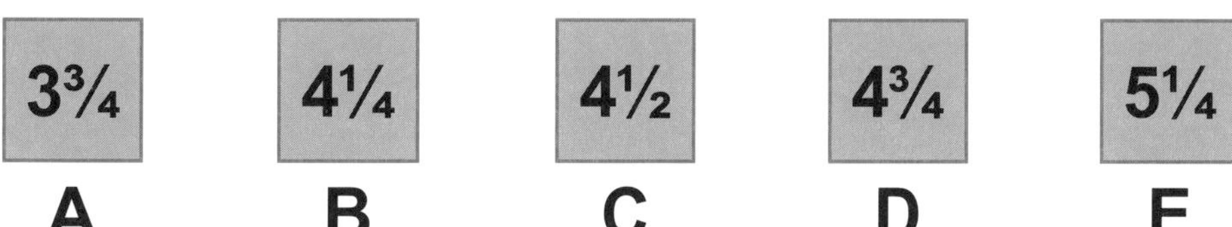

$3\frac{3}{4}$	$4\frac{1}{4}$	$4\frac{1}{2}$	$4\frac{3}{4}$	$5\frac{1}{4}$
A	B	C	D	E

Test 1 – More Challenging

9. What number should replace the question mark to correctly complete the equation?

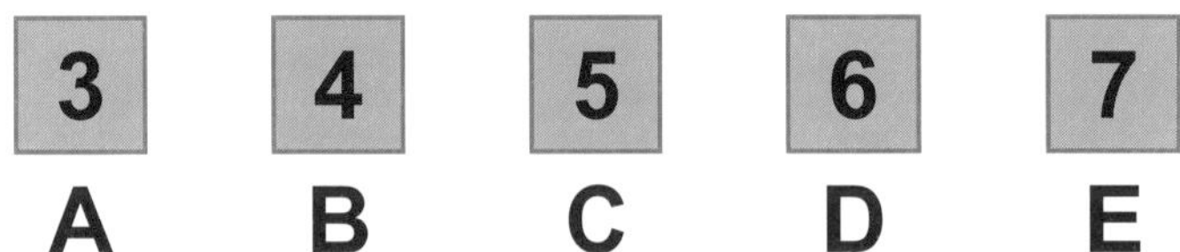

3	?	9	–	1	8	3	=	1	7	6

A	B	C	D	E
3	4	5	6	7

10. What number should replace the question mark to correctly complete the equation?

$4\frac{1}{2}$	+	$2\frac{1}{8}$	+	?	+	$2\frac{1}{4}$	=	1	5	.	2	5

A	B	C	D	E
$6\frac{1}{8}$	$6\frac{1}{4}$	$6\frac{3}{8}$	$6\frac{5}{8}$	$6\frac{3}{4}$

11. $(2^2 + 4 + ?) \times 3 = \frac{735}{7}$

Complete the equation by correctly identifying the missing part of the calculation from the list of options below.

A 7 **B** 8 **C** 23 **D** 8.875 **E** 3^3

Test 1 – More Challenging

12. $725 \div 25 = (167 - \ ?) \times 0.5$

Complete the equation by correctly identifying the missing part of the calculation from the list of options below.

A 109 **B** 111 **C** 75 + 44 **D** 12 x 9 **E** 107

13. 6295 x 3 = 37?7 x 5

Complete the equation by correctly identifying the missing part of the calculation from the list of options below.

A + **B** 7 **C** x **D** 9 **E** 6

14. $? \times \frac{27}{4} = 3.75$

Complete the equation by correctly identifying the missing part of the calculation from the list of options below.

A $\frac{9}{5}$ **B** $\frac{5}{8}$ **C** $\frac{3}{4}$ **D** $\frac{5}{9}$ **E** 44%

15. $\frac{58 \times 12}{3} = 14^2 + ?$

Complete the equation by correctly identifying the missing part of the calculation from the list of options below.

A 2^4 **B** 2^5 **C** 6^2 **D** $\sqrt{49} \times 5$ **E** 2.5 x 14

Test 1 – Difficult

16. $7 \times 12 = ? \times 6$

Complete the equation by correctly identifying the missing part of the calculation from the list of options below.

A 6×3 **B** $(4^2 + 4) - 5$ **C** $\sqrt{121} + \sqrt{16}$ **D** $\frac{45 \times 2}{5}$ **E** $\frac{3 \times 42}{9}$

17. $\frac{44}{?} = 2^3 \times 22$

Complete the equation by correctly identifying the missing part of the calculation from the list of options below.

A 0.25 **B** 0.325 **C** 0.75^2 **D** $\sqrt{1} - 0.5$ **E** $3.6 - 3.475$

18. $\frac{45.5}{? \times 4} = \frac{91}{0.5}$

Complete the equation by correctly identifying the missing part of the calculation from the list of options below.

A 0.0625 **B** 0.025 **C** 0.625 **D** 0.825 **E** 0.0825

Test 1 – Difficult

19. $\dfrac{17}{? \times 8} = (7 \times 2) + (5 \times 4)$

Complete the equation by correctly identifying the missing part of the calculation from the list of options below.

A 0.5^3 **B** 0.325 **C** 0.25^2 **D** 0.675 **E** $\dfrac{12}{15}$

20. $\dfrac{78 - \sqrt{36}}{? \div 1.5} = \dfrac{135}{\sqrt{225}}$

Complete the equation by correctly identifying the missing part of the calculation from the list of options below.

A $\sqrt{169} - 2$ **B** (30% x 40) **C** 492 ÷ 48 **D** $2^2 + 6$ **E** $\dfrac{12^2}{9}$

Brain Fact

The study of other animals suggests a relationship exists between brain size and intelligence levels. The dolphin, for example, has an unusually large brain and is considered one of our planet's most highly intelligent creatures. Human brain size levelled off about 100 thousand years ago. Unlike animals, there is no relationship between brain size and intelligence level in humans.

Test 2

1. Multiply 12 by 9.

2. Divide 132 by 3.

3. What is three quarters of 68?

4. Multiply 9 by 4 by 6.

5. What is 28 divided by 4 added to 16 multiplied by 3?

6. What is 4011 divided by 7?

7. Add 92 + 71 + 13 + 62.

8. What is 65% of 420?

9. What is five ninths of 720?

10. Which is the greatest, five eighths of 192, or seven eighths of 136?

Test 2

11. Add 569 to 887 and divide by 2.

12. Divide 1104 by 12.

13. Multiply 7 x 8 x 11.

14. What is 1.5 x 760?

15. Subtract 374 from 1037.

16. What is 12.75 multiplied by 11?

17. Multiply 642 by 21.

18. What is 1000 less four sevenths of 224?

19. Divide 22.95 by 9.

20. Multiply 39 by 15.

Test 3

1. What number should replace the question mark?

1 11 20 28 35 41 ?

2. What numbers should replace the question marks?

5 10 11 22 23 ? ?

3. What number should replace the question mark?

100 91 73 64 46 37 ?

4. What numbers should replace the question marks?

1 10 3 9 6 7 10 4 ? ?

5. What number should replace the question mark?

56 112 168 224 ?

6. What numbers should replace the question marks?

1000 ? ? 725 600 525 400

7. What numbers should replace the question marks?

1.05 1.55 ? ? 4.55 6.05

8. What number should replace the question mark?

100 97 88 61 ?

9. What numbers should replace the question marks?

5 10 11 22 24 48 51 ? ?

10. What number should replace the question mark?

197 204 208 216 ? 224 228

Solutions – Test 1

1. B.
2. D.
3. E.
4. A.
5. B.
6. D.
7. A.
8. C.
9. C.
10. C.
11. E.
12. A.
13. B.
14. D.
15. C.
16. E.
17. A.
18. A.
19. C.
20. B.

Performance Rating

Score 1 point for each correct answer

Total Score	Rating	Percentage of Population
19 / 20	Genius level	Top 5%
17 / 18	High Expert	Top 10%
15 / 16	Expert	Top 30%
13 / 14	High Average	Top 40%
11 / 12	Middle Average	Top 60%
9 / 10	Low Average	Bottom 40%
7 / 8	Borderline Low	Bottom 30%
5 / 6	Low	Bottom 10%
0 / 4	Very Low	Bottom 5%

Transfer your score to the chart in the Assessment Section on page 302.

Solutions – Test 2

1. 108.

2. 44.

3. 51.

4. 216.

5. 55.

6. 573.

7. 238.

8. 273.

9. 400.

10. Five eighths of 192 = 120 and seven eighths of 136 = 119.

11. 728.

12. 92.

13. 616.

14. 1140.

15. 663.

16. 140.25.

17. 13482.

18. 872.

19. 2.55.

20. 585.

Performance Rating

Score 1 point for each correct answer

Total Score	Rating	Percentage of Population
19 / 20	Genius level	Top 5%
17 / 18	High Expert	Top 10%
15 / 16	Expert	Top 30%
13 / 14	High Average	Top 40%
11 / 12	Middle Average	Top 60%
9 / 10	Low Average	Bottom 40%
7 / 8	Borderline Low	Bottom 30%
5 / 6	Low	Bottom 10%
0 / 4	Very Low	Bottom 5%

Transfer your score to the chart in the Assessment Section on page 302.

Solutions – Test 3

1. 46: Add 10, 9, 8, 7, 6 and 5.
2. 46 and 47: The sequence progresses x2 and +1 repeated.
3. 19: Subtract 9 and 18 alternately.
4. 15 and 0: There are two interwoven sequences: starting at 1 add 2, 3, 4 and 5; starting at 10 subtract 1, 2, 3 and 4.
5. 280: Add 56 each time.
6. 925 and 800: Subtract 75 then 125 alternately.
7. 2.3 and 3.3: Add 0.5, 0.75, 1, 1.25 and 1.5.
8. -20: Subtract 3, 9, 27 and 81.
9. 102 and 106: The sequence progresses x2, +1, x2 +2, x2 +3, x2 and +4.
10. 222: Add the last digit of the previous number each time.

Performance Rating

Score 1 point for each correct answer

Total Score	Rating	Percentage of Population
9 / 10	Genius level	Top 5%
8	High Expert	Top 10%
7	Expert	Top 30%
6	High Average	Top 40%
5	Middle Average	Top 60%
4	Low Average	Bottom 40%
3	Borderline Low	Bottom 30%
2	Low	Bottom 10%
0 / 1	Very Low	Bottom 5%

Transfer your score to the chart in the Assessment Section on page 302.

Puzzles

The puzzles in this section are sometimes referred to as spatial or culture-fair and rely entirely on diagrammatic representation. They are designed not just to make you exercise your powers of logic and your ability to deal with problems in a structured and analytical way, but to make you think laterally and creatively.

The definition of 'spatial' is 'pertaining to space', and spatial abilities mean the perceptual and cognitive abilities that enable a person to deal with spatial relations.

Puzzles of this nature are referred to as culture-fair, or culture-free, as they are designed to be free of any particular cultural bias, so that no advantage can be derived by individuals of one culture to those of another. In other words, they eliminate language factors or other skills that may be closely tied to another culture.

Spatial aptitude involves different thought processes to those which determine verbal or numerical prowess. This is because the left side of the human brain is analytical and functions in a sequential and logical fashion and is the side which controls language, academic studies and rationality. The right side of the brain is creative and intuitive and leads, for example, to the birth of ideas for works of art and music. It is this side of the brain which determines how well we are able to adapt to puzzles and tests involving spatial aptitude.

Brain Fact

The branches of a neuron's dendrite (the dendritic tree) are connected to a thousand neighbouring neurons. It is when one of these neurons fire that a positive or negative charge is received by one of the dendrites. The strengths of all the charges are added together and the aggregate input is then passed to the soma, the cell body. It is just one part of the soma, the axon hillock, which concerns itself with the signal. If the aggregate input is greater than the axon hillock's threshold, this causes the neuron to fire and an output signal is transmitted down the axon.

Example

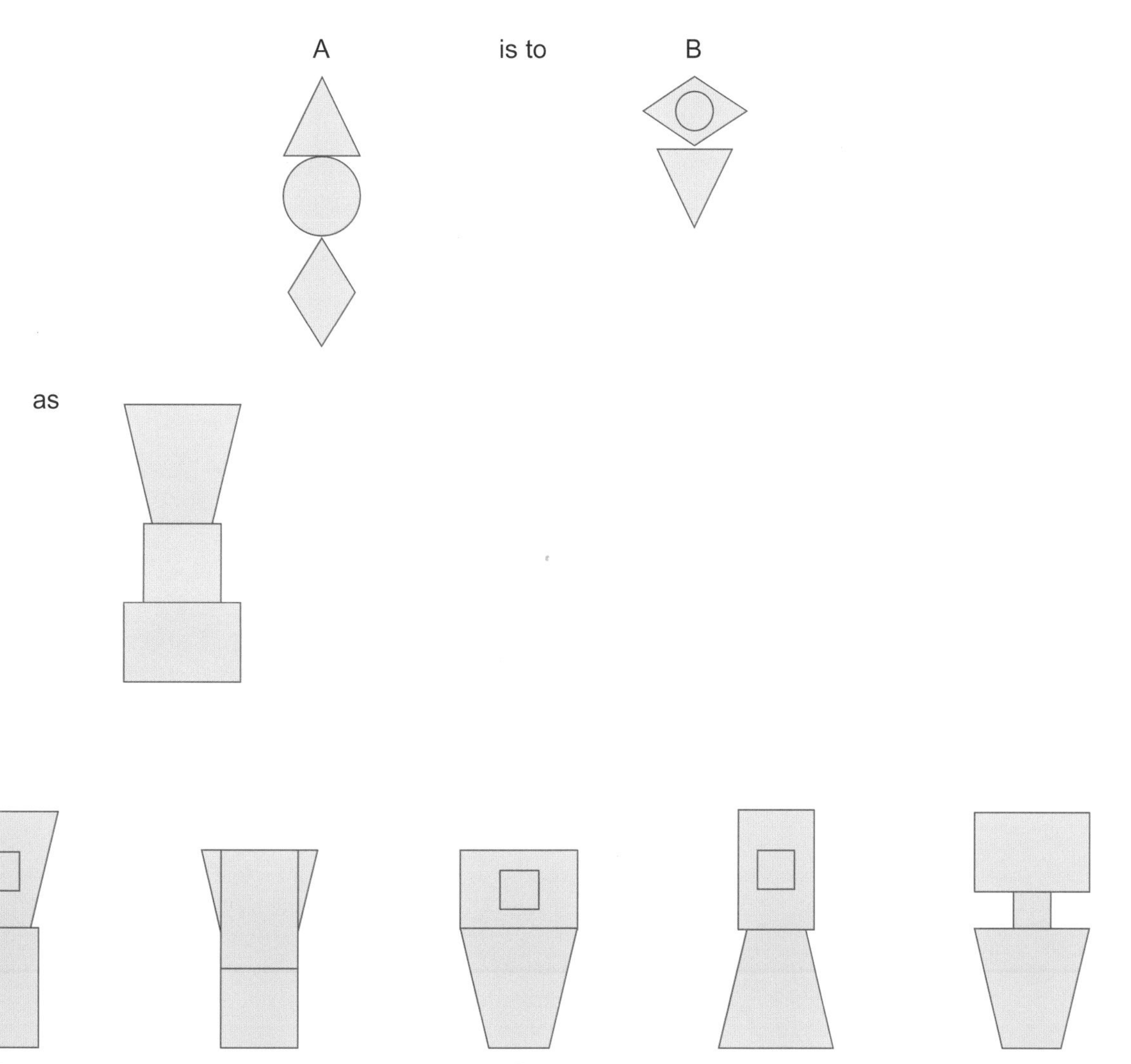

Answer: D – The figures behave in the same way as the figures in the example. The trapezium moves from top to bottom and rotates 180 degrees. The rectangle rotates 90 degrees and goes to the top. The square reduces in size and goes inside the rectangle.

Quick Fire

1.

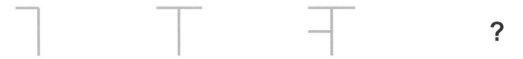

What comes next in the above sequence?

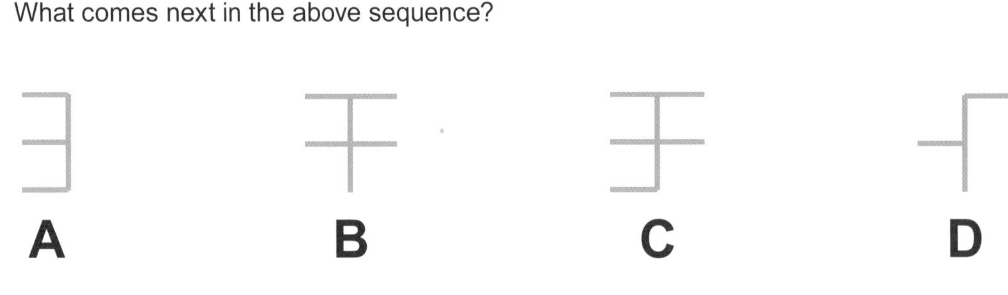

2.

What comes next in the above sequence?

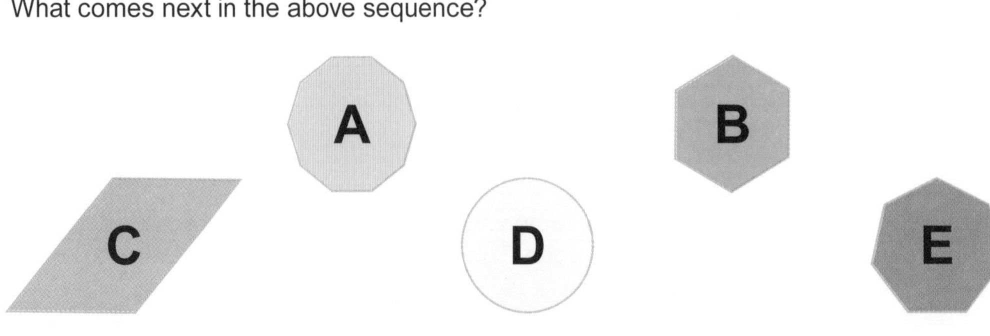

Quick Fire

3.

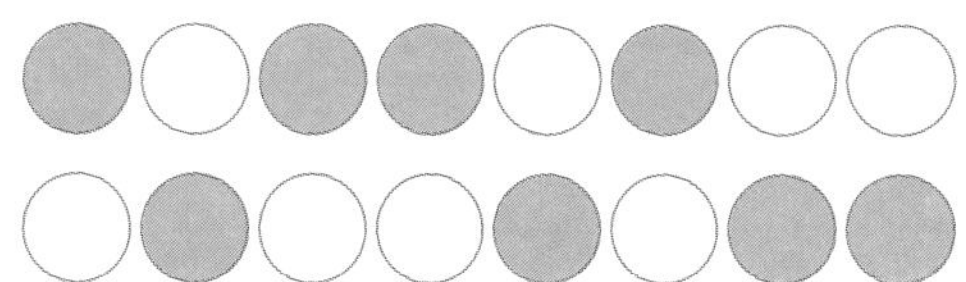

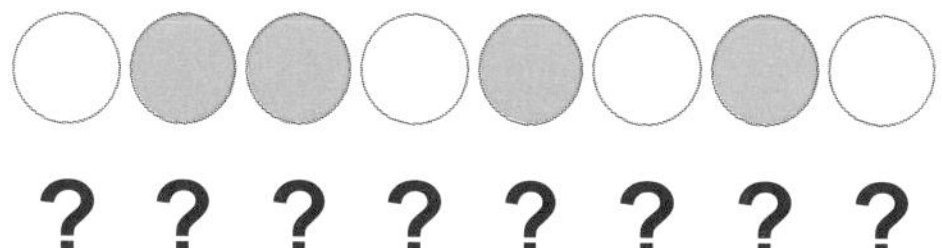

? ? ? ? ? ? ? ?

Which set of circles should replace the question marks?

A 

B 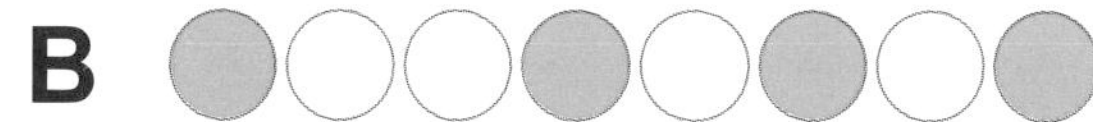

C 

D 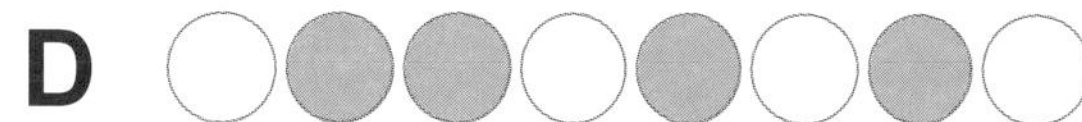

E 

Quick Fire

4.

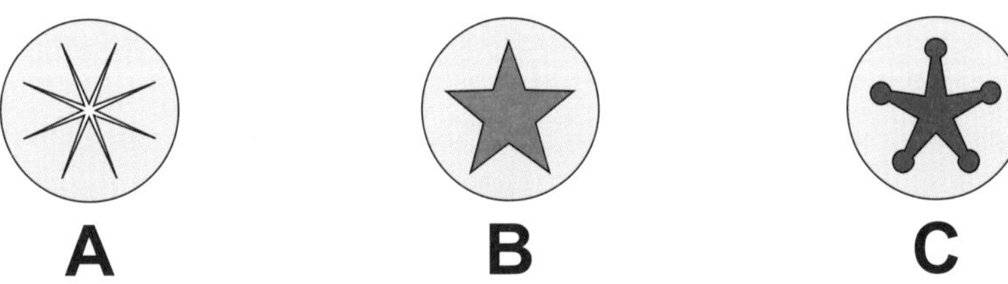

Which of the above symbols should replace the question mark?

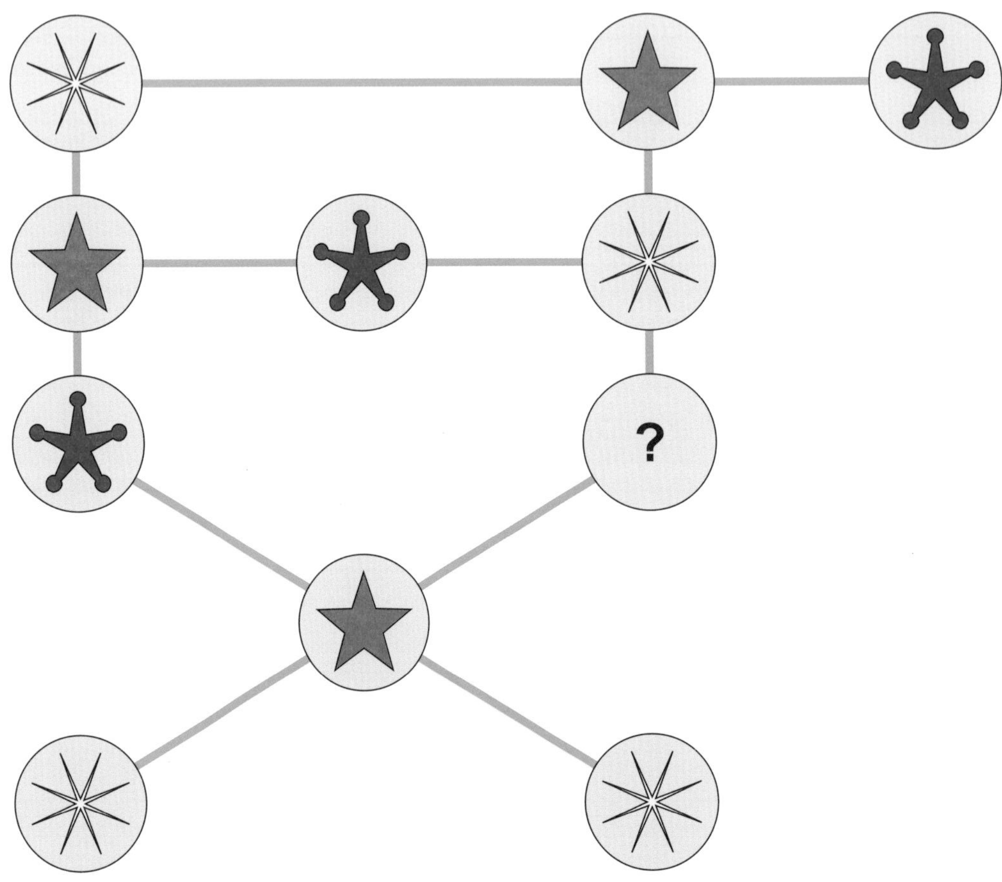

Quick Fire

5.

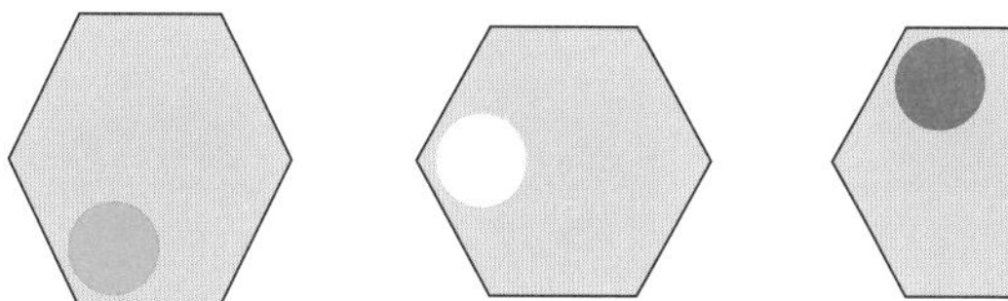

?

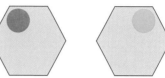

Which hexagon comes next in the above sequence?

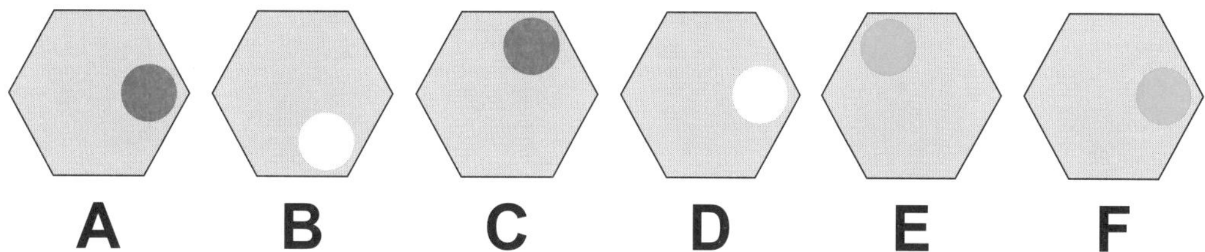

6.

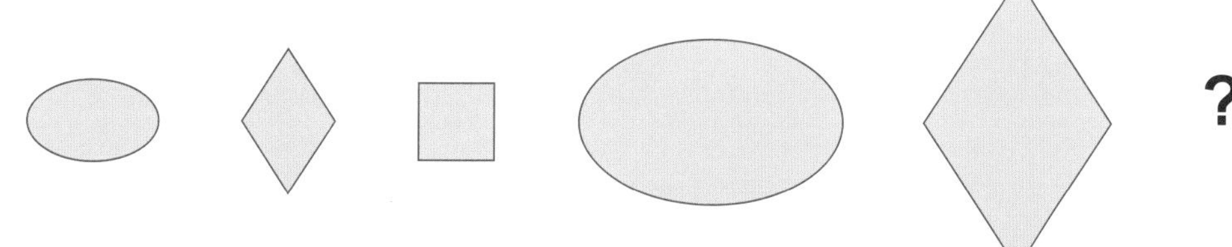

?

What comes next in the above sequence?

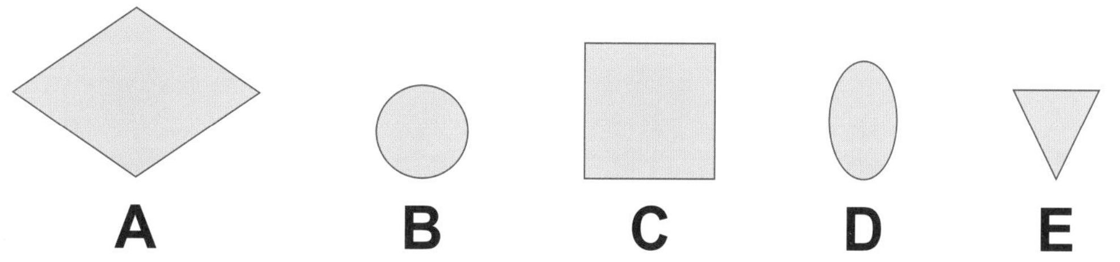

Quick Fire

7.

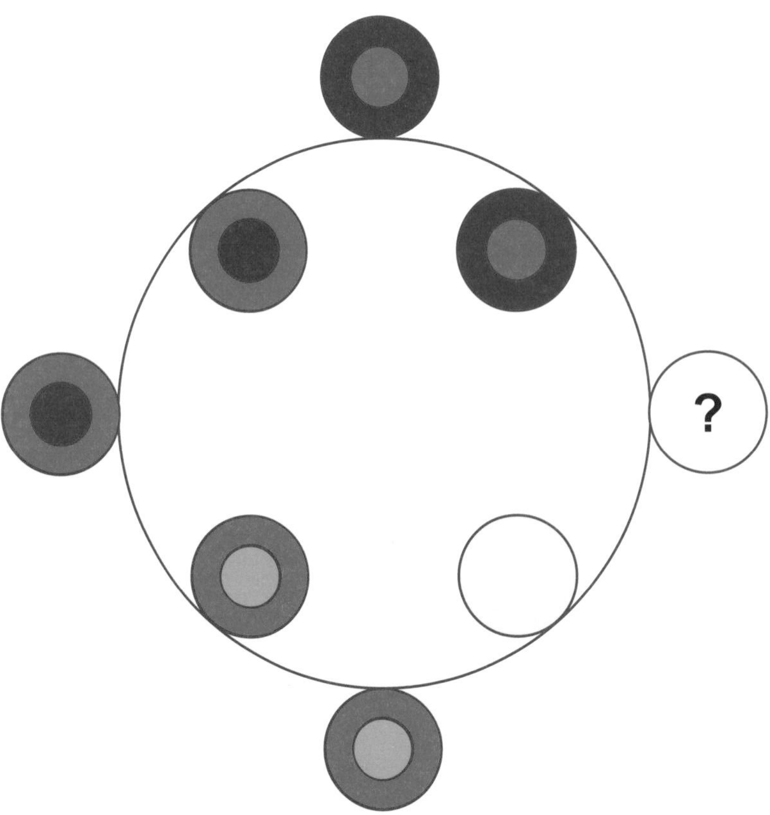

Which circle below should replace the one with the question mark?

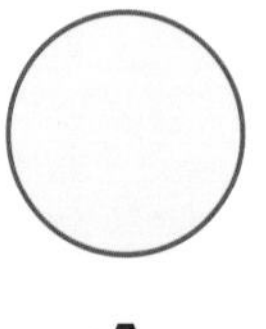

A

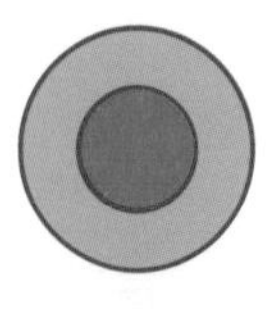

B

C

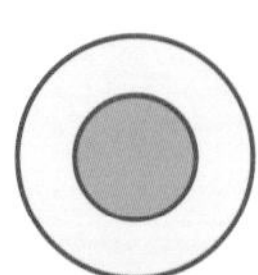

D

Quick Fire

8.

What comes next in the above sequence?

9.

is to

as

is to:

A

B

C

D

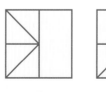

Quick Fire

10.

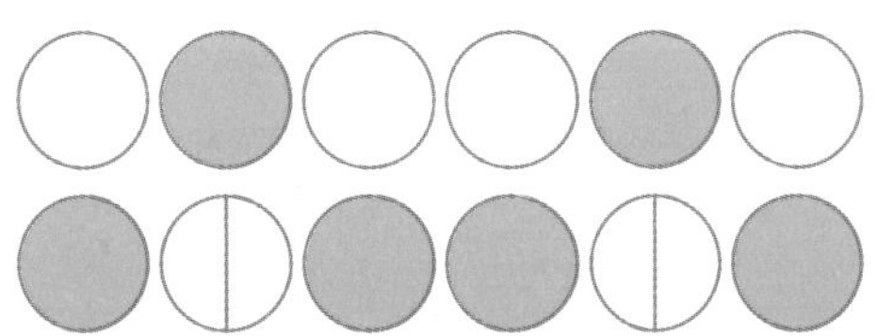

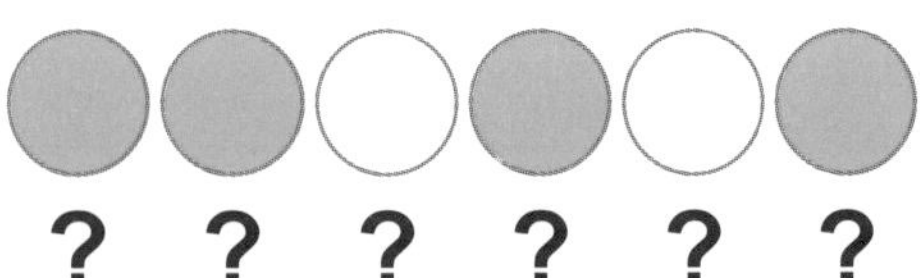

Which set of circles should replace the question marks?

A 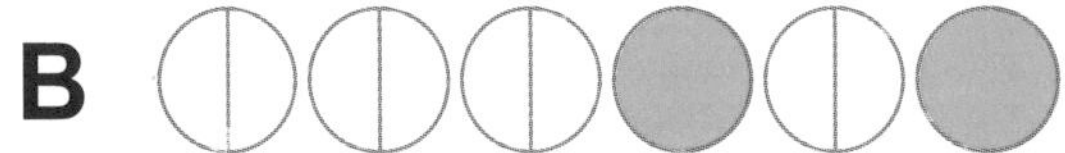

B 

C 

D 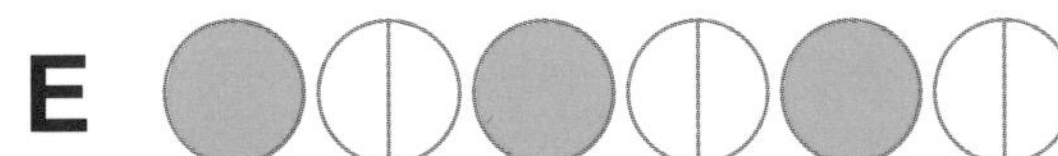

E

Quick Fire

11. Which is the odd one out?

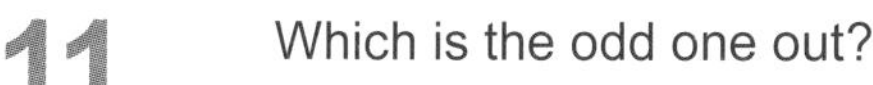

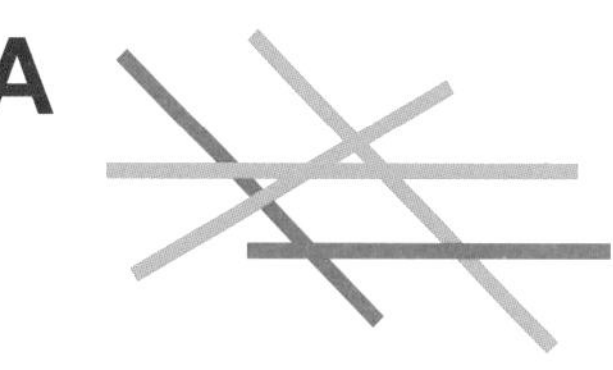

A

B

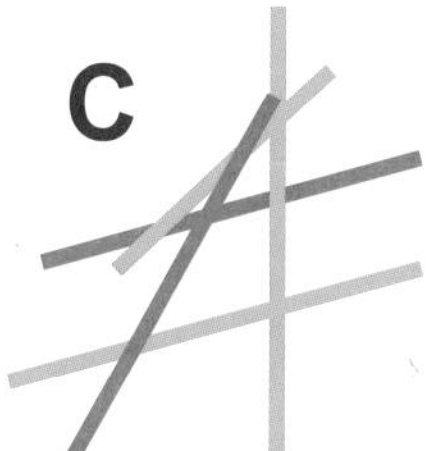

C

D

E

12.

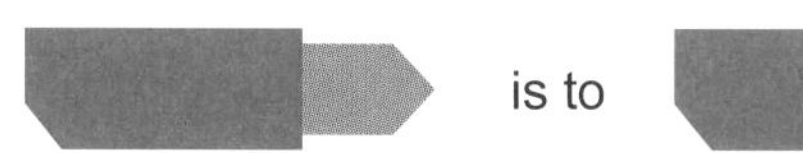

is to

as  is to:

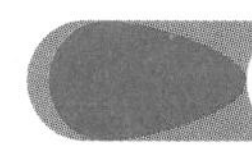

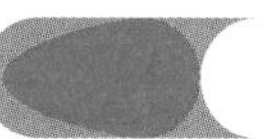

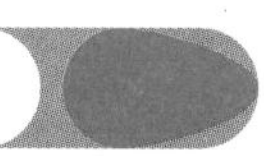

A **B** **C** **D** **E**

Quick Fire

13.

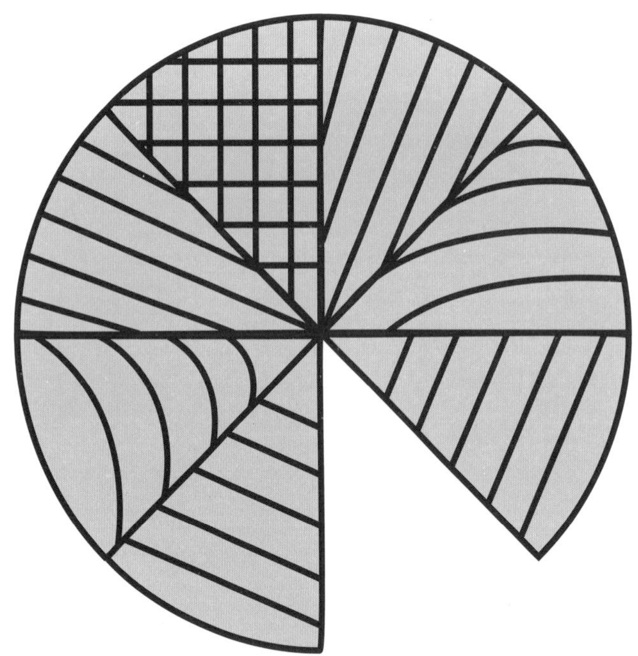

Which is the missing section?

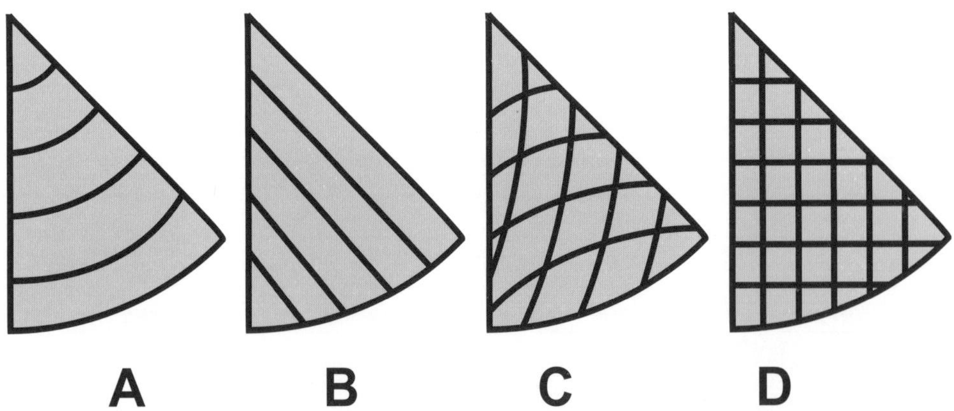

Quick Fire

14. Which is the missing tile?

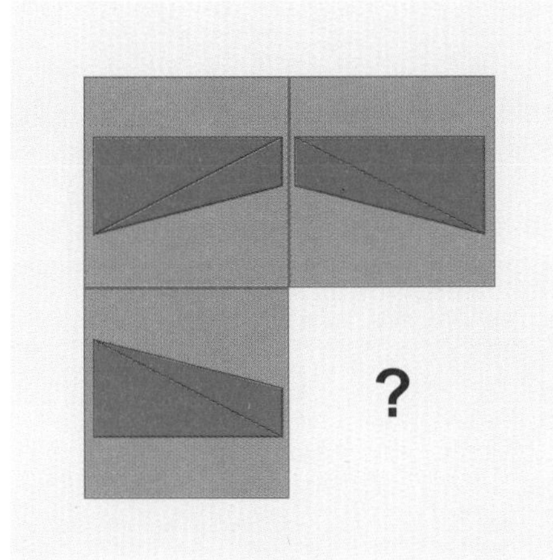

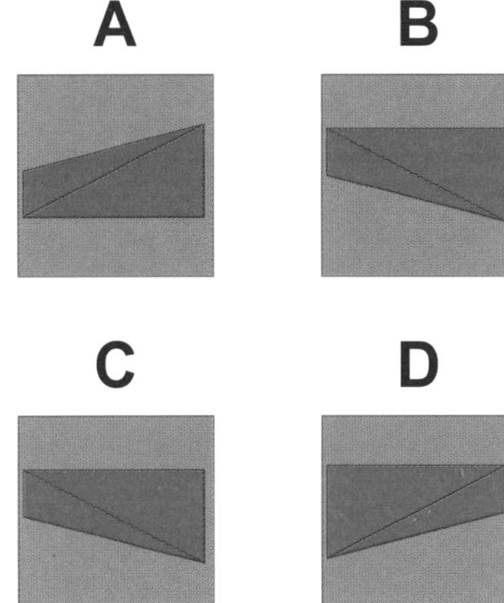

15. Which is the odd one out?

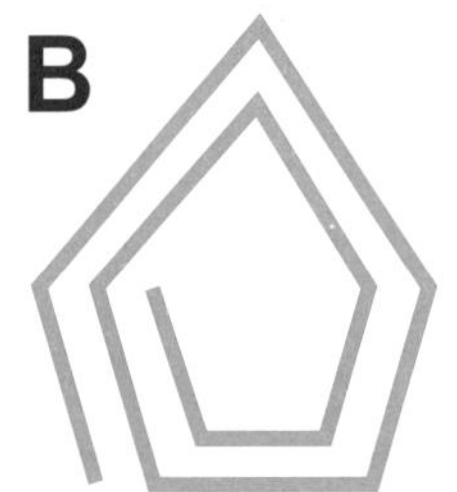

More Challenging

16.

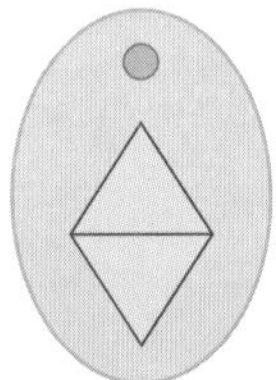 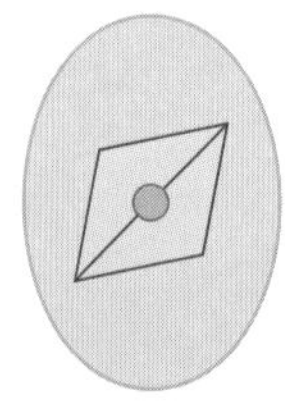 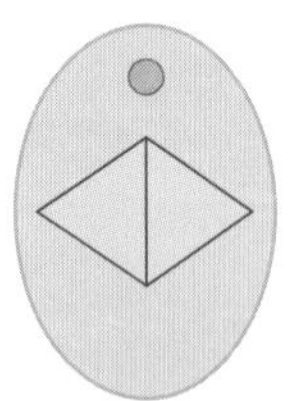 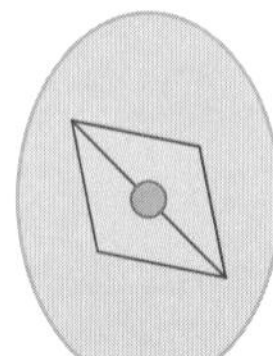 ?

What comes next in the above sequence?

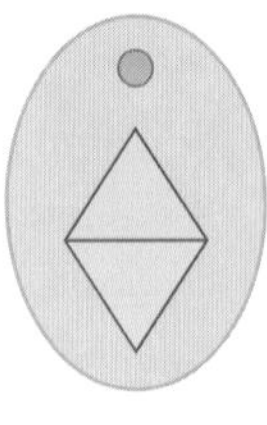 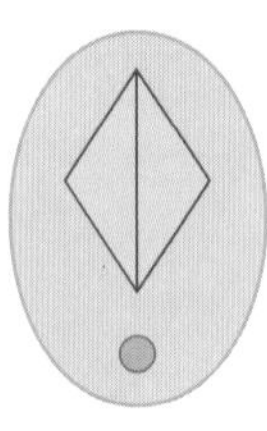 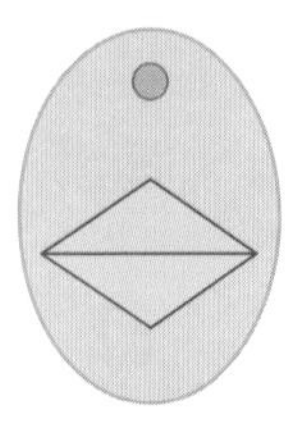 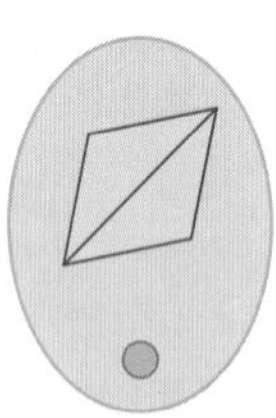 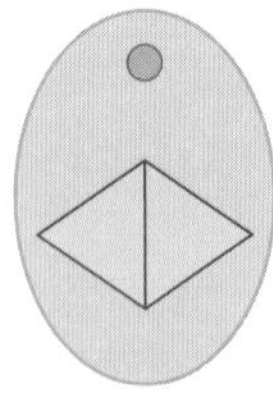

A B C D E

17.

   ?

What comes next in the above sequence?

A B C D E

F G H I

More Challenging

18. Which is the odd one out?

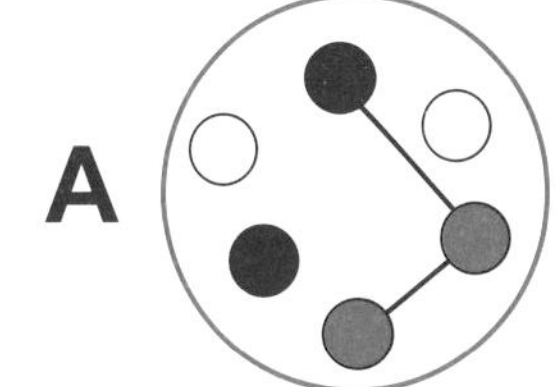

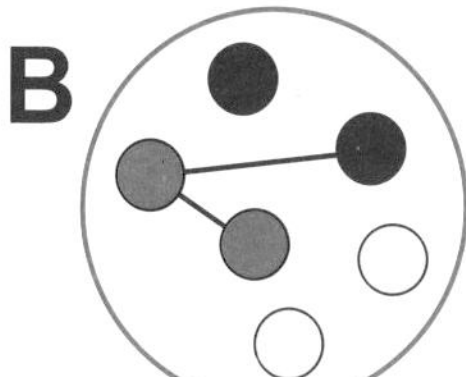

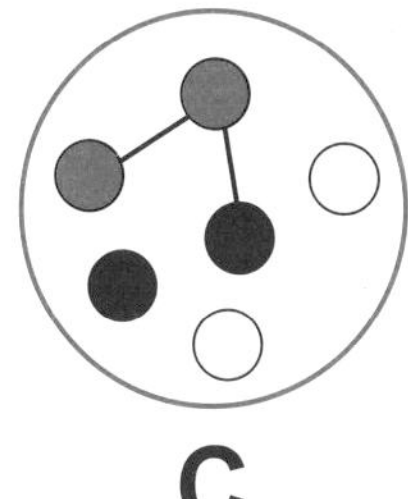

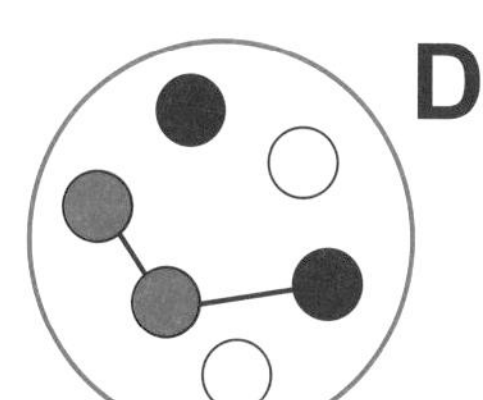

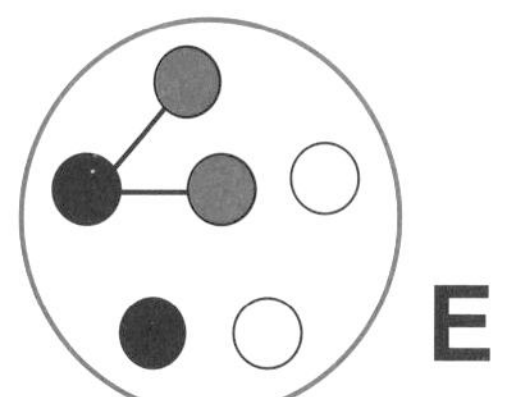

19. Which is the odd one out?

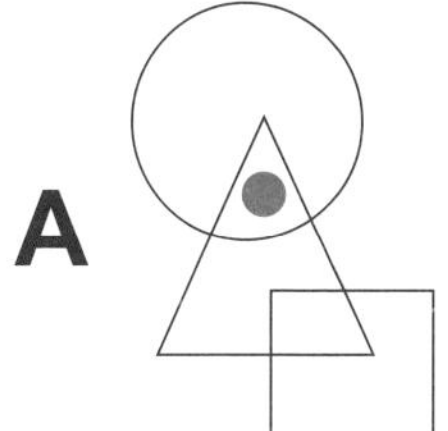

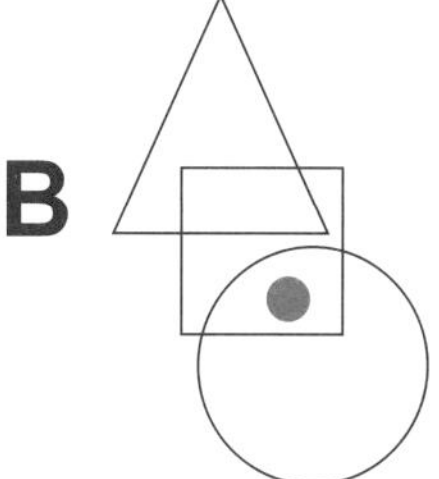

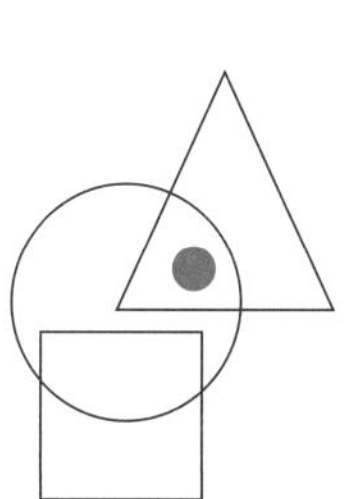

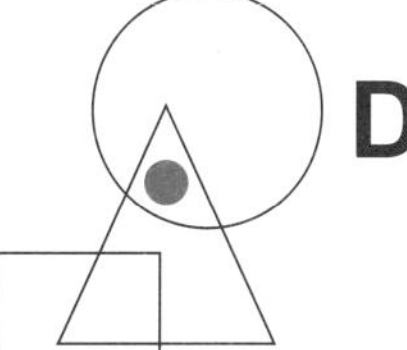

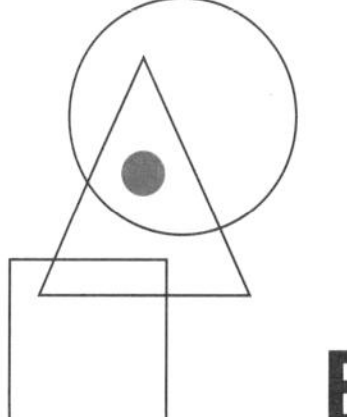

More Challenging

20.

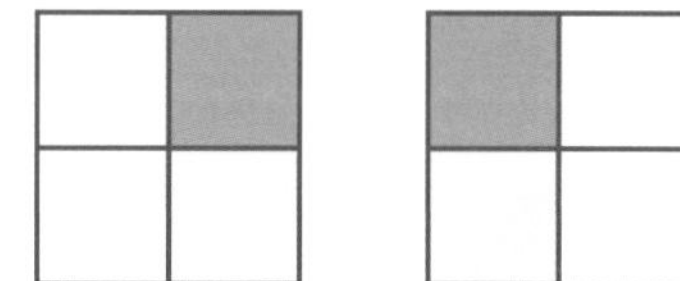
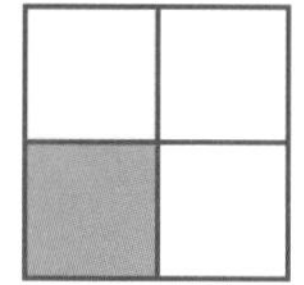
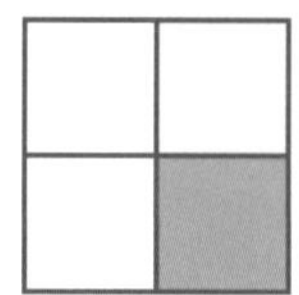

?

What comes next in the above sequence?

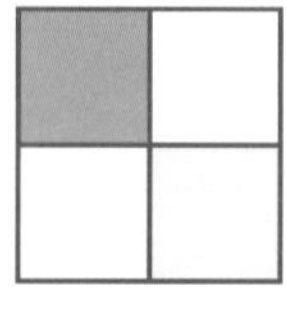
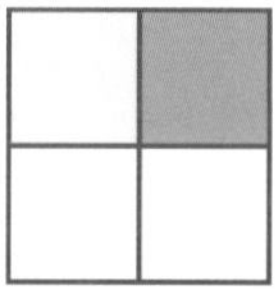
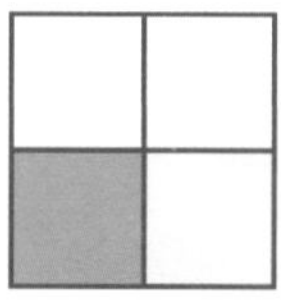
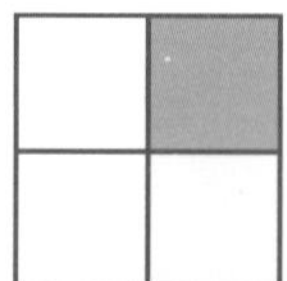
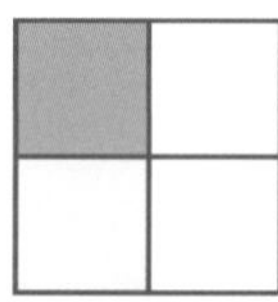

A B C D E

21.

Which is the odd one out?

A

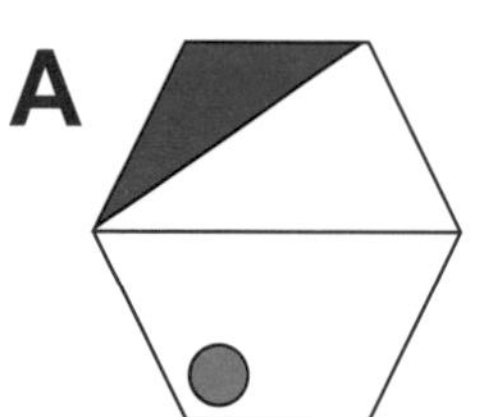

B

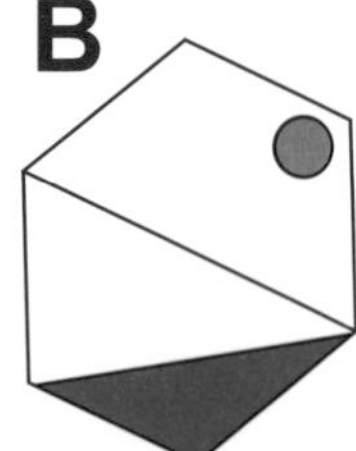

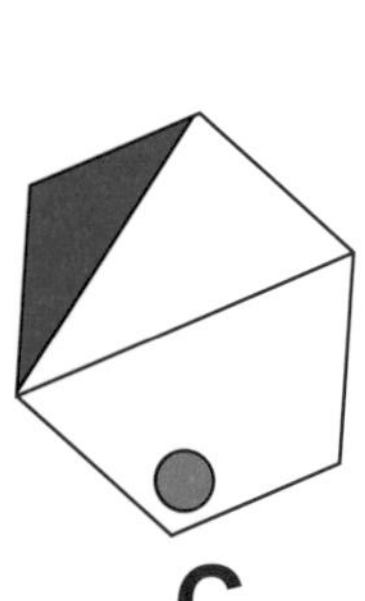

C

D

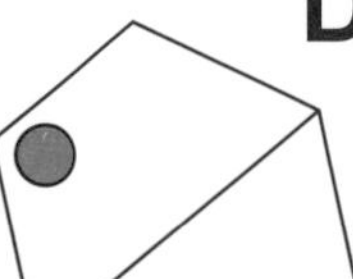

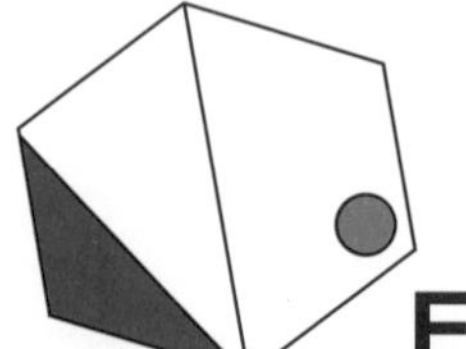

E

More Challenging

22.

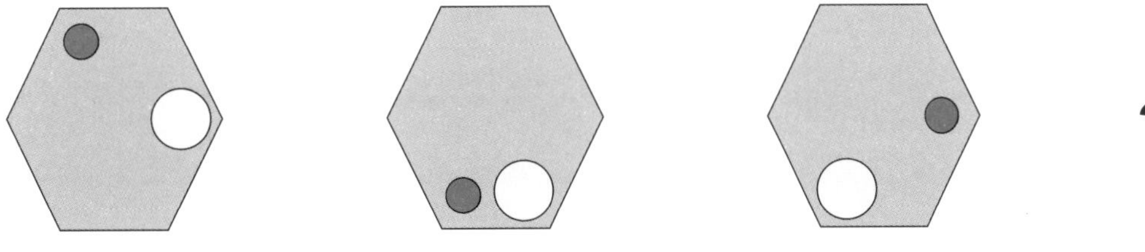

What comes next in the above sequence?

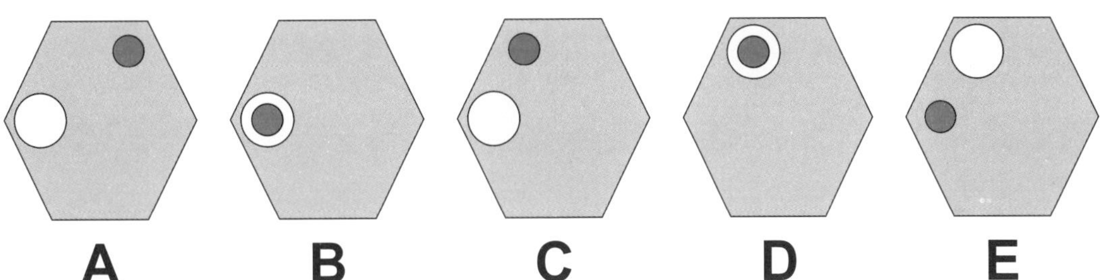

23.

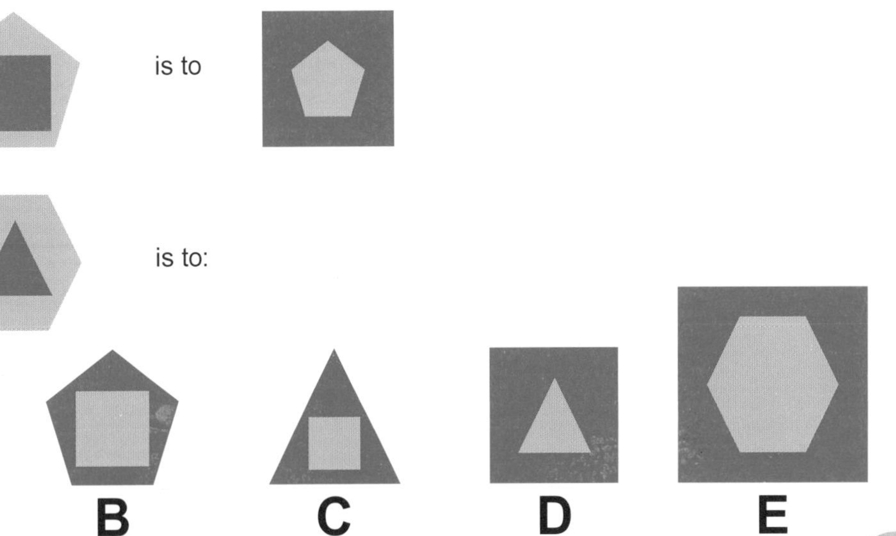

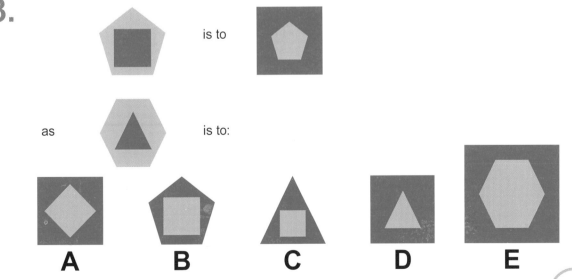

More Challenging

24. Which is the missing box?

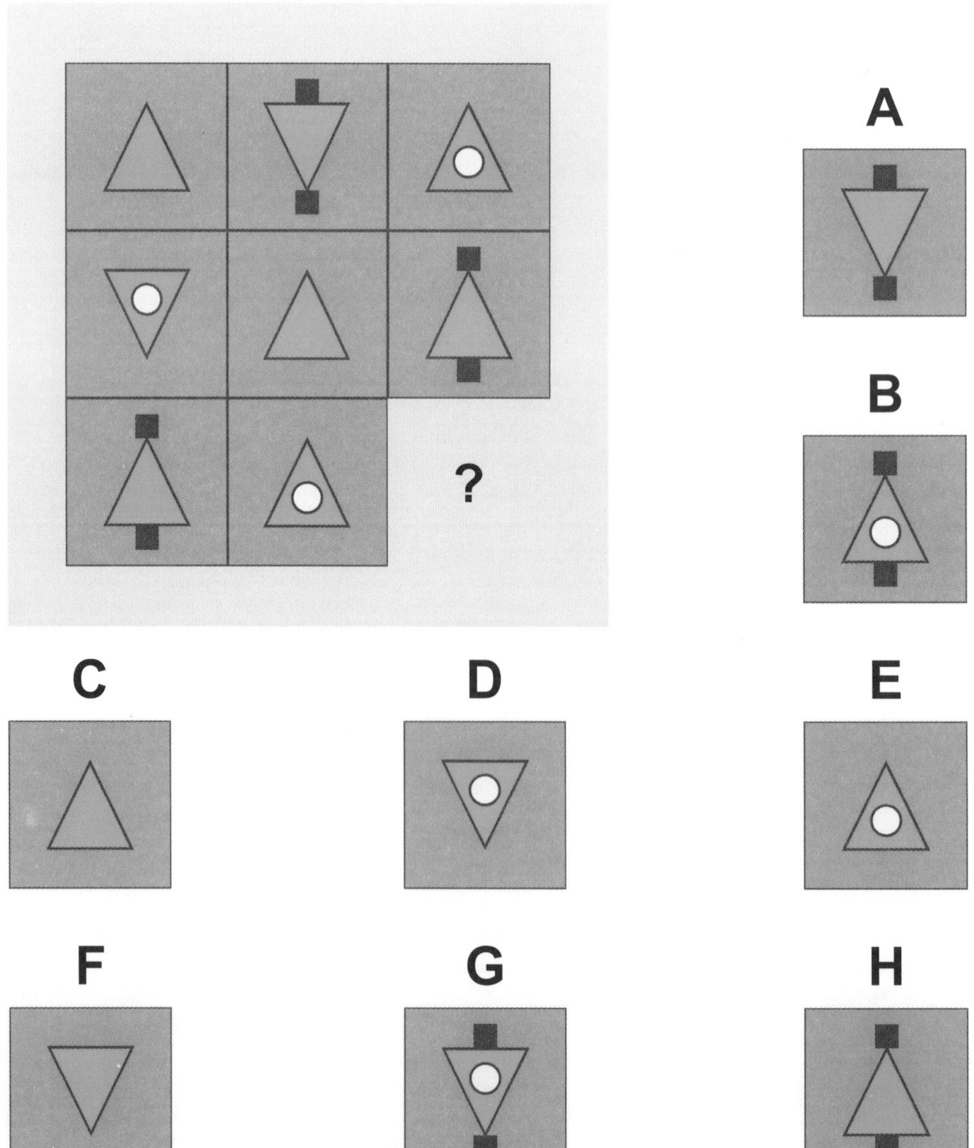

More Challenging

25. Which is the odd one out?

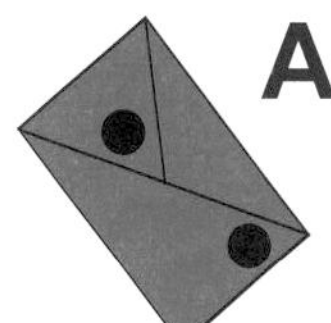

A

B

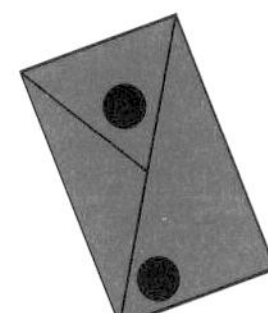

C

D

26.

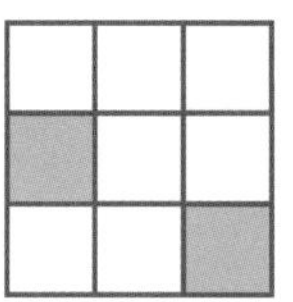

is to

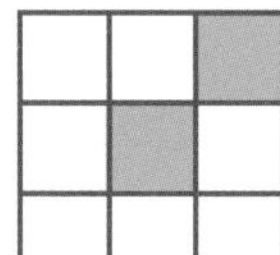

as

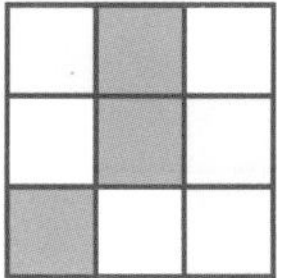

is to:

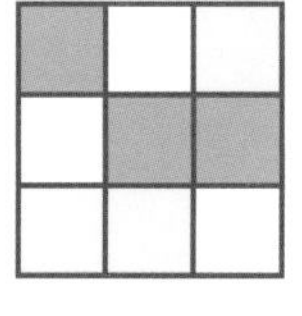

A

B

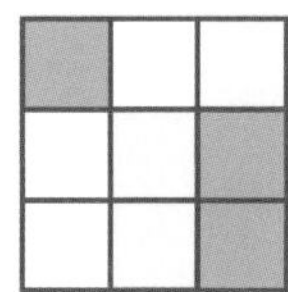

C

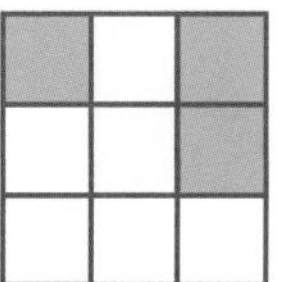

D

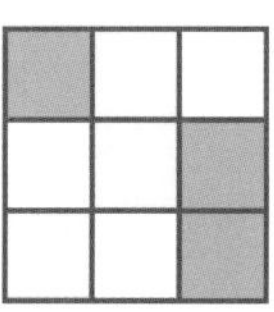

E

More Challenging

27.

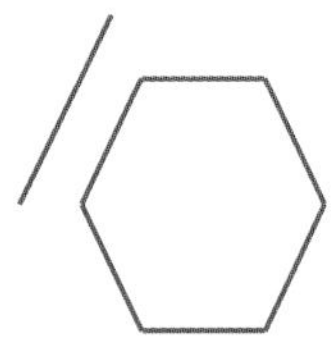   ?

What comes next in the above sequence?

 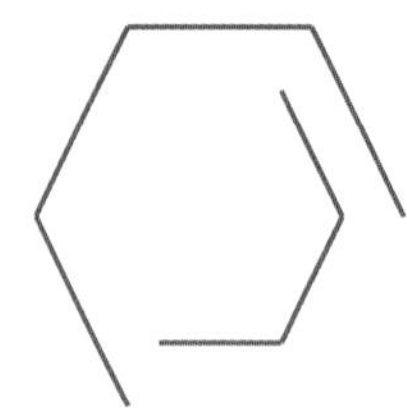 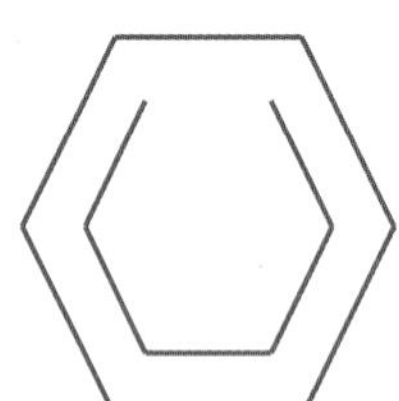 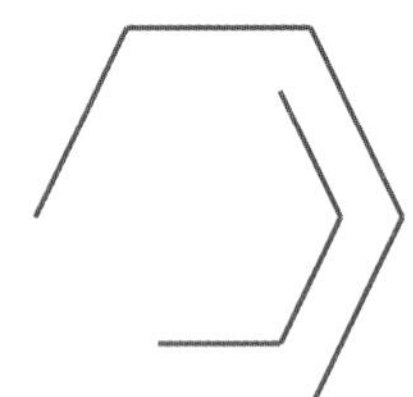

A **B** **C** **D** **E**

28.

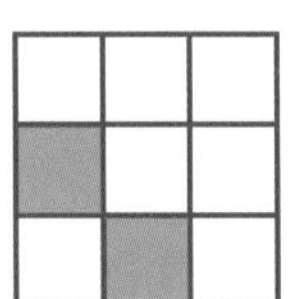 is to 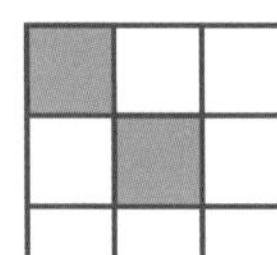

as 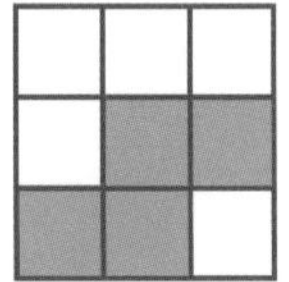 is to:

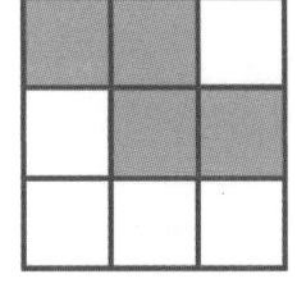 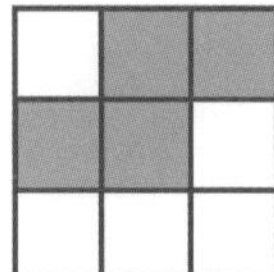 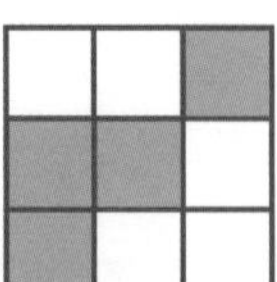 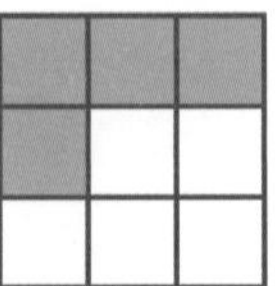

A **B** **C** **D** **E**

More Challenging

29.

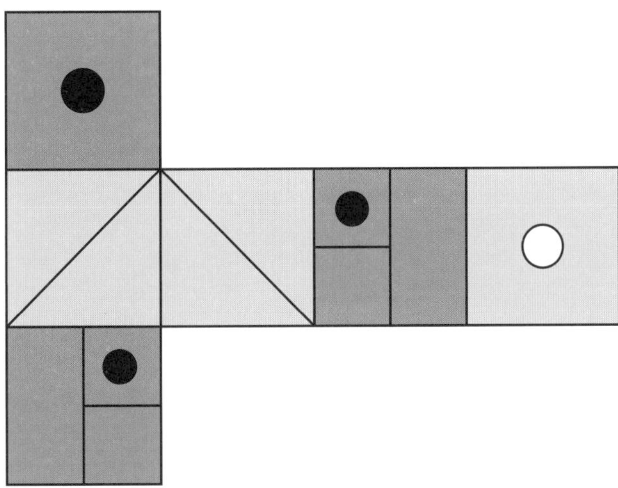

When the above is folded to form a cube, which is the only one of the following that **cannot** be produced?

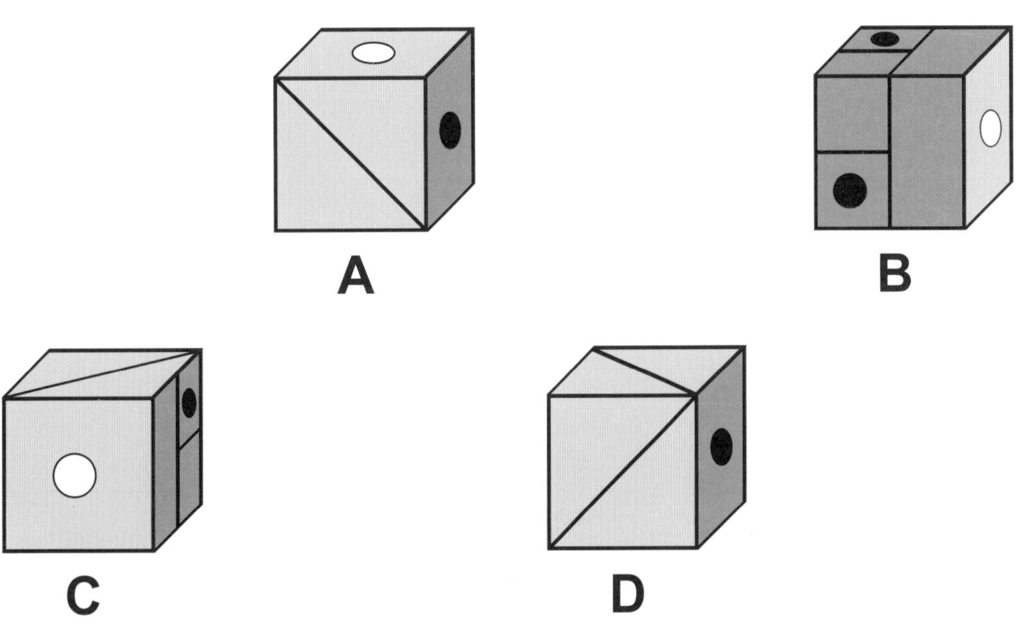

More Challenging

30.

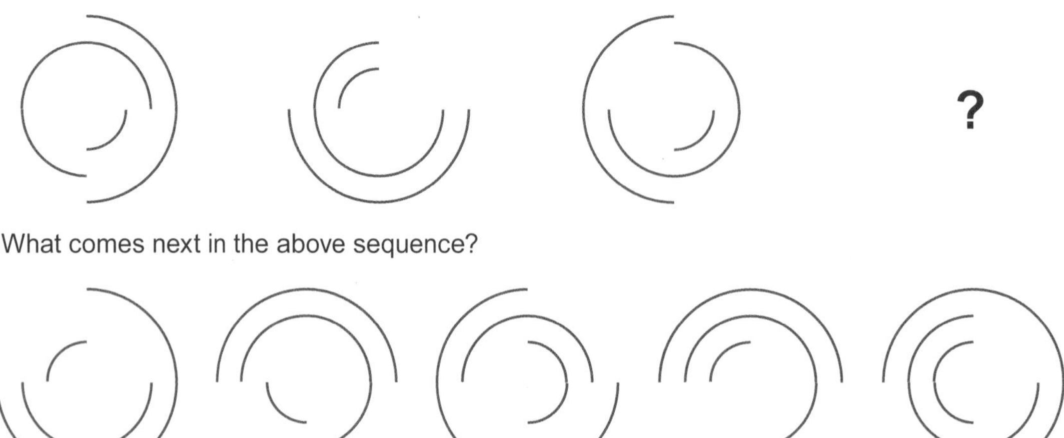

What comes next in the above sequence?

31.

Which is the odd one out?

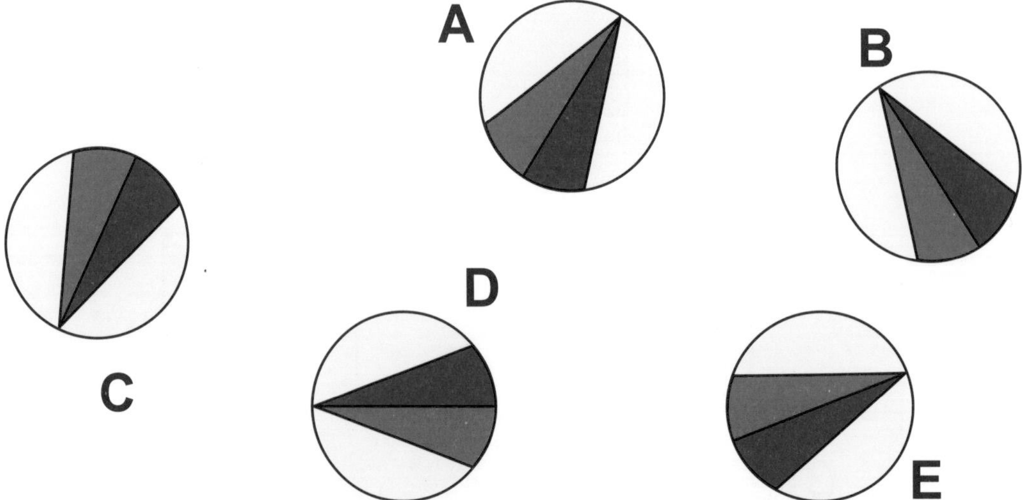

More Challenging

32.

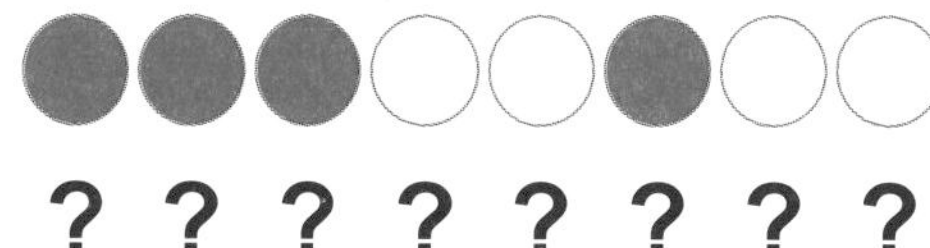

Which set of circles should replace the question marks?

A 

B 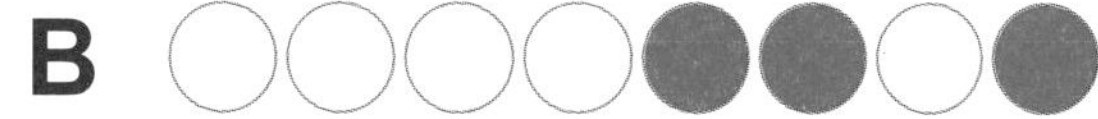

C 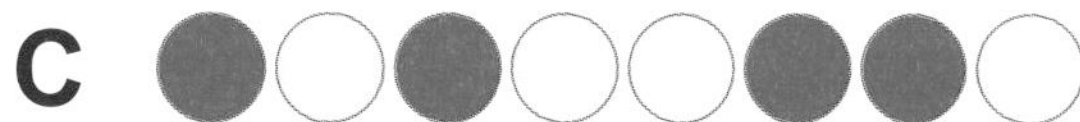

D 

E 

More Challenging

33. Which three of the four pieces below can be fitted together to form the figure on the right?

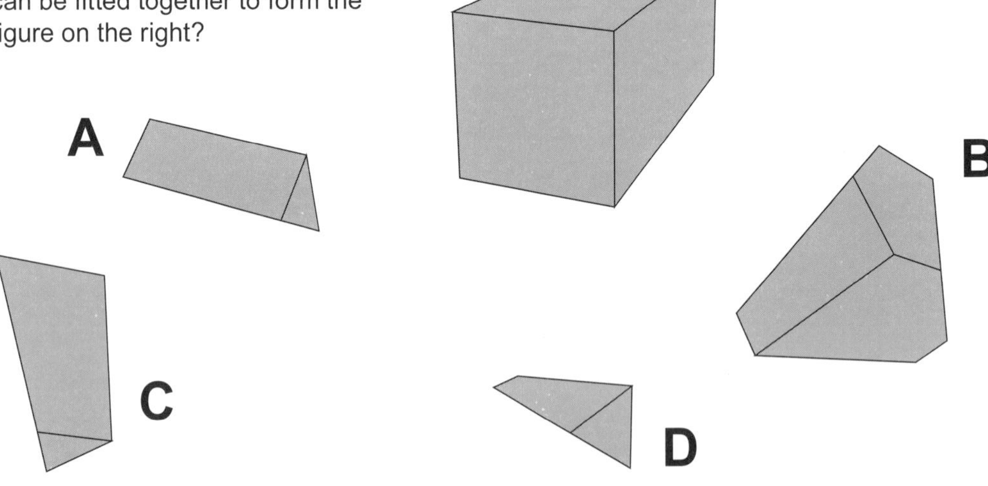

34.

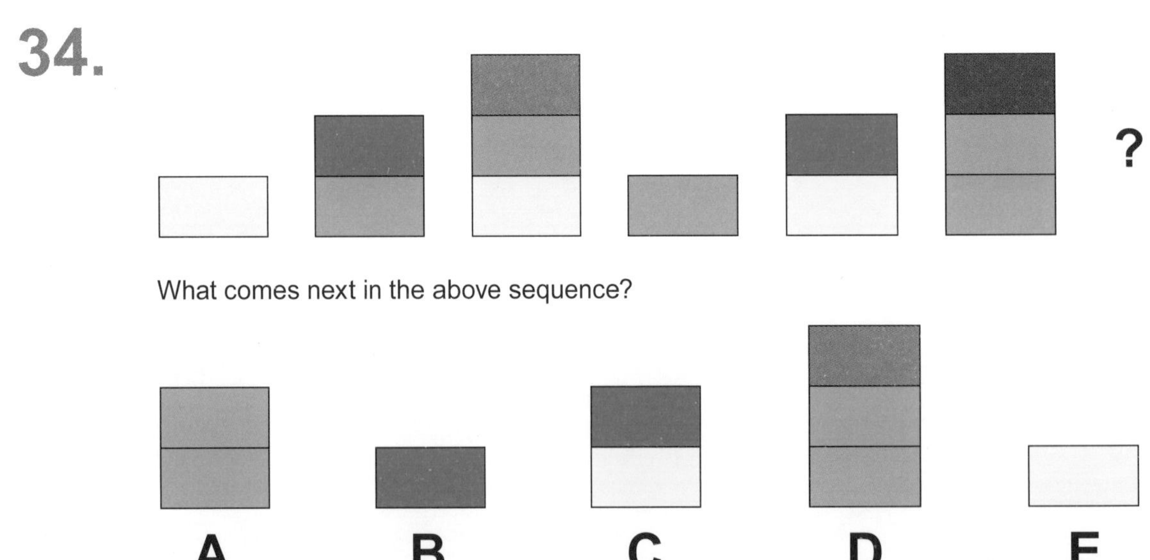

What comes next in the above sequence?

More Challenging

35.

   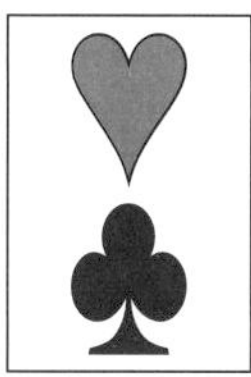  ?

Which option below completes the above set?

A

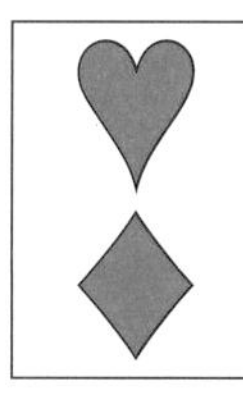
B

C

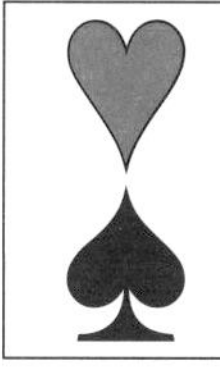
D

E

36.

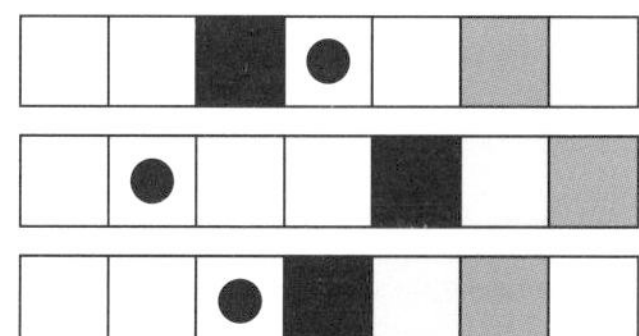

What comes next in the above sequence?

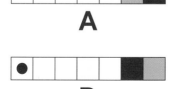

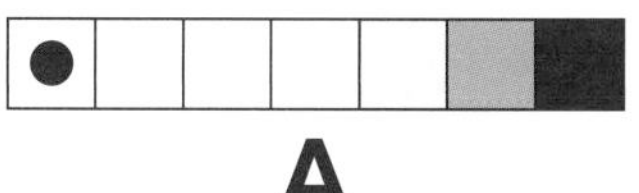
A

B

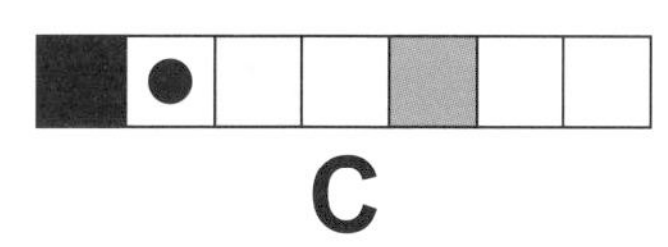
C

D

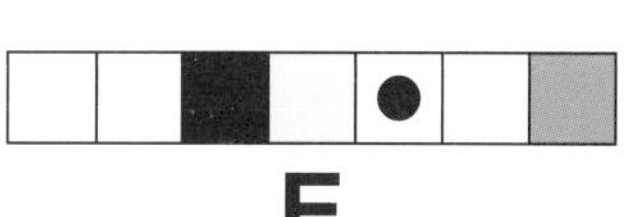
E

More Challenging

37.

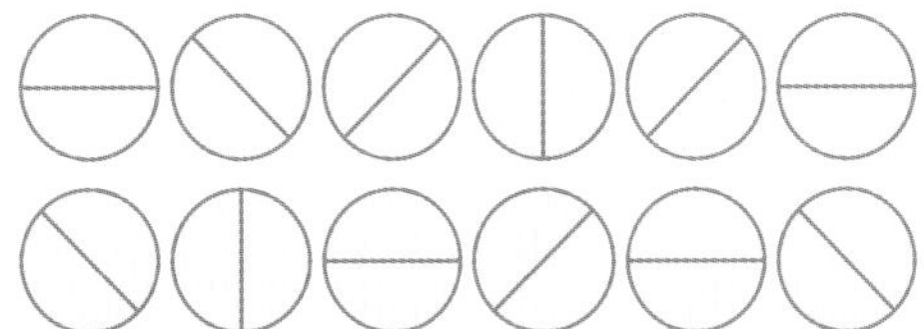

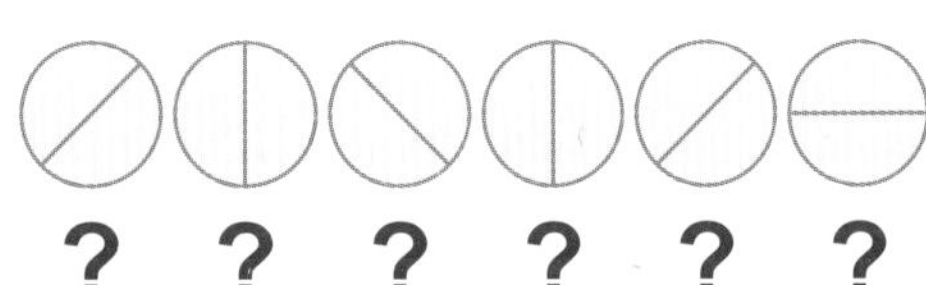

Which set of circles should replace the question marks?

A

B 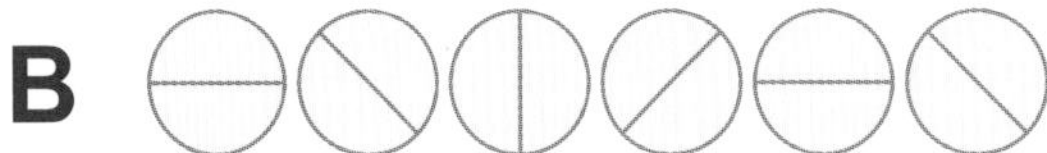

C

D

E 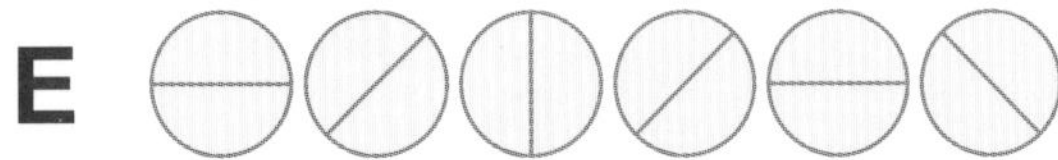

More Challenging

38. Which is the odd one out?

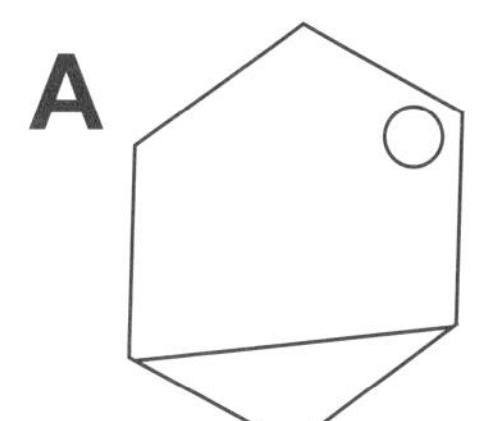

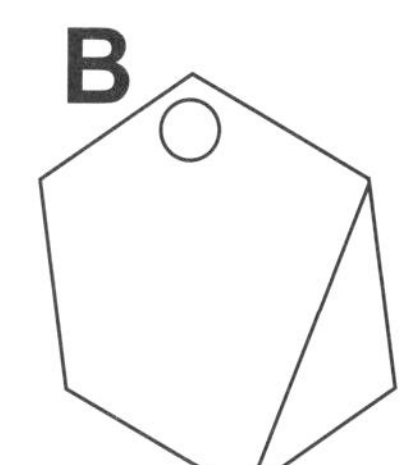

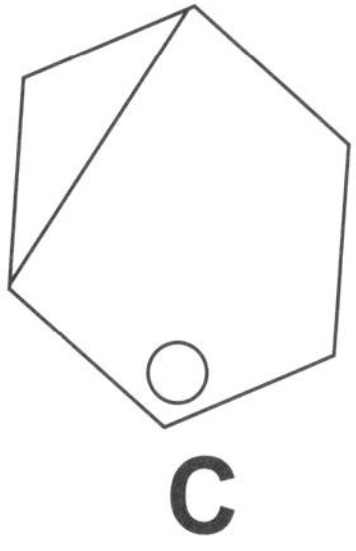

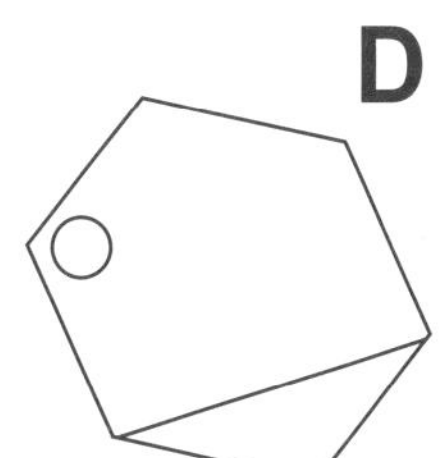

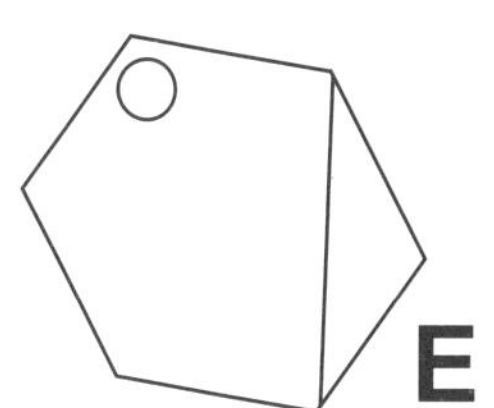

39. Which is the odd one out?

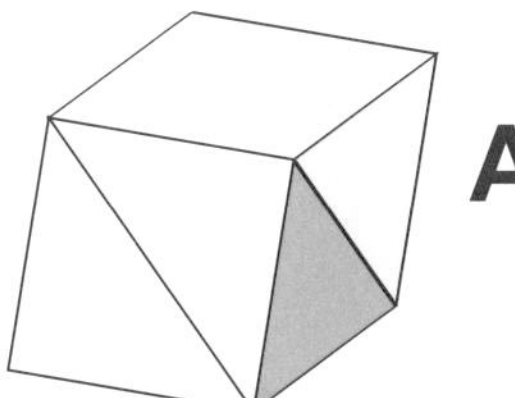

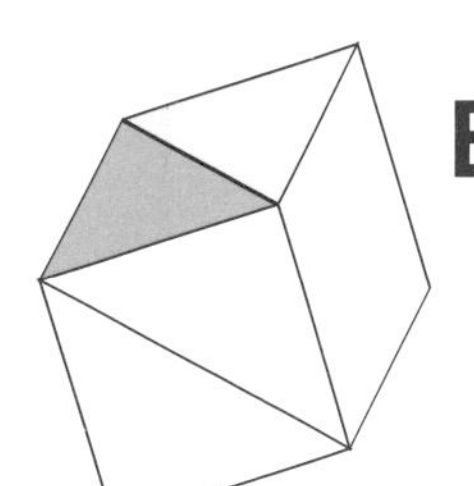

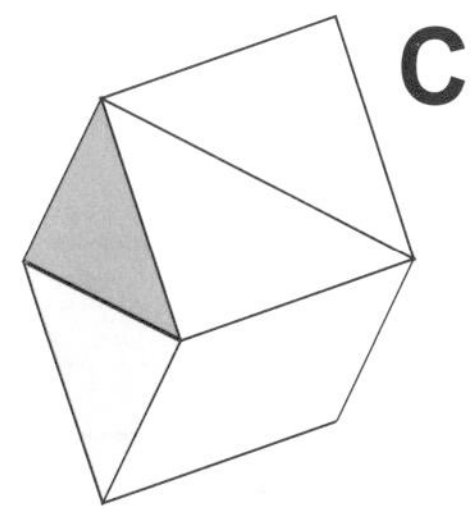

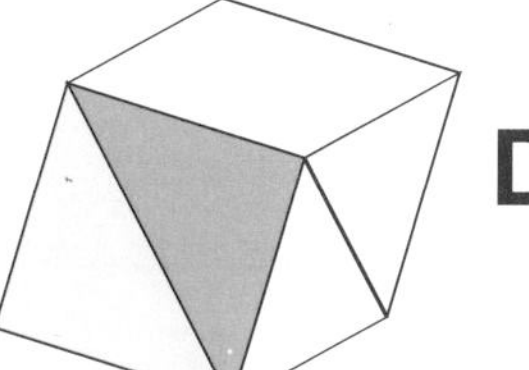

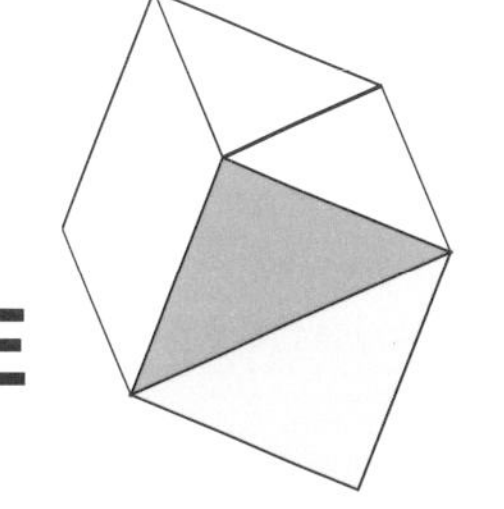

More Challenging

40.

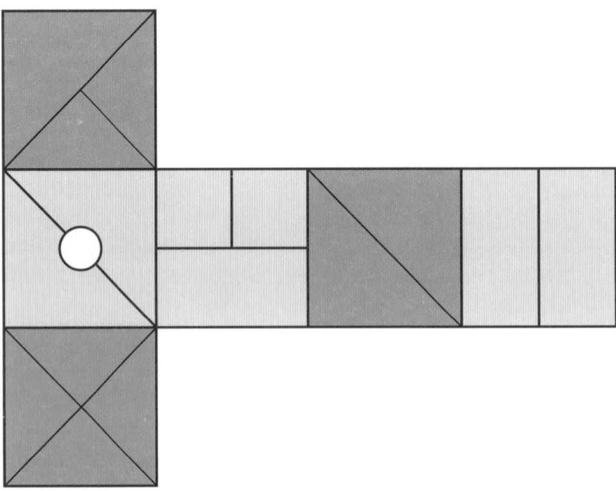

When the above is folded to form a cube, which is the only one of the following that **can** be produced?

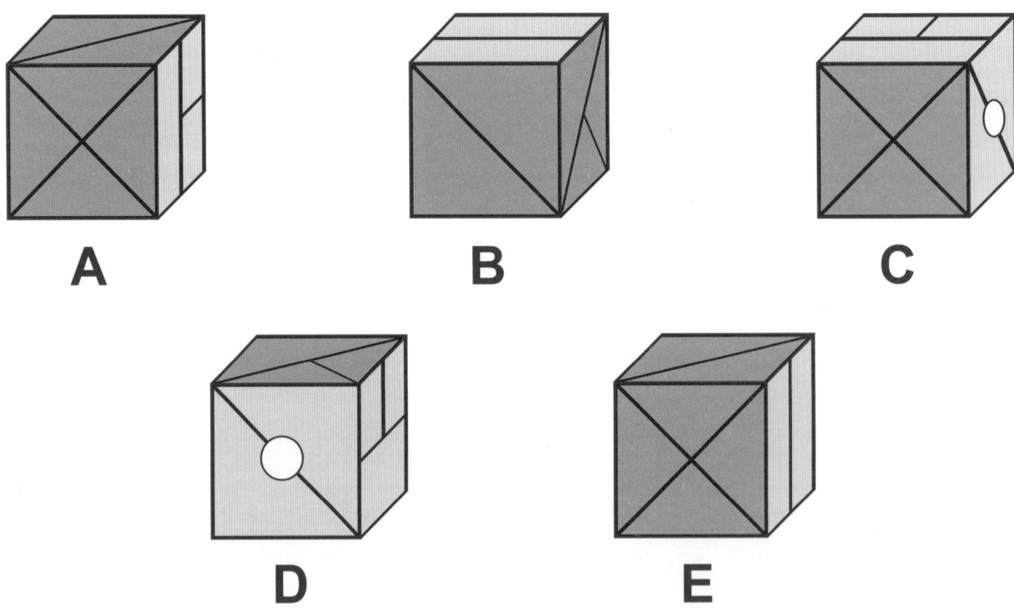

More Challenging

41.

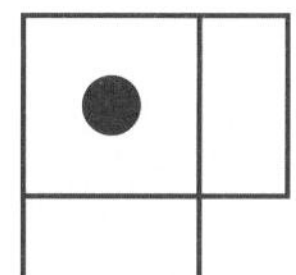
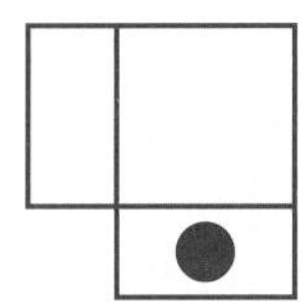
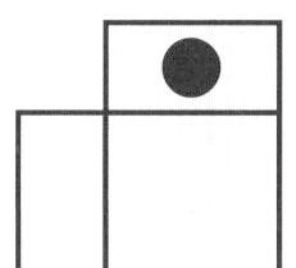

?

What comes next in the above sequence?

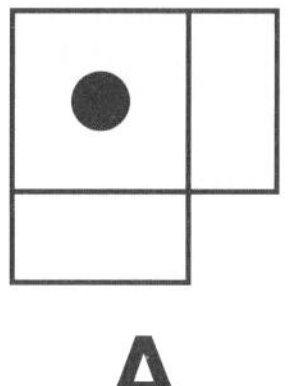
A

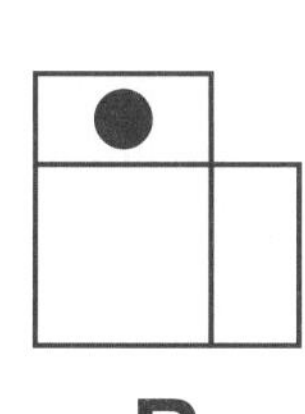
B

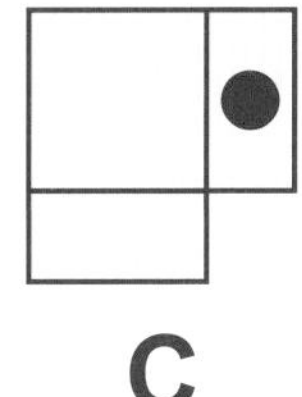
C

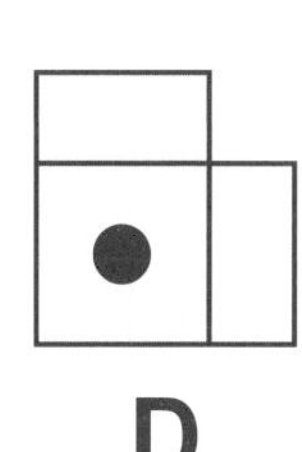
D

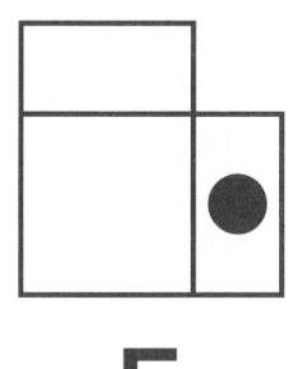
E

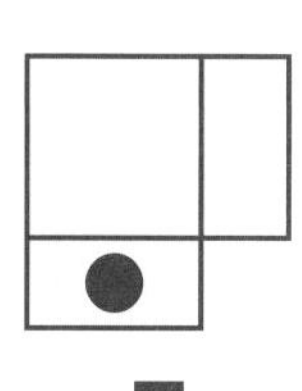
F

42.

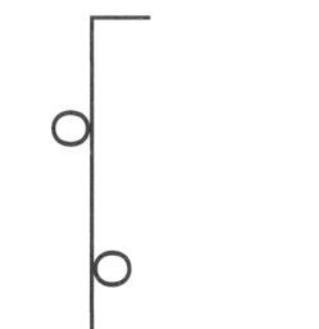

is to

as  is to:

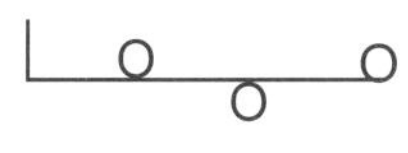
A

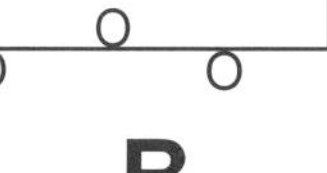
B

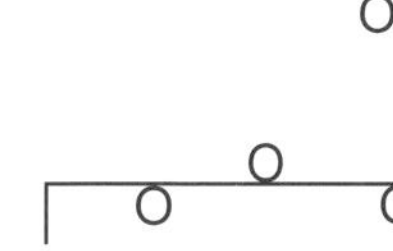
C

D

E

More Challenging

43. Which is the odd one out?

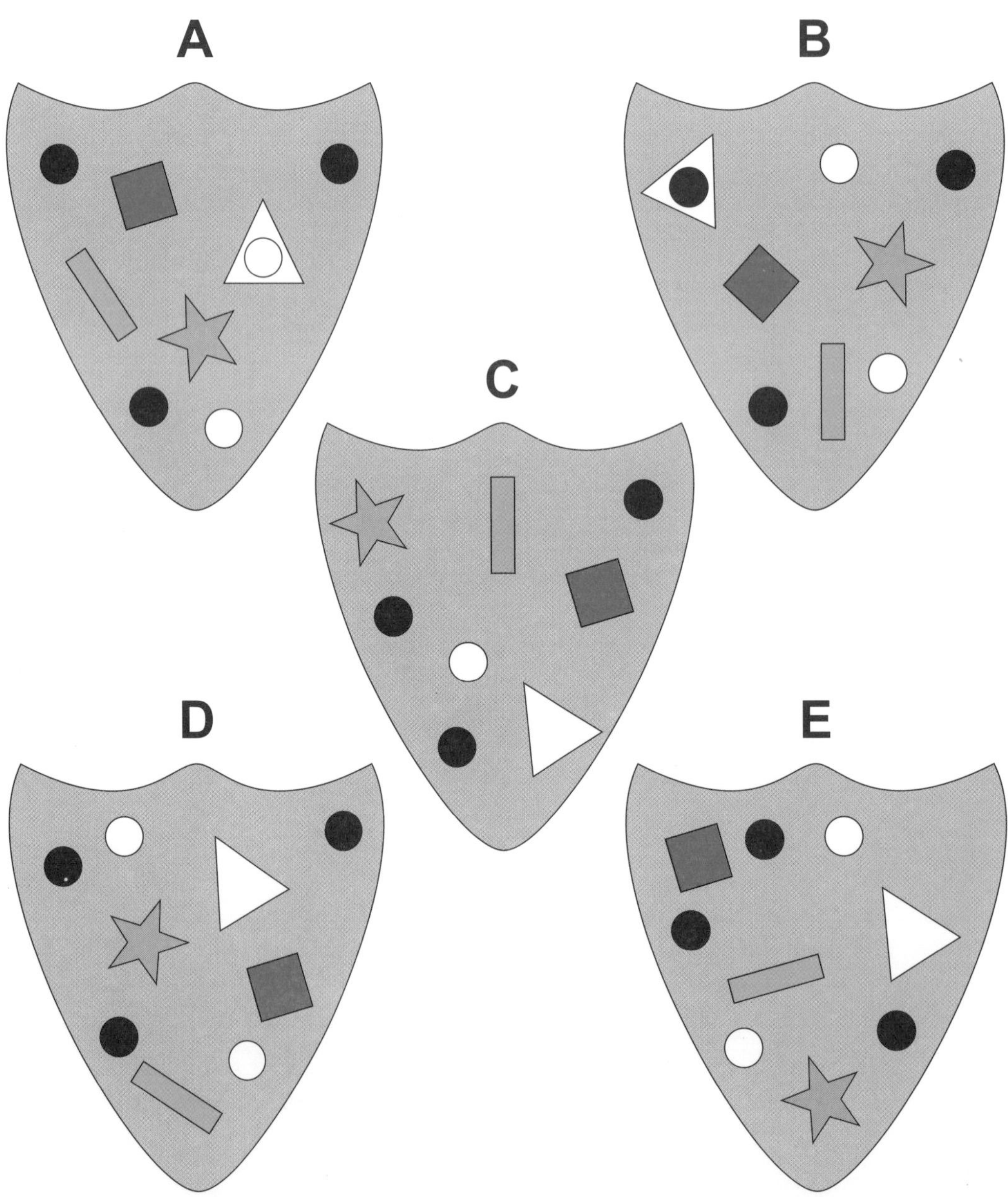

More Challenging

44.

 is to 

as 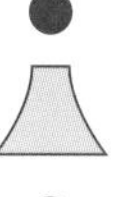 is to:

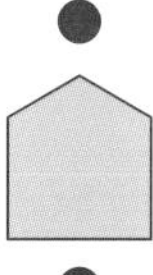

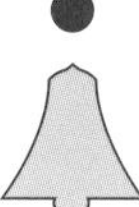

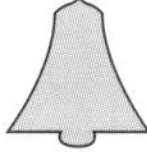

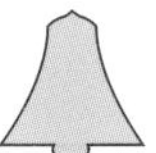

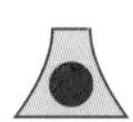

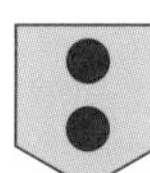
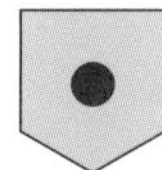
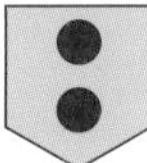

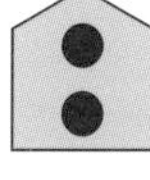
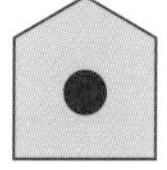

A **B** **C** **D** **E** **F**

More Challenging

45.

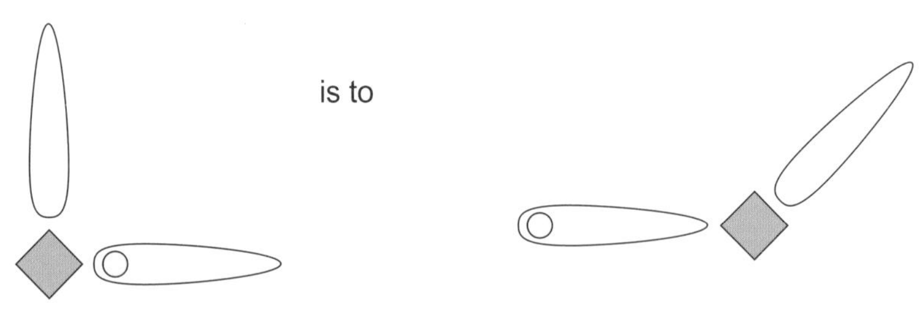

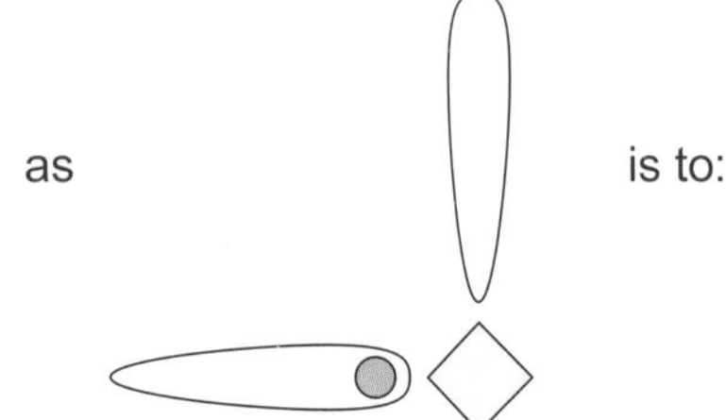

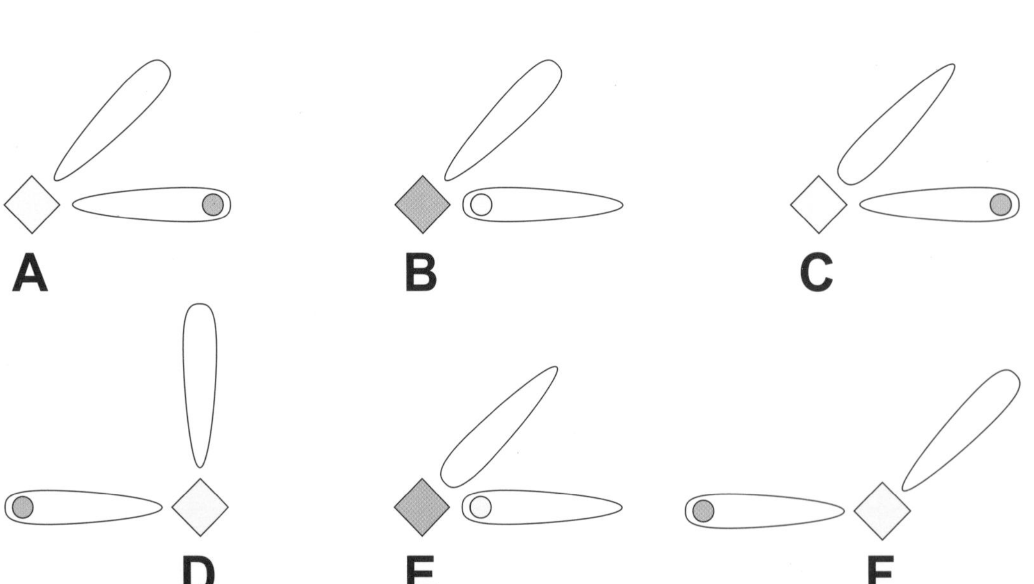

Difficult

46. Which is the odd one out?

A

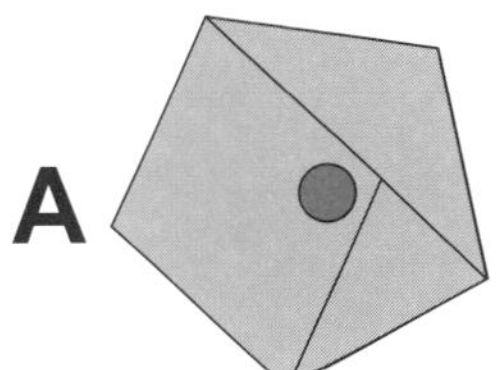

B

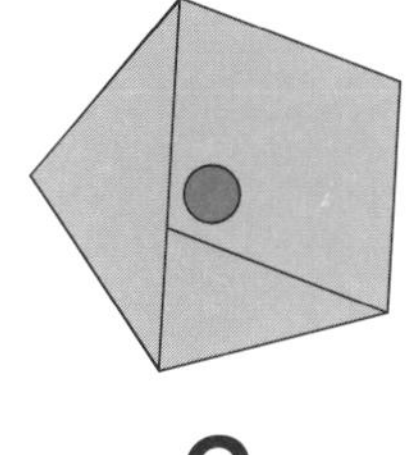

C

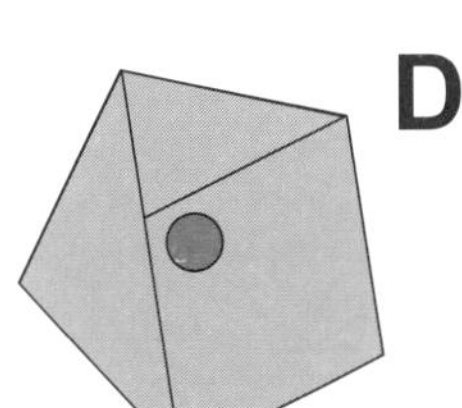

D

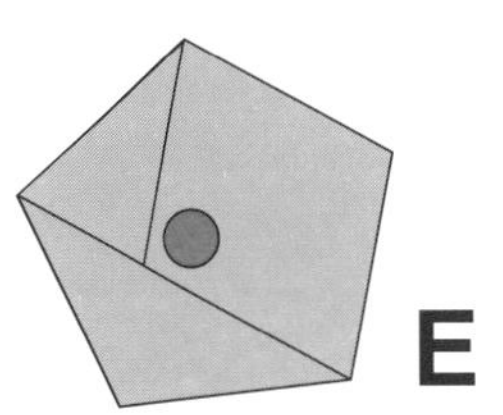

E

47.

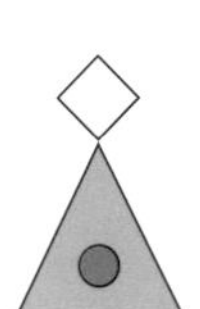

is to

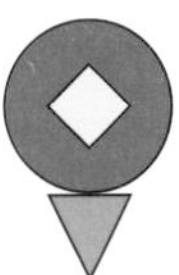

as

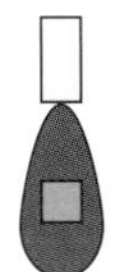

is to:

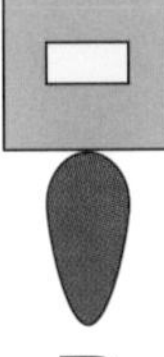

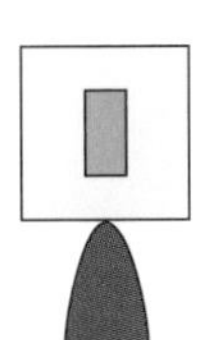

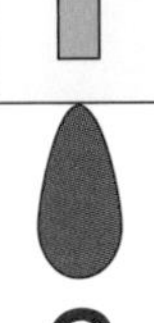

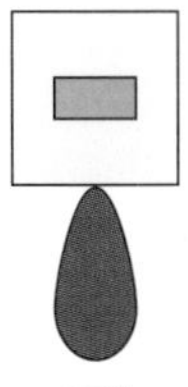

A **B** **C** **D** **E**

Difficult

48.

?

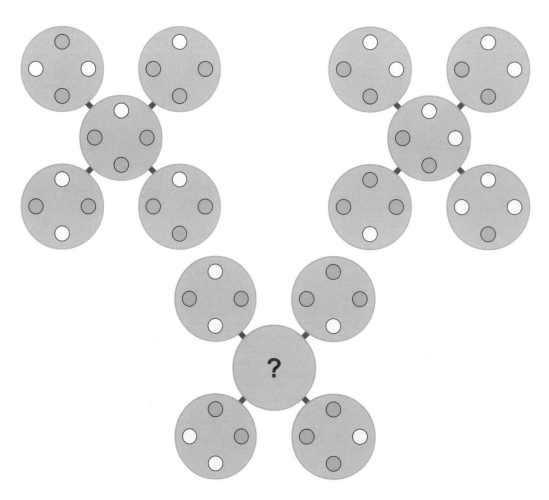

Which circle below should replace the one with the question mark?

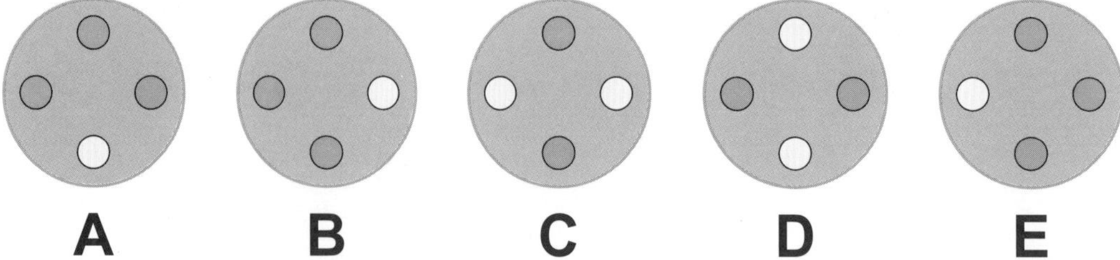

Difficult

49.

Which is the odd one out?

50.

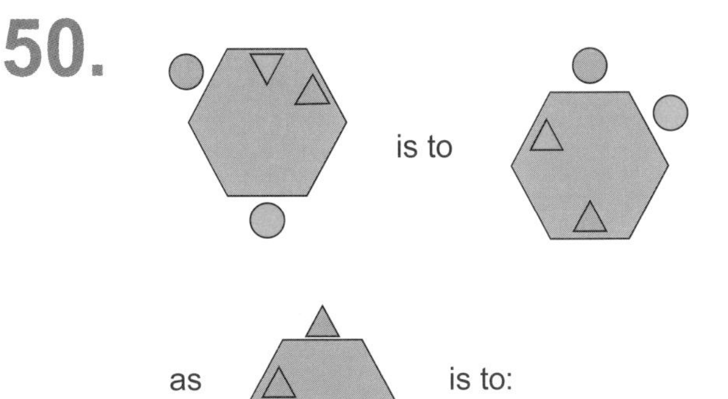

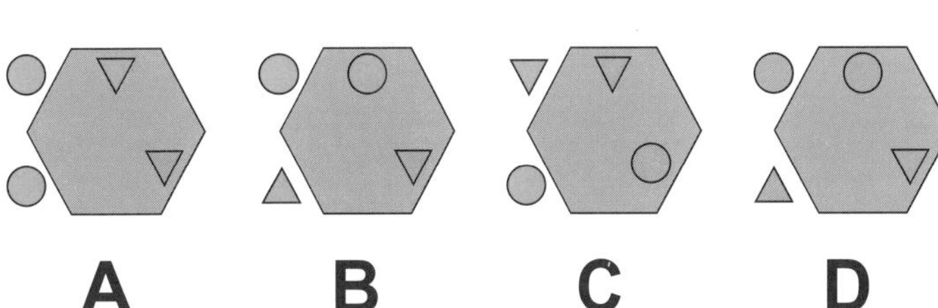

Difficult

51. Which is the odd one out?

A
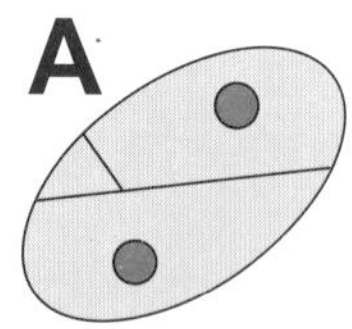

B
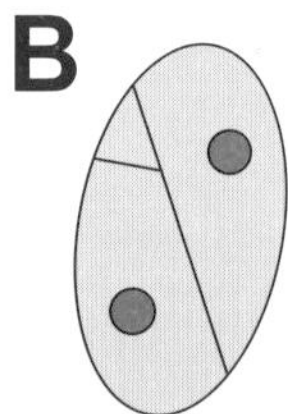

C
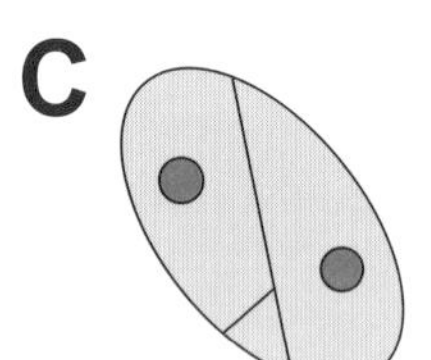

D
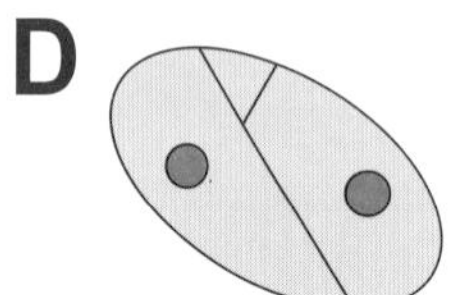

E
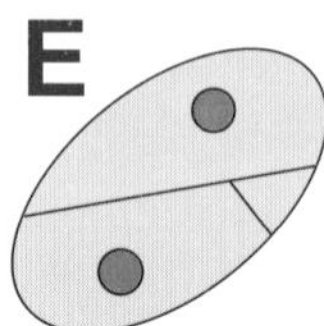

52.

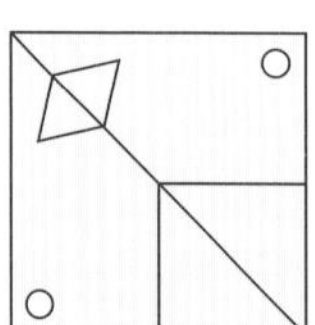

Which box below has most in common with the box above?

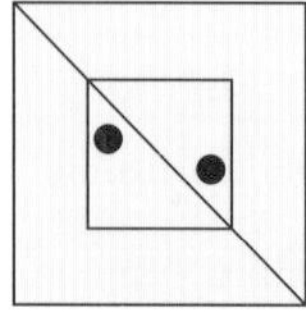
A

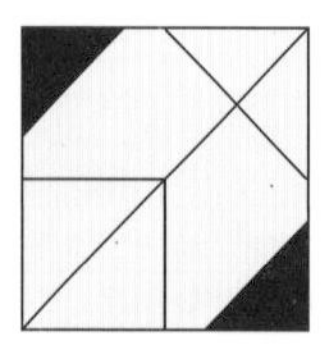
B

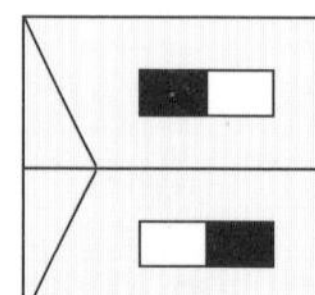
C

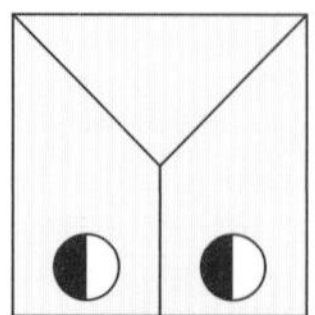
D

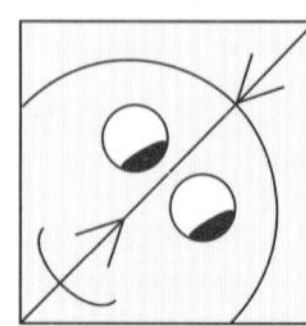
E

Difficult

53.

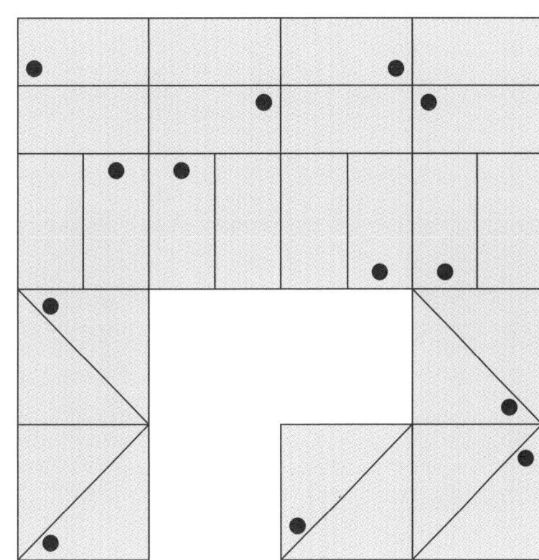

Which section is missing?

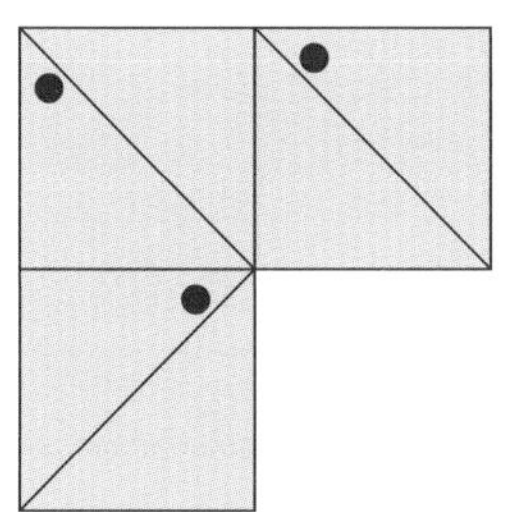

A

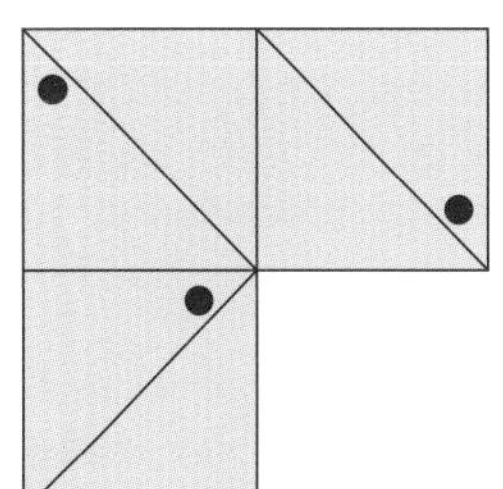

B

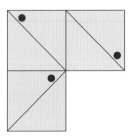

C

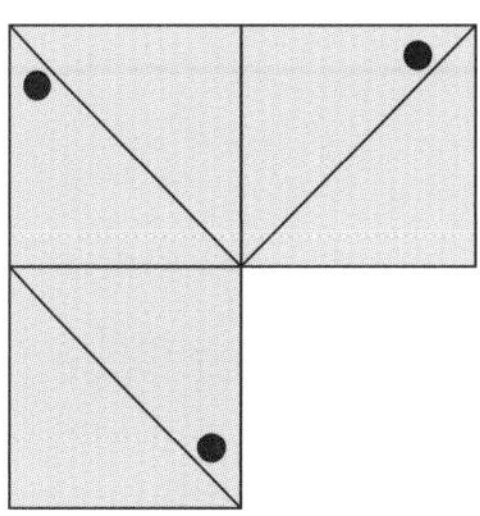

D

Difficult

54. The staff building the winner's podium decided to lay the blocks in a logical system. What design of block should replace the question mark?

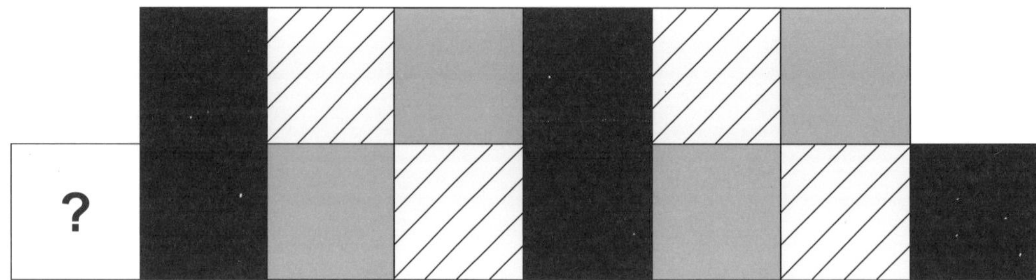

55. Replace the question mark by drawing the contents of the middle tile in accordance with the rules of logic already established.

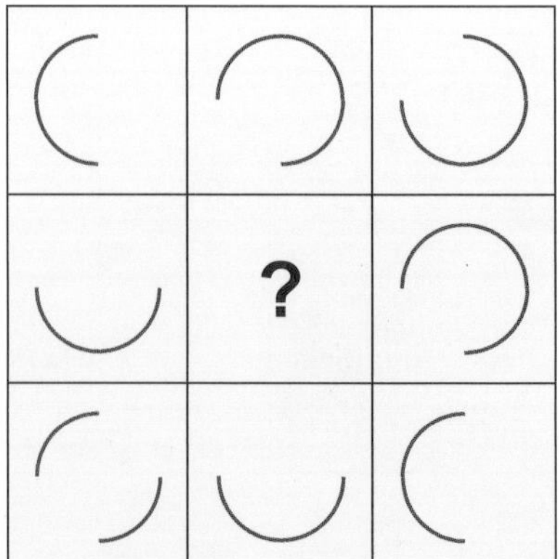

Difficult

56.

Which is the odd one out?

A

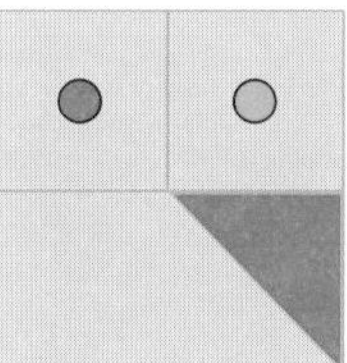

B

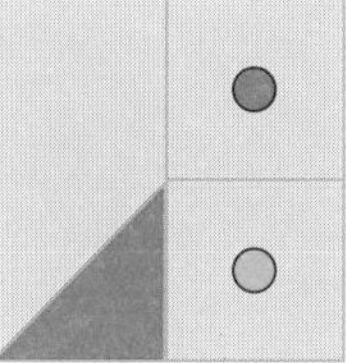

C

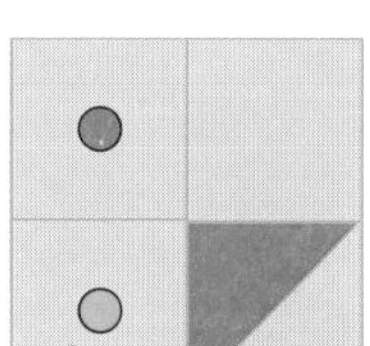

D

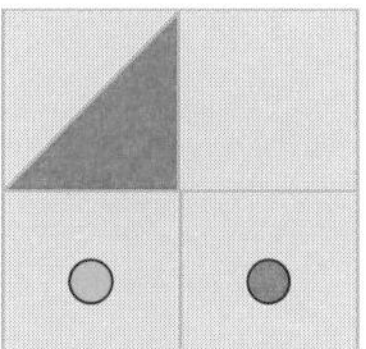

E

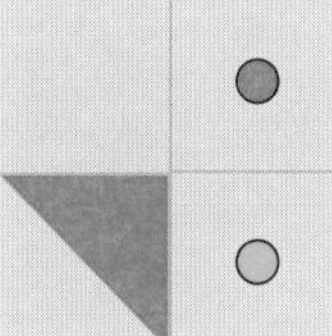

57.

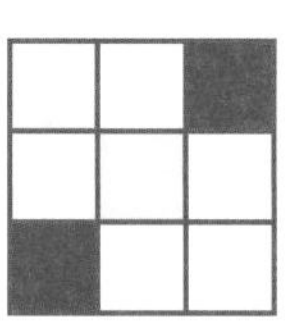

is to

as

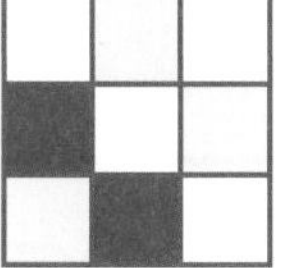

is to:

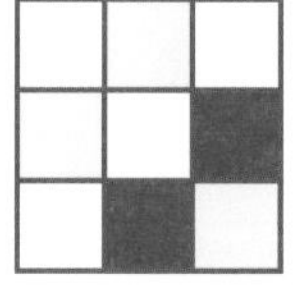

A

B

C

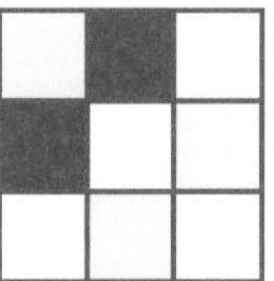

D

E

Difficult

58. Consider the three trominoes below:

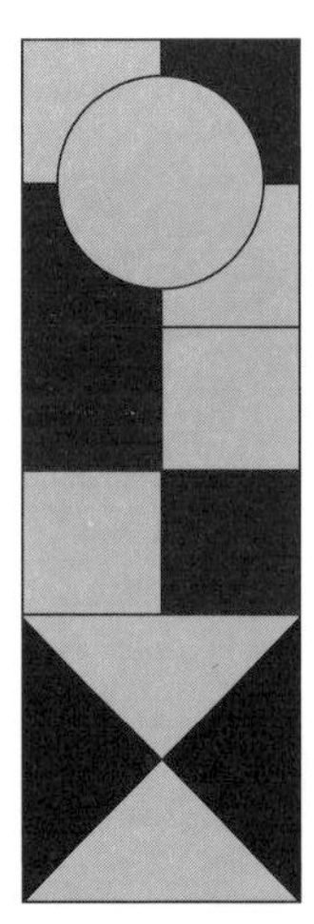

Now choose one of the following to accompany the above:

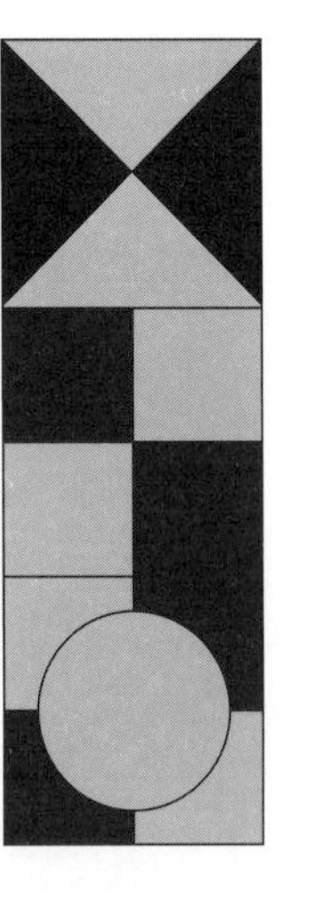

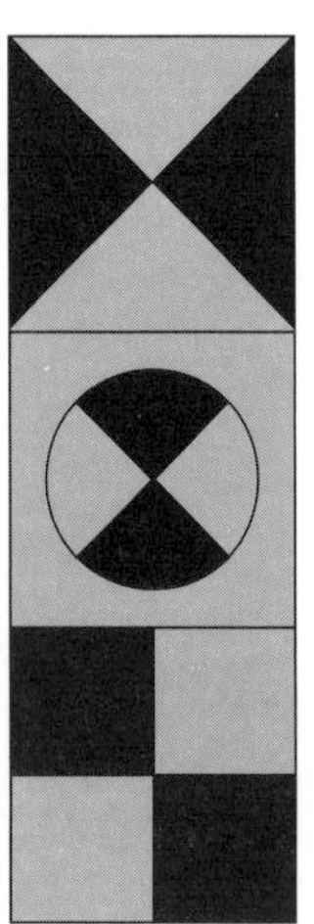

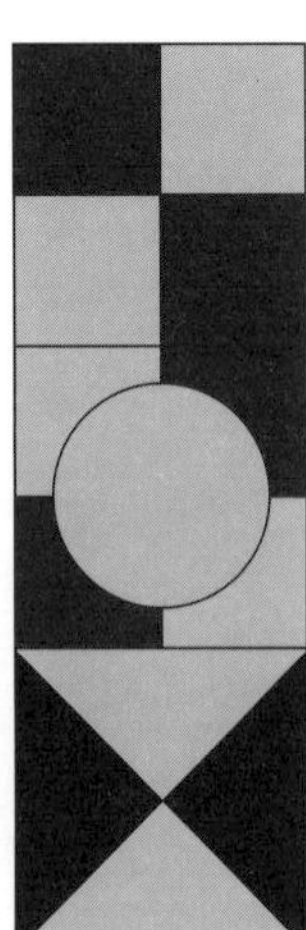

A B C D E

Difficult

59.

Which is the odd one out?

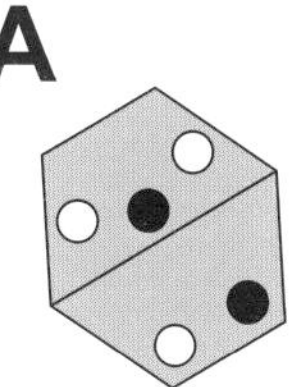

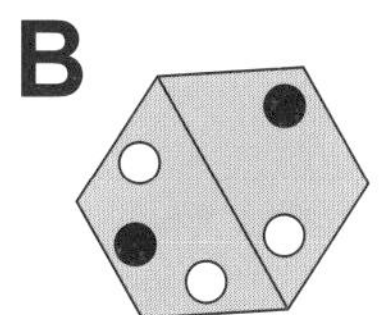

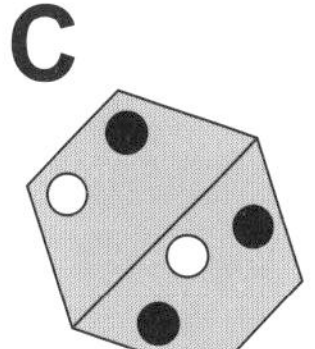

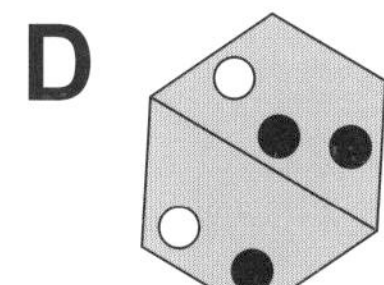

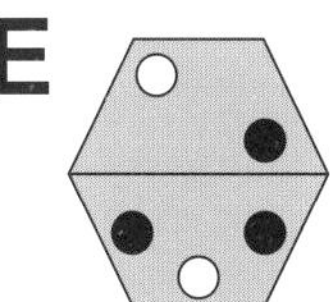

60.

Replace the question mark by drawing the contents of the lowest hexagon in accordance with the rules of logic already established.

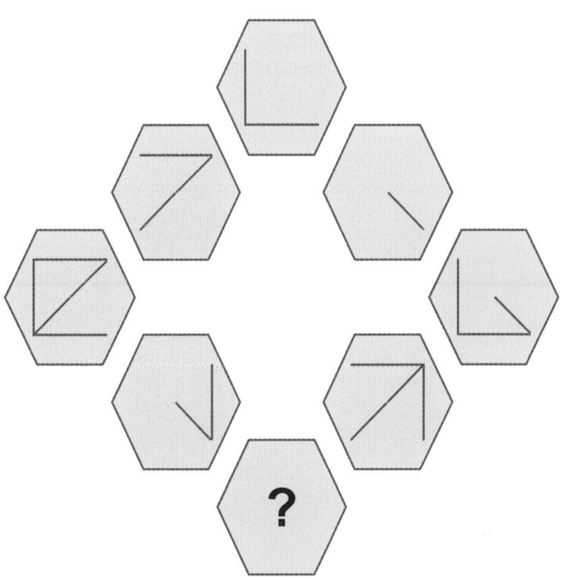

Difficult

61.

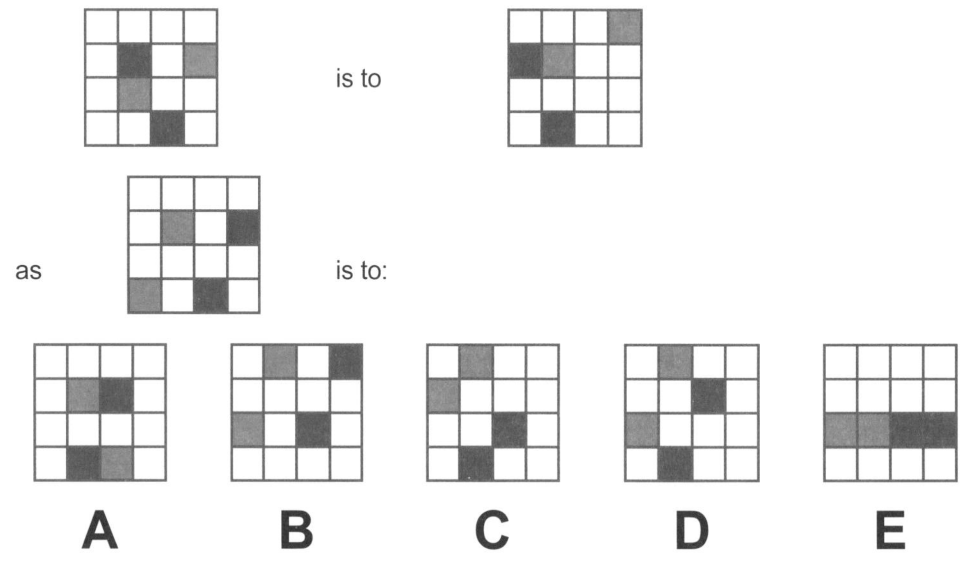

62. Draw the largest possible ring inside the square that will not touch any other ring nor overlap the edge of the square.

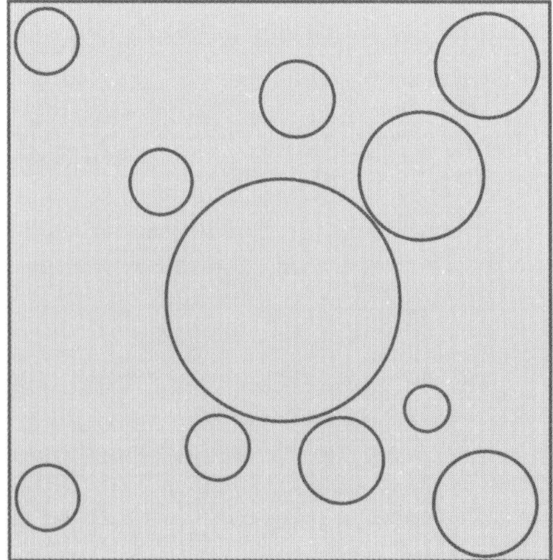

Difficult

63.

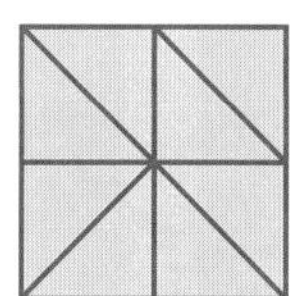

is to

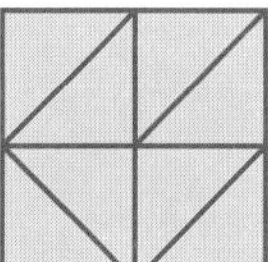

as

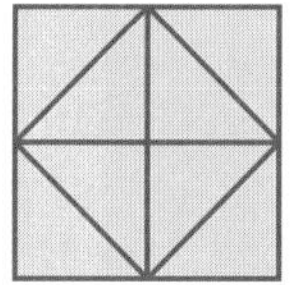

is to:

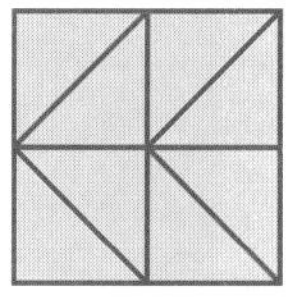

A **B** **C** **D** **E**

64. Which is the odd one out?

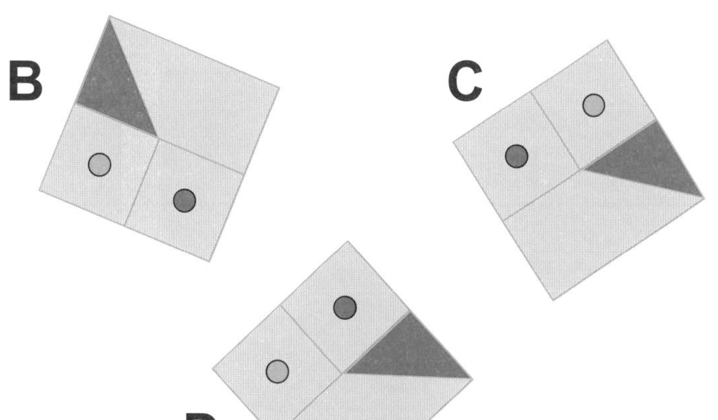

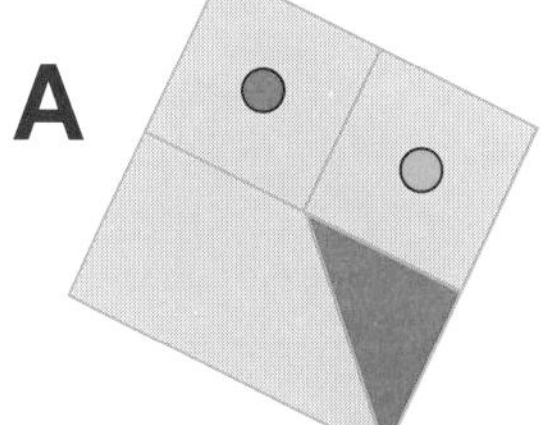

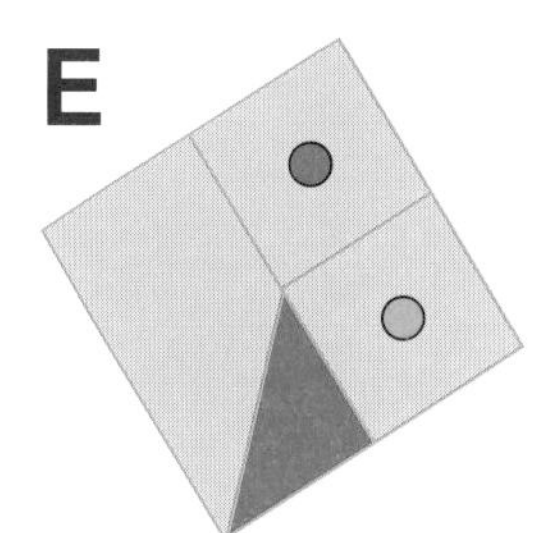

Difficult

65.

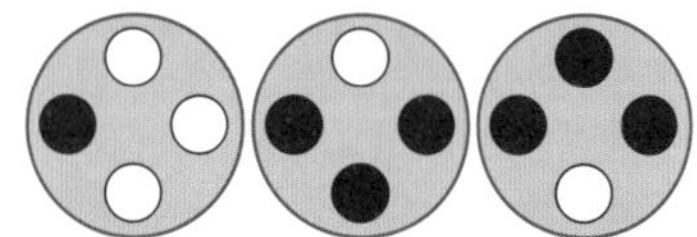 is to 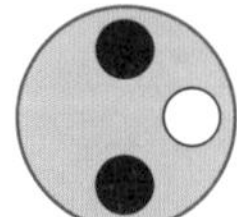

as is to:

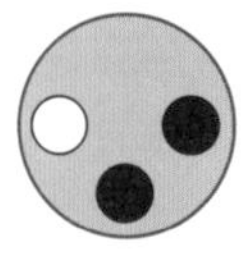 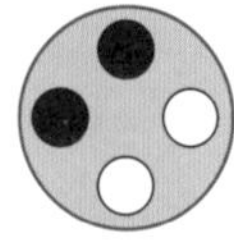 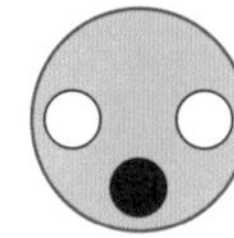 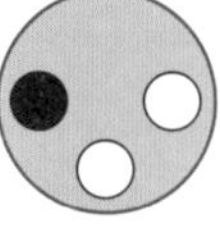

A **B** **C** **D** **E** **F**

66. Which is the odd one out?

A

B

C

D

E

Difficult

67.

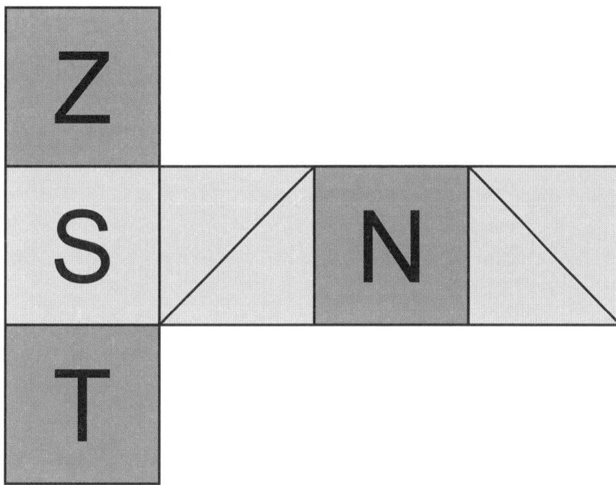

When the above is folded to form a cube, which are the only two of the following that can be produced?

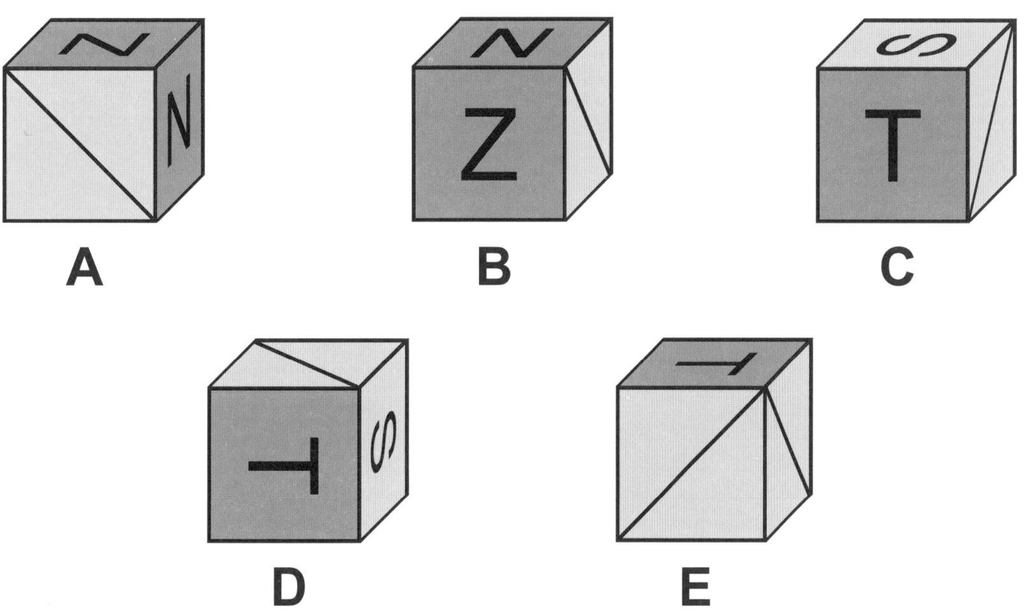

Difficult

68.

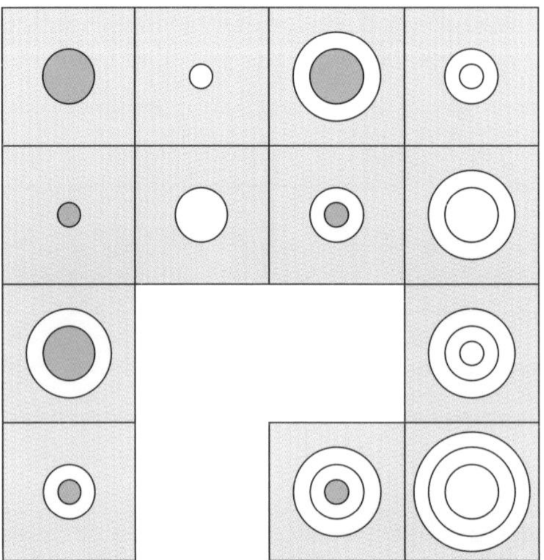

Which section is missing?

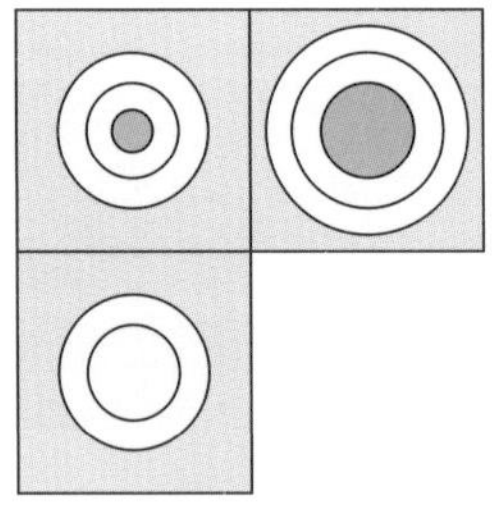

A

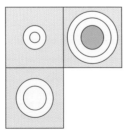

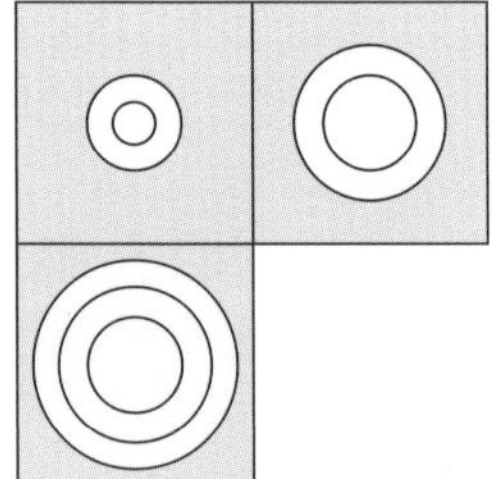

B

C

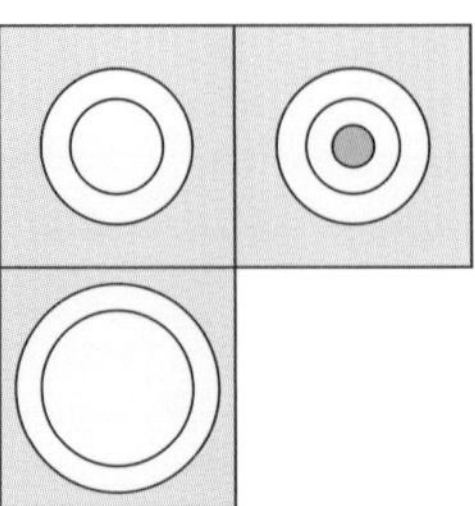

D

Difficult

69.

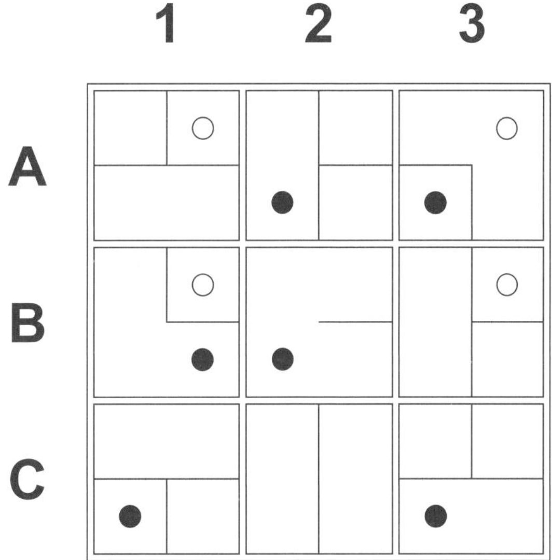

Looking at lines across and down, if the contents of the first two tiles are combined to produce the third tile, with the exception that identical lines and circles are cancelled out, which of the above tiles is incorrect, and with which of the tiles below should it be replaced?

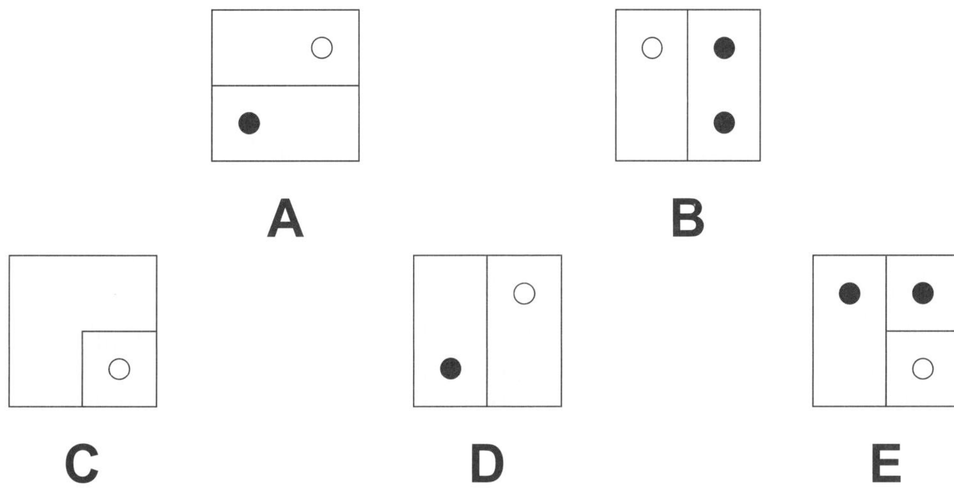

Difficult

70.

When the above is folded to form a cube, which is the only one of the following that can be produced?

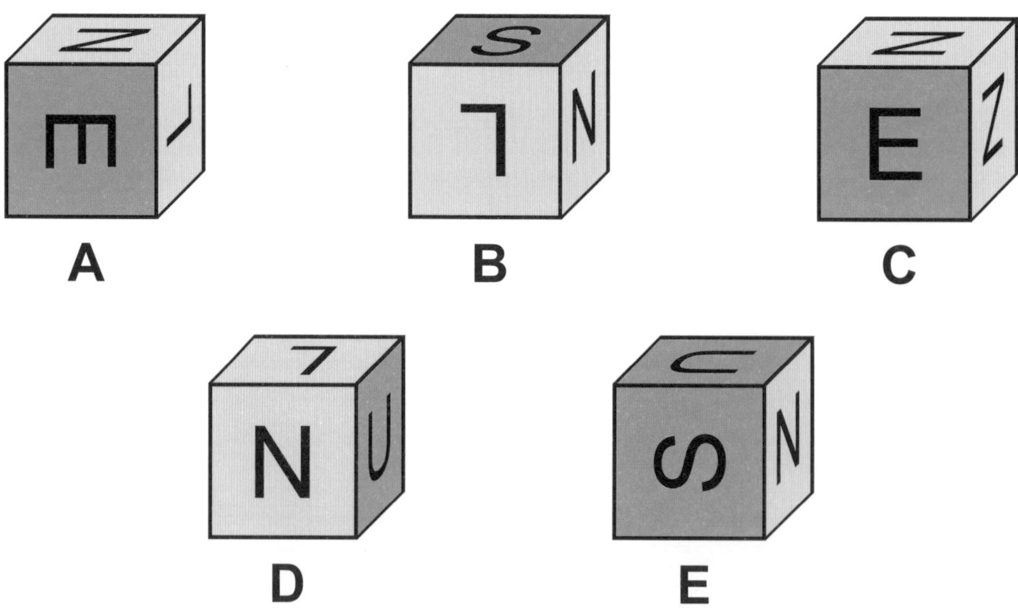

Difficult

71.

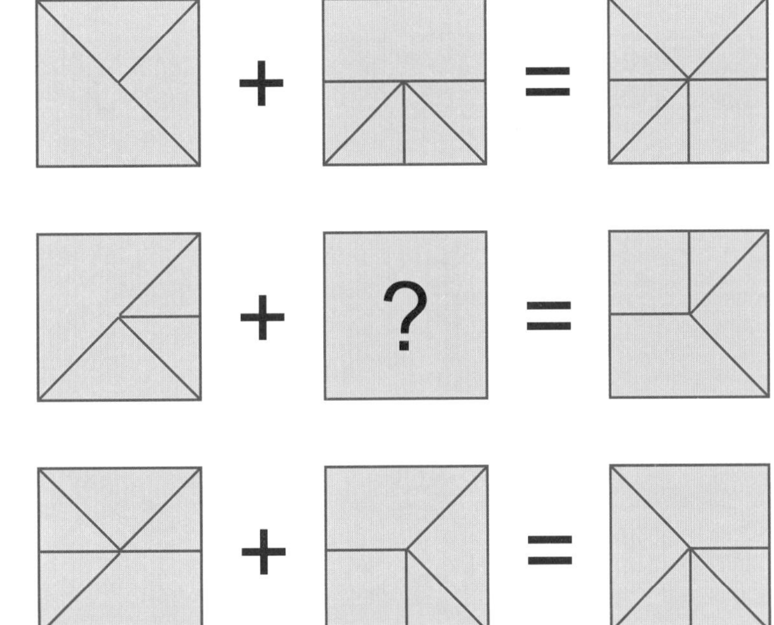

Which is the missing square?

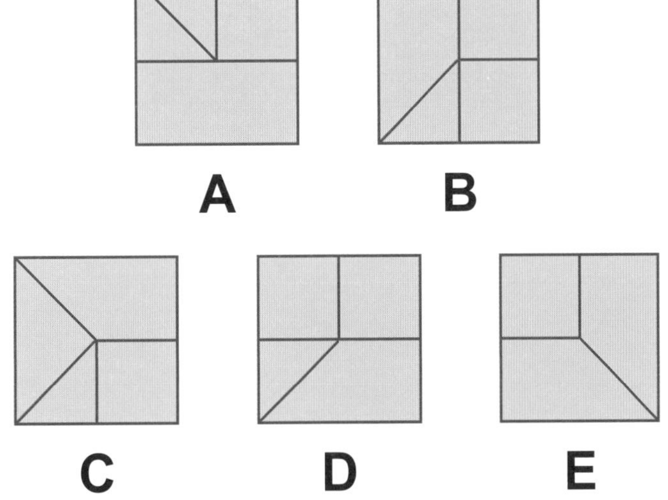

Difficult

72.

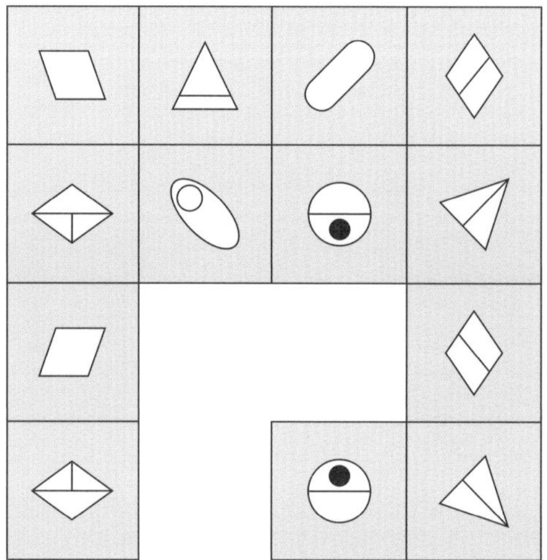

Which section is missing?

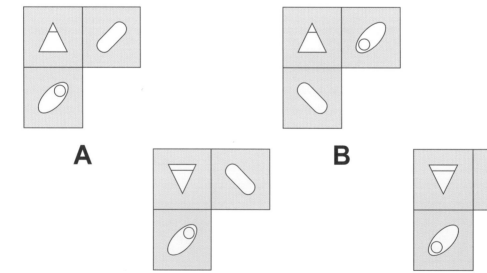

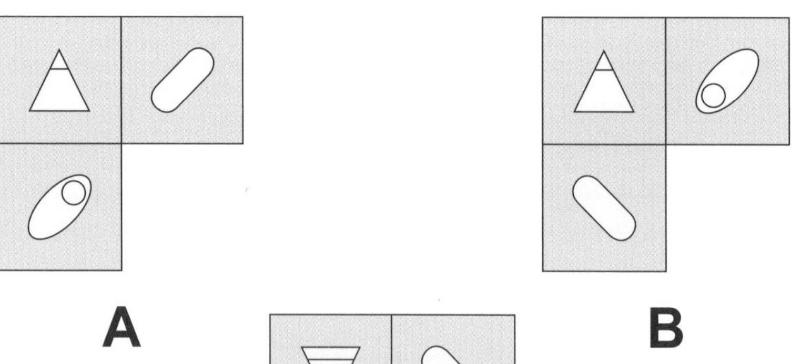

C

D

Difficult

73.

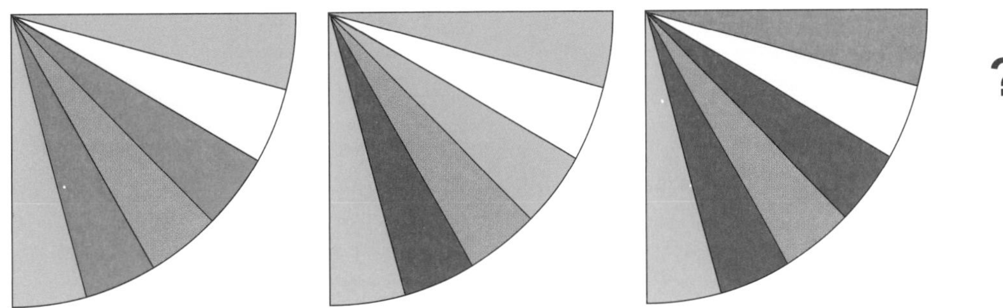

What comes next in the above sequence?

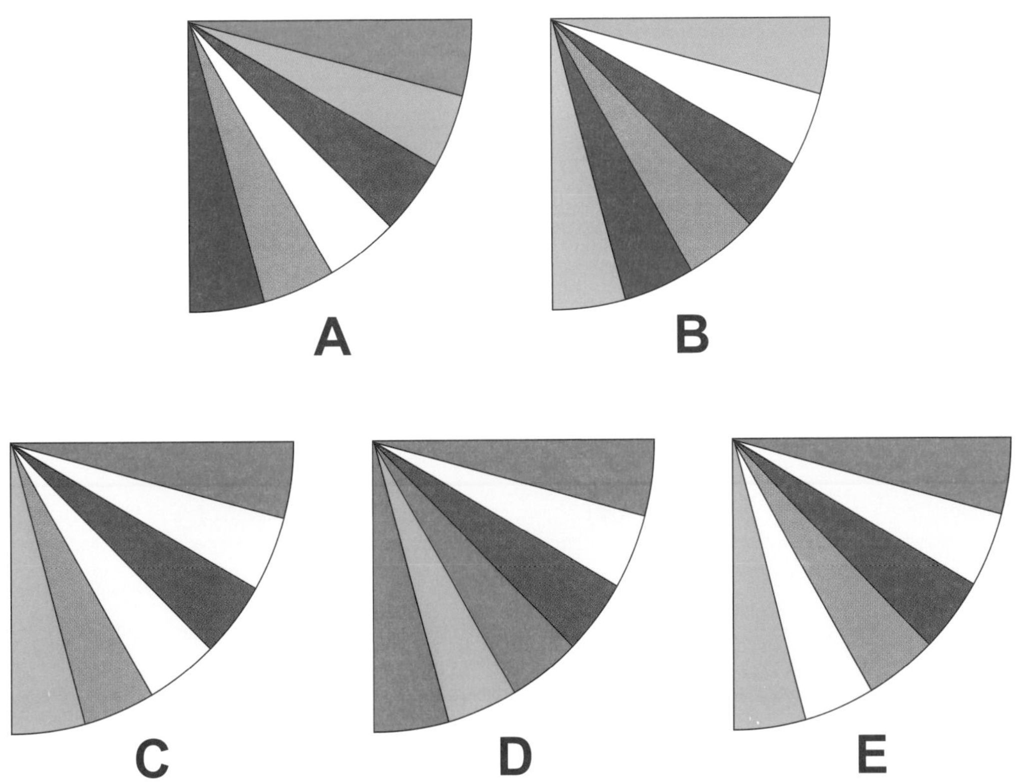

Difficult

74.

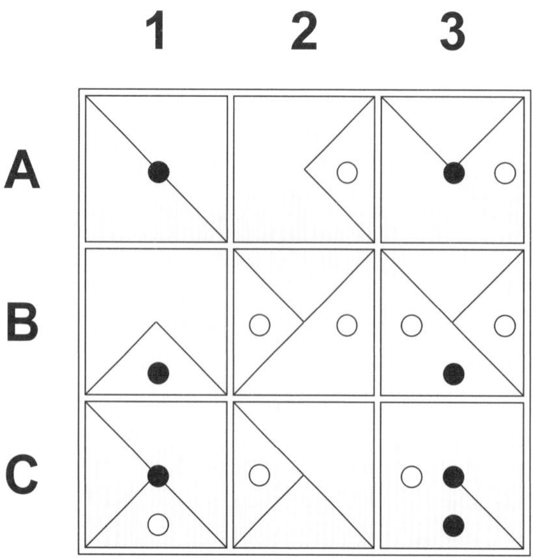

Looking at lines across and down, if the contents of the first two tiles are combined to produce the third tile, with the exception that identical lines and circles are cancelled out, which of the above tiles is incorrect, and with which of the tiles below should it be replaced?

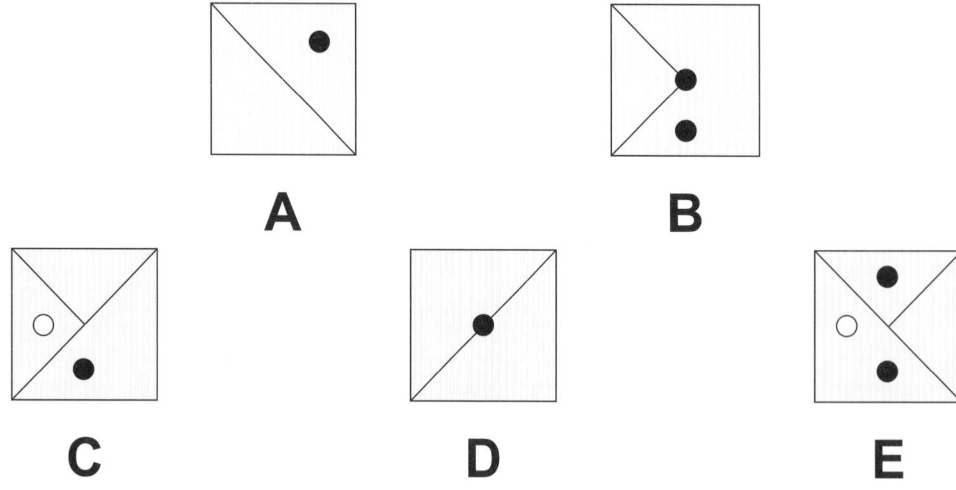

Difficult

75.

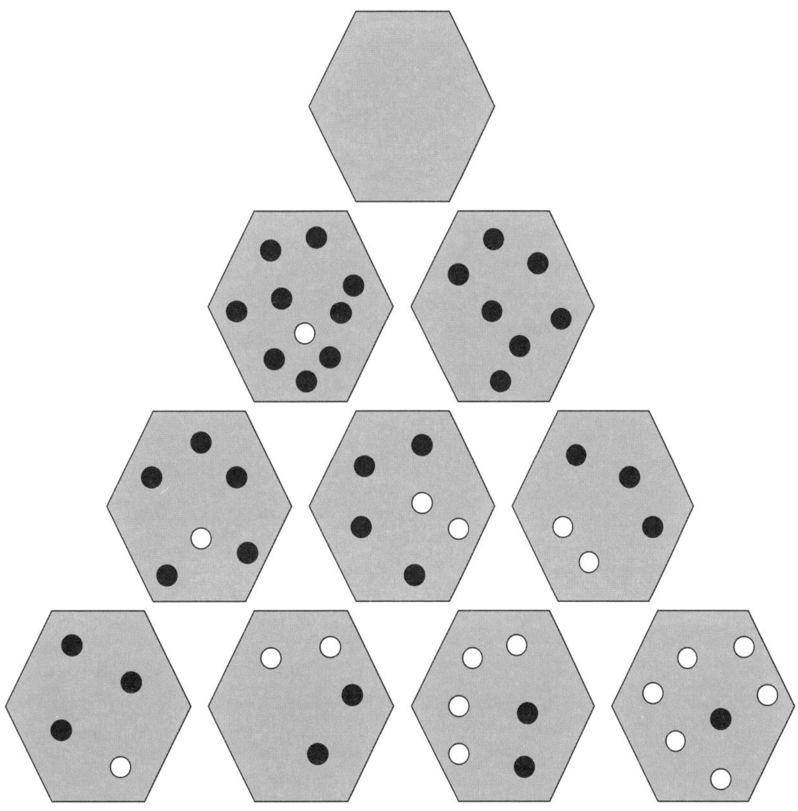

Which hexagon should appear at the top of the pyramid?

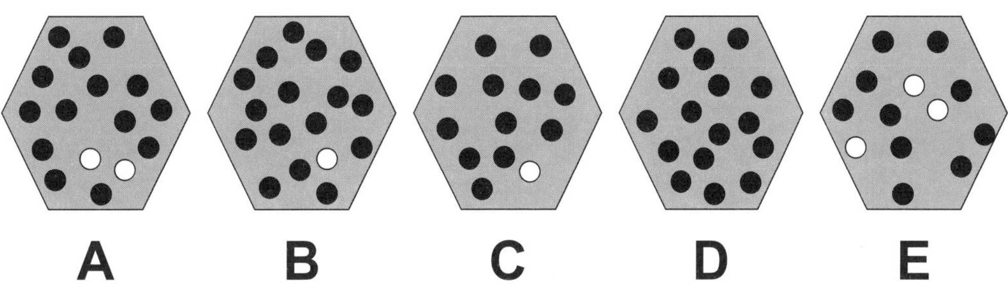

Solutions – Quick Fire

1. B – Working from the top, a line is added to the left side then right side alternately.
2. E – The number of sides in each figure increases by one every time.
3. B – Looking from top to bottom, in the left-hand set the orange circles change to white and vice versa; therefore, in the right-hand set the blue circles change to white and vice versa.
4. C – Each connected straight row of three figures contains one each of the three different symbols.
5. D – The dot is moving one corner clockwise at each stage and alternates blue, yellow and red in turn.
6. C – The first three figures are being repeated, but twice as large.
7. A – Looking clockwise the circles are in pairs (one inside and one outside the large ring).
8. A – The figure is rotating 45 degrees anticlockwise.
9. D – The figures are mirror images of each other.
10. C – From top to bottom, the white circles change to blue and the blue circles change to a circle with a vertical line.
11. B – It has three red and two green lines: the rest have three green and two red lines.
12. D – The right-hand part folds on top of the left-hand part.
13. D – In opposite sections all lines are rotated 90 degrees. This effectively means that option D is the same as its opposite section.
14. A – The bottom figures are a mirror image of the top figures and the left-hand figures are a mirror image of the right-hand figures.
15. D – It rotates anticlockwise from the outside: all the others rotate clockwise from the outside.
16. A – The diamond rotates 45 degrees clockwise at each stage and the line alternates between the shortest and longest corners: the dot alternates in and out of the diamond.

Solutions – More Challenging

17. F – There are three types of arrow which are repeated. The arrow alternates between blue and black and moves 45 degrees clockwise at each stage.

18. E – In the string of connected dots the black dot is in the middle: in the others it is at the end.

19. B – The dot is in the square and circle: in all the others it is in the circle and triangle.

20. D – The green section is moving one corner anticlockwise at each stage and the yellow section is moving one corner clockwise.

21. D – The others are all the same figure rotated.

22. C – The red dot moves two corners anticlockwise at each stage and the yellow circle moves one corner clockwise.

23. B – The number of sides in the outer figure reduces by one and the number of sides in the inner figure increases by one.

24. F – Each line across and down contains one inverted triangle, one yellow circle and two brown squares above and below a triangle.

25. A – All the rest are the same figure rotated.

26. E – All yellow squares become green and vice versa.

27. E – The outer hexagon is appearing one line at a time clockwise: the inner hexagon is disappearing one line at a time clockwise.

28. C – All the green squares move up one place.

29. C.

30. D – At each stage the large arc moves 90 degrees clockwise, the middle arc moves 90 degrees anticlockwise and the small inner arc moves 180 degrees.

31. C – The rest are all the same figure rotated, but in C the red and blue sectors are reversed.

Solutions – More Challenging

32. D – The circles at the bottom are in the same sequence as the ones at the top except that they are reversed.

33. B, C and D. 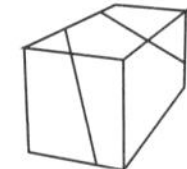

34. E – The columns appear in the sequence one/two/three blocks high which is repeated: the colour sequence of the bottom block is yellow/blue, the sequence of the middle block is red/green and the sequence of the top block is grey/brown.

35. A – to complete every possible pairing of the four different suits: hearts, clubs, diamonds, spades.

36. D – At each stage, the black dot is moving two places back and one forward, the black square is moving two forward and one back, the green square is moving one forward and one back, and the yellow square is moving one back.

37. E – From top to bottom each line moves 45 degrees clockwise.

38. D – The rest are the same figure rotated.

39. B – A and C are alike, as are D and E.

40. D.

41. D – The figure is rotating 90 degrees clockwise and the dot is moving to a different section clockwise each time.

42. C – The circles change to lines and vice versa.

43. C – It contains one white dot only: the rest contain two white dots.

44. C – The symbol at the bottom moves to the top: the other two symbols rotate 180 degrees and move down one place. Two of the dots move inside the bottom symbol and the other dot moves inside the middle symbol.

45. A – The figure with the dot slides from left to right; the other figure rotates 45 degrees clockwise.

46. C – The rest are the same figure rotated.

Solutions – Difficult

47. B – All shapes retain the same colour. The brown shape rotates 180 degrees and goes to the bottom; the rectangle rotates 90 degrees and goes inside the square, which increases in size.

48. A – Looking at the four outer circles, only when the same coloured dot appears in the same position in three of the outer circles is it transferred to the middle circle.

49. E – D is the same as A but with black/white reversal, and C is the same as B with black/white reversal.

50. B – Symbols change from inside to outside the hexagon and vice versa, and orange circles change to blue triangles and vice versa.

51. B – The rest are the same figure rotated.

52. B – The lines and symbols at either side of the line which divides the box are a mirror image of each other.

53. B – Looking across each line contains the same direction line, but with the dot in four different positions.

54. Patterns start at the bottom left from left to right, followed by the top row from right to left in the sequence yellow striped/black/blue repeated.

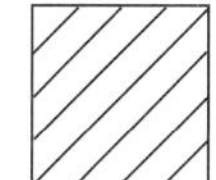

55. Looking both across and down, the contents of the third tile are determined by the contents of the first two tiles. Lines are carried forward from these first two tiles to the third tile, except when two lines appear in the same position, in which case they are cancelled out.

56. C – E is the same figure as D rotated and B is the same as A rotated.

57. A – The left box is a mirror image of the right box.

58. D – This completes every possible different grouping in threes of the four different symbols.

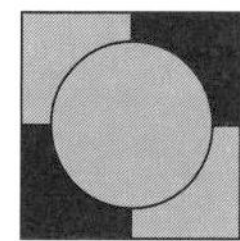  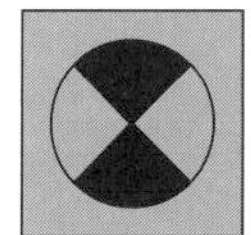 

Solutions – Difficult

59. D – C is the same as A but with black/white reversal, and E is the same as B but with black/white reversal.

60. Looking at each line of three hexagons: from the top down to the centre left, from the top down to the centre right, from the centre left down to the bottom, and from the centre right down to the bottom, the contents of the first two combine to form the content of the third hexagon.

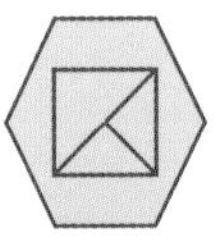

61. D – Blue squares move one place to the left, and red squares move one place upwards.

62.

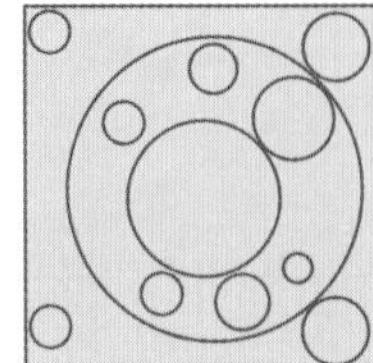

63. E – All lines rotate 90 degrees from the left to the right box.

64. D – The rest are the same figure rotated.

65. F – Only dots which appear just once in the same position in the first three circles are transferred to the fourth circle.

66. C – The rest are the same figure rotated; C contains the same figures as the others, but they go round in the opposite direction.

67. B and D.

68. C – Alternate circles are identical, except for the addition of an outer circle.

69. Tile 1B is incorrect and should be replaced by tile D.

70. A.

71. D – Lines are carried forward from the first two tiles to the third tile, except when two lines appear in the same position, in which case they are cancelled out.

Solutions – Difficult

72. D – The third line is a mirror image of the first line and the fourth line is a mirror image of the second line.

73. E – When two identically coloured segments appear in a figure they are replaced by two differently coloured segments at the next stage.

74. Tile 1C is incorrect and should be replaced by tile B.

75. B – the contents of each hexagon are determined by the contents of the two hexagons immediately below it. The number of black dots is added together, but the number of white dots is the difference between the numbers of white dots in the two hexagons immediately below.

Brain Fact

One of the most effective ways of keeping your brain active is to try puzzles. Word puzzles, such as crosswords, are exceptionally good for building vocabulary and word fluency. Calculation and computational skills can be sharpened up using number puzzles, while jigsaws and three-dimensional puzzles expand the ability to visualize relationships in space.

Brain Fact

The more connections there are among the brain's hundred billion neurons, the more efficiently it will work. Connections form as a result of two elements; inherited growth patterns, and in response to external and internal stimuli. Large amounts of brain activity, the kind that goes on in a healthy and active brain, can stimulate growth of new dendroids, fostering further connections between neurons and improving overall brain function.

Tests

This section consists of three separate tests which are all timed and assessed.

You should keep strictly within the time limits otherwise your score will be invalidated.

The three tests are culture-fair and rely totally on diagrammatic representation. They are designed to test your spatial appreciation as well as your powers of logical analysis.

It is recommended that you study the examples provided before attempting the tests.

Symbolic Odd One Out Test

This test consists of 20 questions which are designed to make you think laterally and creatively as well as spatially. The questions in the test gradually increase in difficulty from Quick Fire to Difficult.

You are allowed 45 minutes in which to solve the 20 questions.

Brain Fact

The brain stem is all the structures lying between the cerebrum and the spinal cord and is divided into several components including the Thalamus, Hypothalamus, Midbrain, Medulla Oblongata, Pons, Limbic System and Cranial Nerves. These components regulate, or are involved in, many vital activities necessary for survival. The Hypothalamus, for example, is concerned with eating, drinking, temperature regulation, sleep, emotional behaviour and sexual activity, and within the Medulla are the vital control centres for cardiac and respiratory functions as well as other reflex activities.

Example

Which is the odd one out?

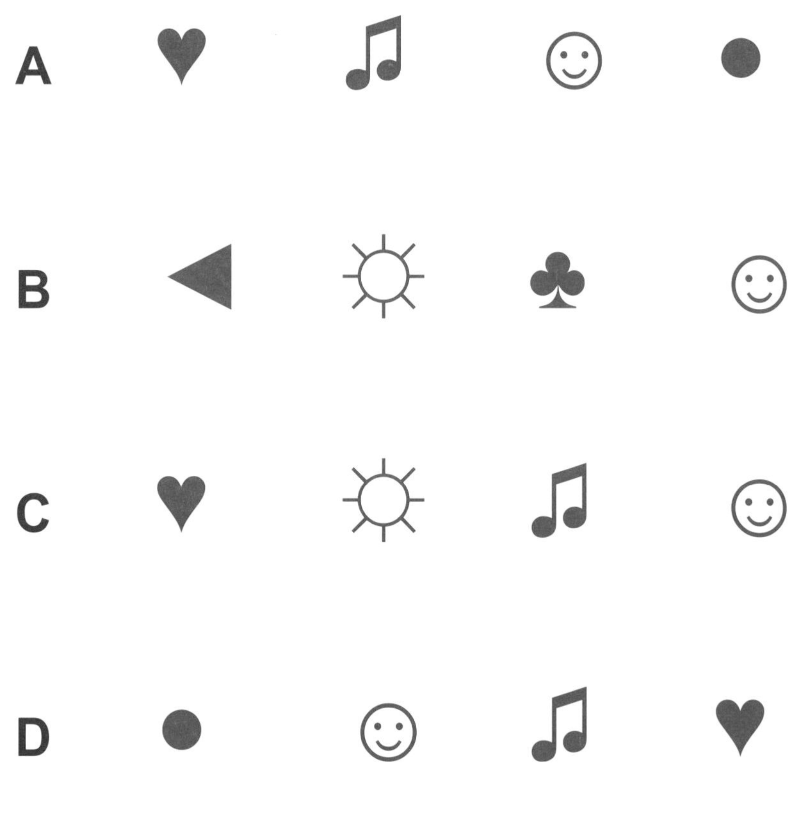

Answer: C – A is the same as D in reverse; B is the same as E in reverse.

Quick Fire

1. Which is the odd one out?

2. Which is the odd one out?

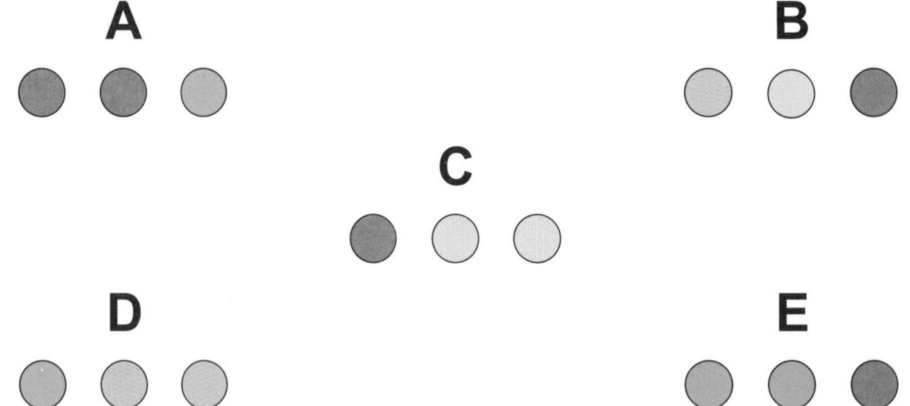

Quick Fire

3. Which is the odd one out?

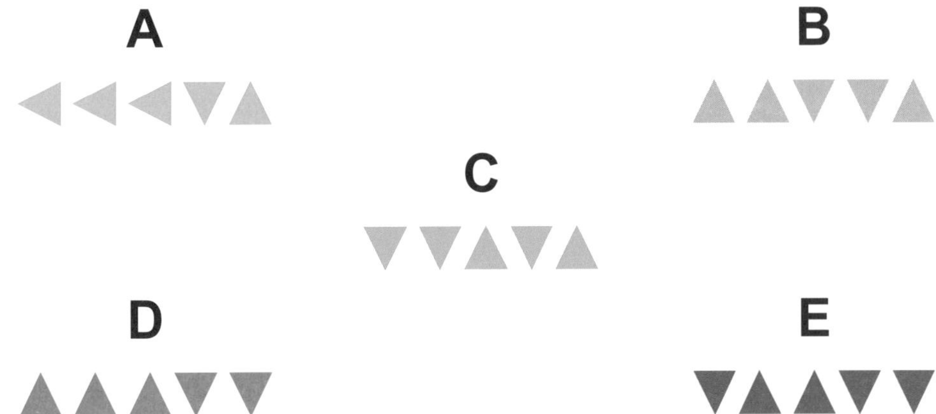

4. Which is the odd one out?

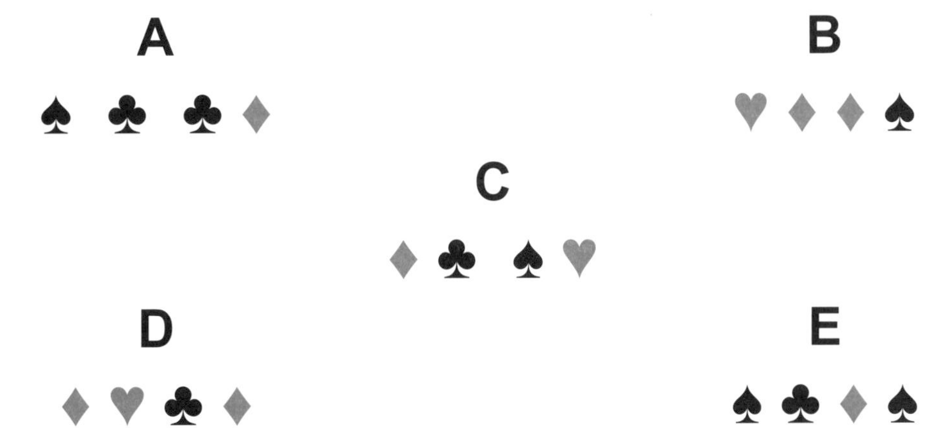

Quick Fire

5. Which is the odd one out?

A

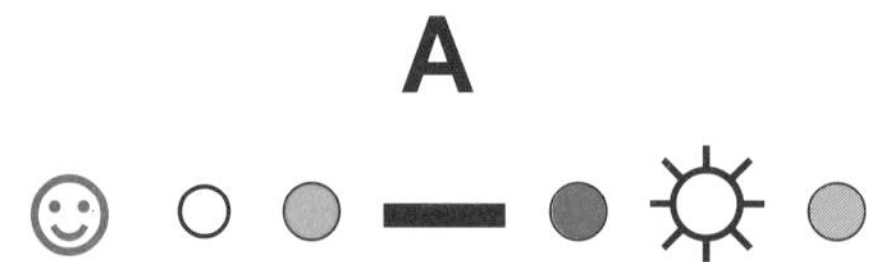

B

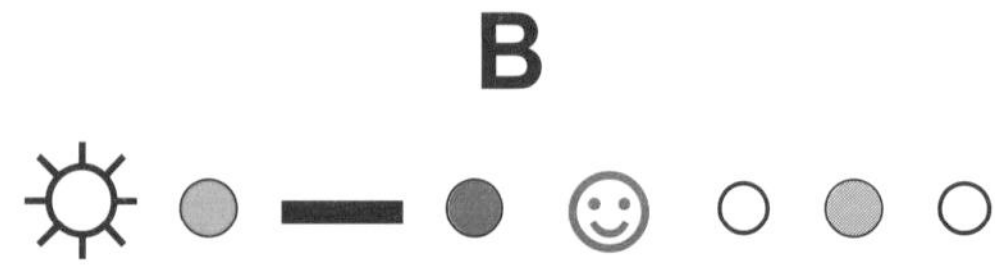

C

D

E

Quick Fire

6. Which is the odd one out?

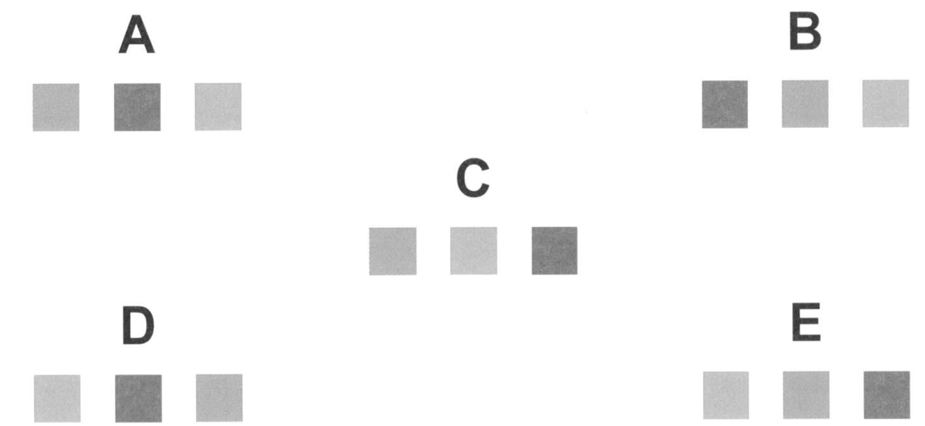

7. Which is the odd one out?

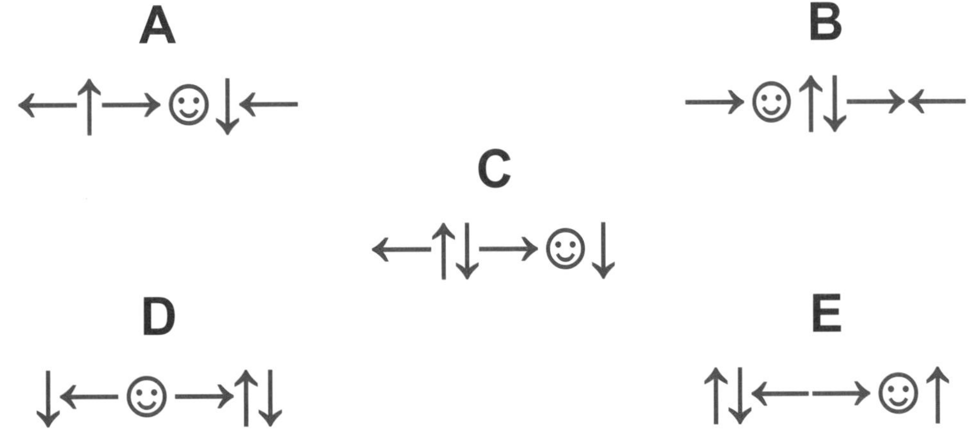

More Challenging

8. Which is the odd one out?

A

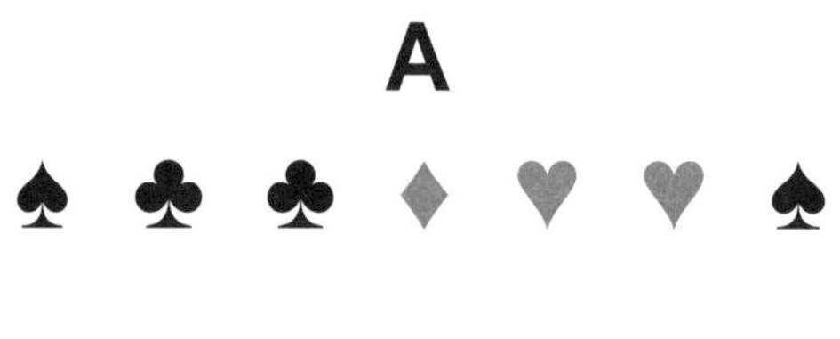

B

C

D

E

More Challenging

9. Which is the odd one out?

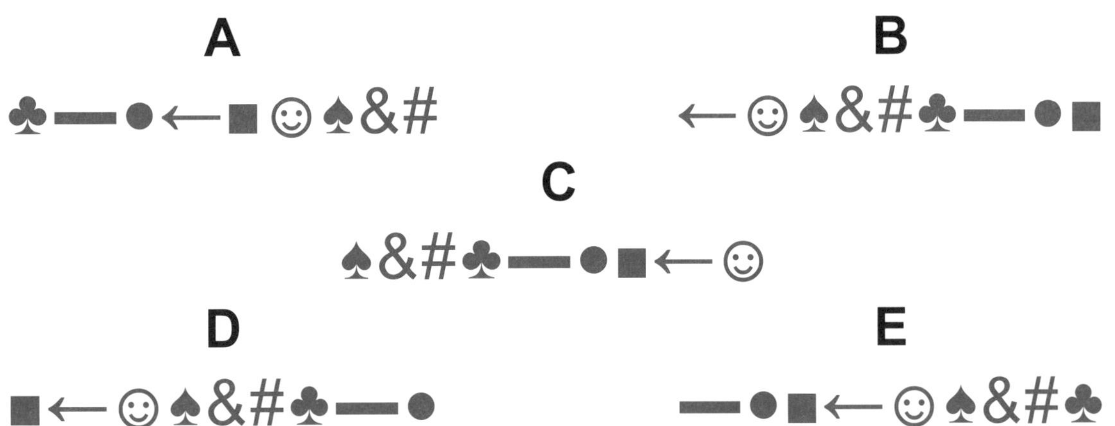

10. Which is the odd one out?

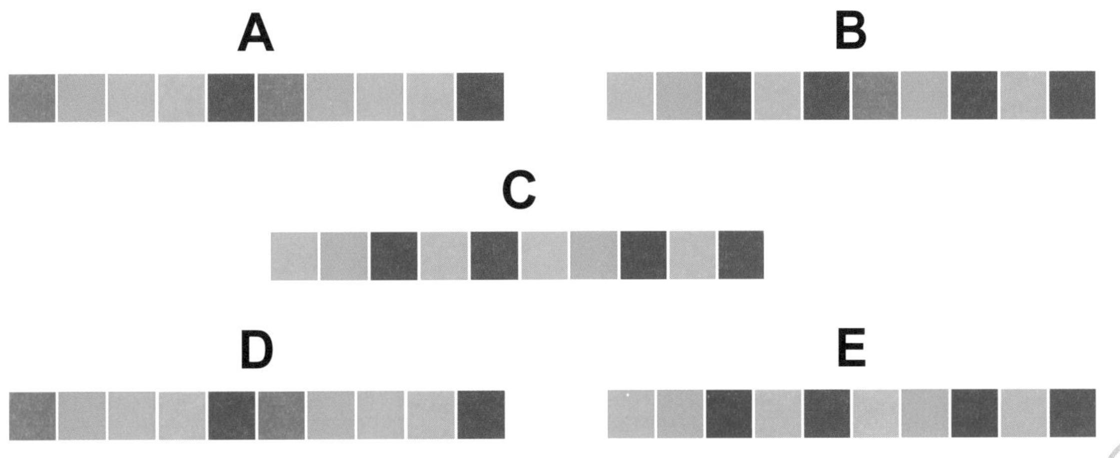

More Challenging

11. Which is the odd one out?

A

B

☺ — ☺ ☺ — ☺ — ☺ ☺

C

☺ ☺ ☺ ☺ — ☺ ☺ ☺ — ☺ ☺

D

☺ ☺ — ☺ ☺ ☺ — ☺ ☺ — ☺

E

☺ ☺ — ☺ — ☺ ☺ — ☺

More Challenging

12. Which is the odd one out?

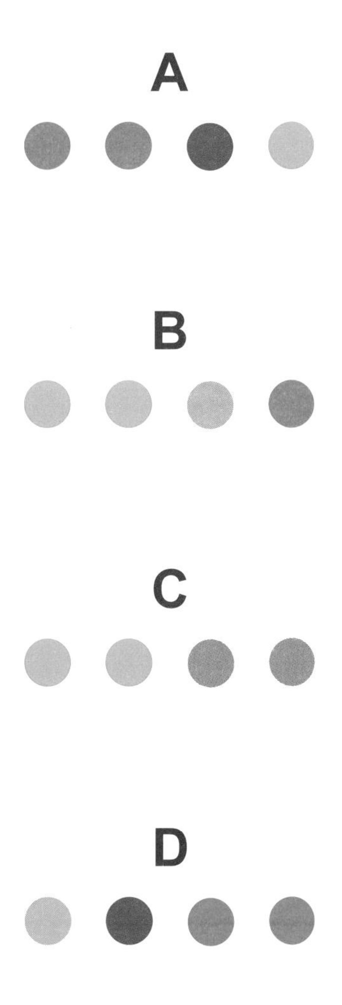

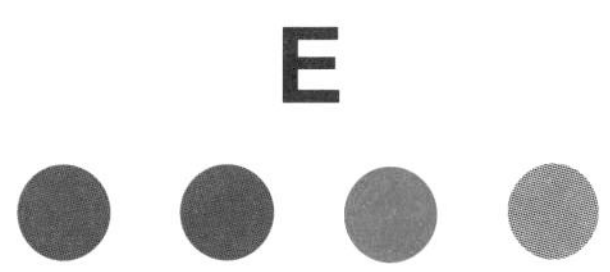

More Challenging

13. Which is the odd one out?

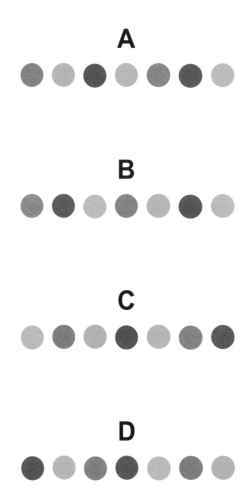

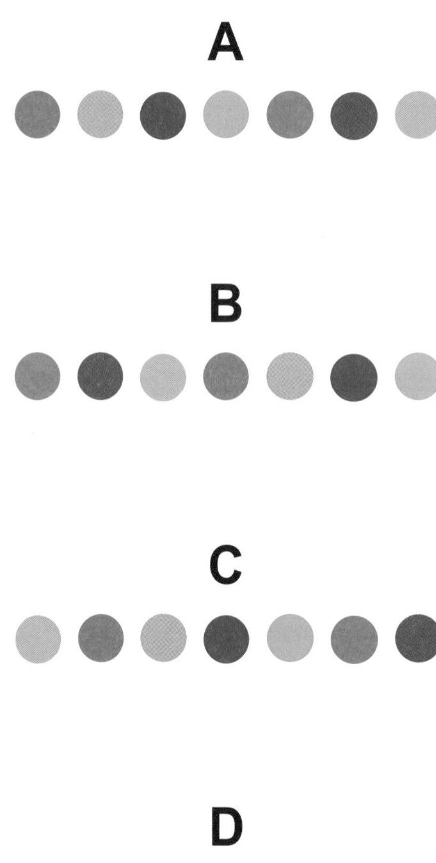

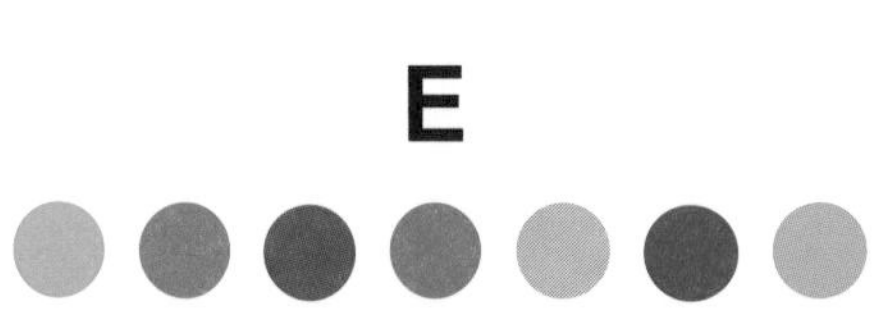

More Challenging

14. Which is the odd one out?

A

← ← ↑ ↑ → → ☺ ↓ ↓ ← →

B

← ← ↑ ↑ → ← ☺ ↓ ↓ → →

C

← ← ☺↑ ↑ → → ↓ ↓ ← →

D

← ← → ↑ ↑ → → ☺ ↓ ↓ ←

E

→ ← ↑ ↑ → → ☺ ↓ ↓ ← ←

More Challenging

15. Which is the odd one out?

A

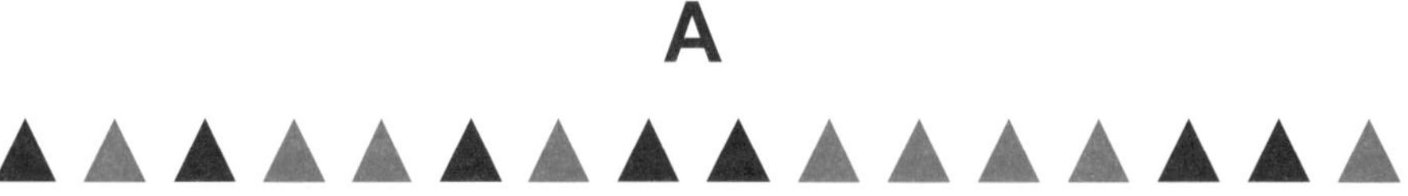

B

C

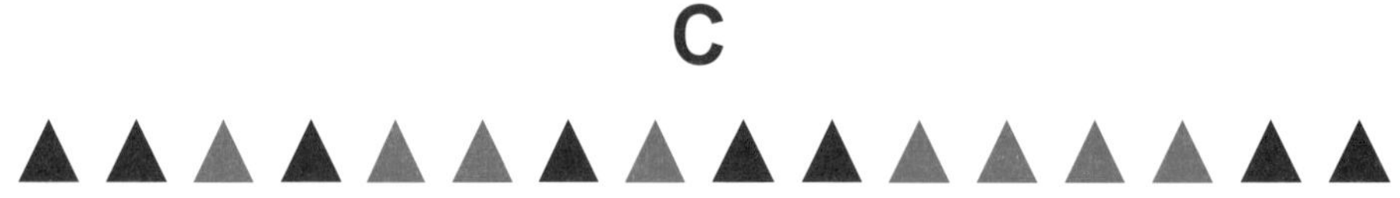

D

E

Difficult

16. Which is the odd one out?

A

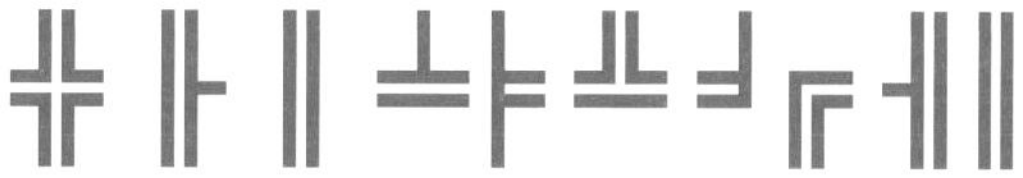

B

C

D

E

Difficult

17. Which is the odd one out?

A

● ☺ ♠ ♥ ♪ ▲ ▬ ■ ▓ ♫

B

♥ ■ ♦ ▬ ∑ Ω ↔ £ ɸ $

C

$ ɸ £ ↔ Ω ∑ ▬ ♦ ■ ♥

D

☺ $ ▲ ▓ Ω ↔ ■ ♦ ▬ £

E

♫ ▓ ■ ▬ ▲ ♪ ♥ ♠ ☺ ●

Difficult

18. Which is the odd one out?

A

B

C

D

E

Difficult

19. Which is the odd one out?

A

¢ ☼ ¥ — ♪ § © « ® µ ¶ ☺ ● £

B

£ ☺ ● — ¥ § © « ® µ ¶ ♪ ¤ ¢

C

♪ § © « ® µ ¶ ☺ ● — ¢ £ ¤ ¥

D

® µ ¶ ☺ ● — ¢ £ ¤ ♪ ¥ § © «

E

¤ ¥ « ® µ ¶ ☺ ● § © ¢ £ — ♪

Difficult

20. Which is the odd one out?

A

☼ ♀ ﬂ ▲ ♫ ● # & ╣ ∏ Ω £

B

☼ ∏ Ω £ ▲ ♫ ● # & ♀ ﬂ ╣

C

● # £ ☼ ♀ ♫ & ╣ ∏ Ω ﬂ ▲

D

☼ £ ﬂ ▲ ♫ ● # & ╣ ∏ Ω £

E

£ ♀ ﬂ ▲ ♫ ● # ∏ ☼ Ω & ╣

Solutions – Quick Fire

1. E – It contains two double notes: the rest only contain one.
2. B – It contains three different coloured circles: the rest all contain one pair of identical coloured circles.
3. A – It contains three triangles pointing left (◀): the rest contain triangles pointing up and down.
4. C – It contains two black suits and two red suits: the rest either contain three black and one red suit or three red and one black suit.
5. D – The two circles either side of the line are red and blue. In all the others they are blue and red.
6. C – In all the others the red and green squares are next to each other. In C they are separated by the blue square.
7. D – In all the others the face is immediately preceded by an arrow pointing to the right (⟶☺).

More Challenging

8. B – It contains a black diamond, whereas all other diamonds are red.
9. A – In the rest the symbols are in the same order, albeit starting with a different symbol.
10. B – A and D are identical, as are C and E.
11. D – A is the same as C in reverse; B is the same as E in reverse.
12. C – It contains two pairs of the same-coloured circle: the rest all contain just one pair.
13. E – The rest are in the same order, albeit starting with a different coloured circle.
14. C – In all the others the face appears immediately in front of two downward facing arrows (☺↓↓).
15. A – More than half the triangles are red. In the rest it is a 50/50 split between red and black.

Solutions – Difficult

16. E – In the rest the symbols are in the same order, albeit starting with a different symbol.

17. D – A is the same as E in reverse; B is the same as C in reverse.

18. C – In all the others the symbols are in the same order, albeit starting with a different symbol.

19. A – The rest contain the same 14 symbols. Option A contains a ☼ instead of a ¤.

20. D – It contains a repeated symbol (£). The rest contain the same 12 symbols.

Performance Rating

Score 1 point for each correct answer

Total Score	Rating	Percentage of Population
19 / 20	Genius level	Top 5%
17 / 18	High Expert	Top 10%
15 / 16	Expert	Top 30%
13 /14	High Average	Top 40%
11 / 12	Middle Average	Top 60%
9 / 10	Low Average	Bottom 40%
7 / 8	Borderline Low	Bottom 30%
5 / 6	Low	Bottom 10%
0 / 4	Very Low	Bottom 5%

Transfer your score to the chart in the Assessment Section on page 302.

Symbolic Complete the Sequence Test

This test consists of 10 questions, increasing in difficulty from Quick Fire to Difficult.

In each question you have to find, from the list of options provided, which symbol will continue the sequence of figures illustrated to a set pattern or rule.

You have 30 minutes in which to complete the 10 questions.

Brain Fact

In addition to 100 billion neurons, there are about 10 to 50 times that many glial cells in the brain. These small cells account for about half the brain's weight and are sometimes referred to as the brain's housekeepers. Their functions include providing physical and nutritional support for neurons by cleaning up brain debris, transporting nutrients to neurons and holding neurons in place.

Brain Fact

The cerebellum lies in the back part of the cranium beneath the cerebral hemispheres and is composed of two hemispheres connected by white fibres called the vermis. Three other bands of fibres (the cerebellar peduncles) connect the cerebellum to other parts of the brain. The cerebellum is essential to the control of movement of the human body and acts as a reflex centre for coordination and maintenance of equilibrium. It is this part of the brain which controls all activity, from manipulating a pair of knitting needles to a batsman smashing a ball to the boundary.

Example

Which figure should replace the question mark?

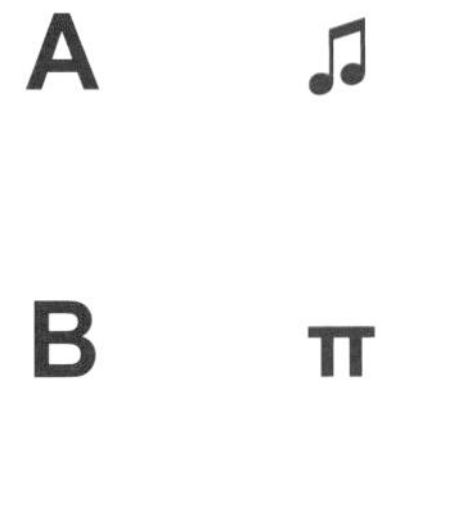

A ♫

B π

C ☺

D π

E ♫

Answer: D – The figures are in the sequence ☺, π, and ♫; and alternate between small and large when they appear.

Quick Fire

1.

Which figure should replace the question mark?

A B C D

2.

Which figure should replace the question mark?

A B C D

Quick Fire

3.

?

Which figure should replace the question mark?

A B C D

4.

?

Which figure should replace the question mark?

A B C D

More Challenging

5.

Which figure should replace the question mark?

6.

Which figure should replace the question mark?

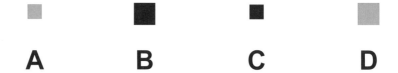

More Challenging

7.

¶ £ ¥ § Ψ ₣ ¶ £ ¥ § Ψ ₣ ¶ £ ¥ § Ψ ₣ ¶ ?

Which figure should replace the question mark?

£	¥	£	¥
A	**B**	**C**	**D**

8.

☼ ♀ ♂ ○ ● ☼ ♀ ♂ ? ● ☼ ♀ ♂ ○ ● ☼

Which figure should replace the question mark?

		♀	○
A	**B**	**C**	**D**

Difficult

9.

?

Which figure should replace the question mark?

A **B** **C** **D**

Difficult

10.

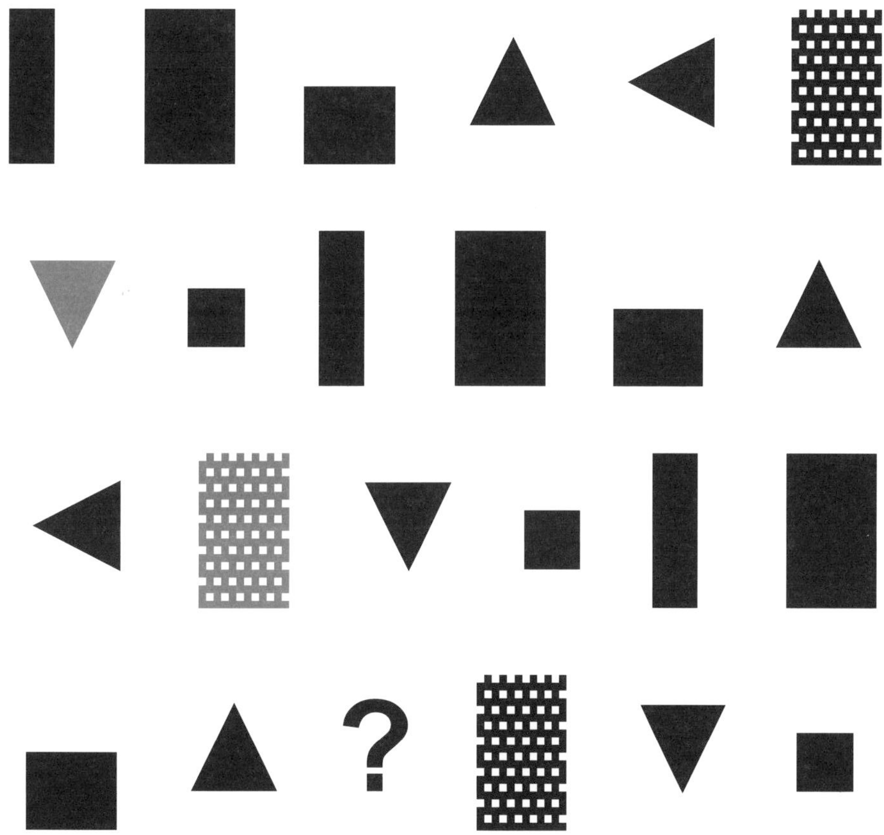

Which figure should replace the question mark?

Solutions – Quick Fire

1. B – The sequence progresses one square, black line, two squares, black line, etc. The first square after each black line is red.

2. C – The sequence progresses red/blue/blue/orange/pink repeated.

3. B – The sequence progresses one of each note, two of each note, three of each note. Every alternate note is red.

4. B – The sequence progresses one black followed by one blue, two blacks followed by one blue, three blacks followed by one blue, etc.

More Challenging

5. D – Every third square is large and every fourth square is blue.

6. A - The sequence progresses one black, three red, one black, two red, one black, one red, repeated. Every third circle is large.

7. A – The sequence consists of the symbols ¶ £ ¥ § Ψ ₣ repeated. Every fifth symbol is red.

8. D – The sequence ☼ ♀ ♂ ○ ● is repeated and every third symbol is large.

Solutions – Difficult

9. C – Reading left to right along each row from top to bottom, the sequence ╖ ╨ ╫ ╬ ╝ ╤ ╡ ╟ ╪ ╞ is repeated twice.

10. A – Reading left to right along each row from top to bottom, the sequence ▐ █ ▄ ▲ ◄ ▓ ▼ ■ is repeated three times and every seventh symbol is red.

Performance Rating

Score 1 point for each correct answer

Total Score	Rating	Percentage of Population
9 / 10	Genius level	Top 5%
8	High Expert	Top 10%
7	Expert	Top 30%
6	High Average	Top 40%
5	Middle Average	Top 60%
4	Low Average	Bottom 40%
3	Borderline Low	Bottom 30%
2	Low	Bottom 10%
0 / 1	Very Low	Bottom 5%

Transfer your score to the chart in the Assessment Section on page 302.

Brain Fact

As a result of work carried out in the 1960s by the American neurologist Roger Wolcott Sperry (1913-1994) it became apparent that the creative functions of human beings are controlled by the right-hand hemisphere of the human brain. This is the side of the brain which is under-used by the majority of people, as opposed to the thought processes of the left-hand hemisphere, which is characterized by order, sequence and logic; and is responsible for such functions as numerical and verbal skills.

Symbolic Sequence Test

This test consists of 20 questions, increasing in difficulty from Quick Fire to Difficult, in which a repeated sequence is provided, but with a missing element.

From the choice of options provided, you must determine which element or elements are missing from the sequence.

You have 60 minutes in which to complete the 20 questions.

Brain Fact

If we were to remove a brain from the skull we would see that it is made up of two almost identical hemispheres.

These two hemispheres are connected by a bridge, or interface, of millions of nerve fibres called the corpus callosum which allows them to communicate with each other.

In order to work to its full potential each of these hemispheres must be capable of analysing its own input first, only exchanging information with the other half, by means of the interface, when a considerable amount of processing has taken place. Because both hemispheres are capable of working independently, human beings are able to process two streams of information at once.

The brain then compares and integrates the information to obtain a broader and more in depth understanding of each concept.

Example

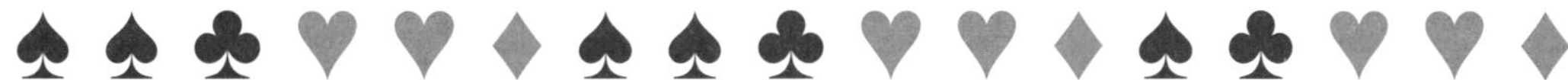

Which is the missing symbol?

B

C

D

E

Answer: B – The sequence comprises of six repeated symbols:

The symbol (ie a spade) should, therefore, appear twice before the final four symbols and not just once.

Quick Fire

1.

Which is the missing symbol?

A **B** **C** **D**

2.

Which is the missing symbol?

A **B** **C** **D**

Quick Fire

3.

● ●

Which is the missing symbol?

●	●	●	●
A	B	C	D

4.

& $ $ * # & $ $ * # & $ $ # & $ $ * #

Which is the missing symbol?

*	$	#	$	&
A	B	C	D	E

Quick Fire

5.

Which is the missing symbol?

6.

Which is the missing symbol?

Quick Fire

7.

Which is the missing symbol?

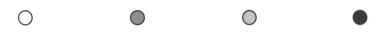

A **B** **C** **D**

More Challenging

8.

Which two symbols are missing?

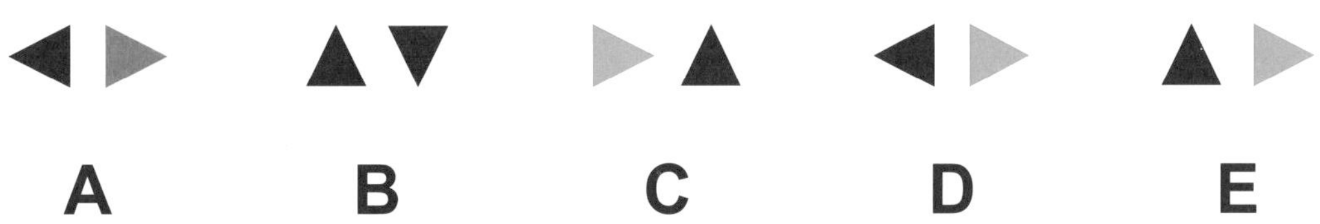

More Challenging

9.

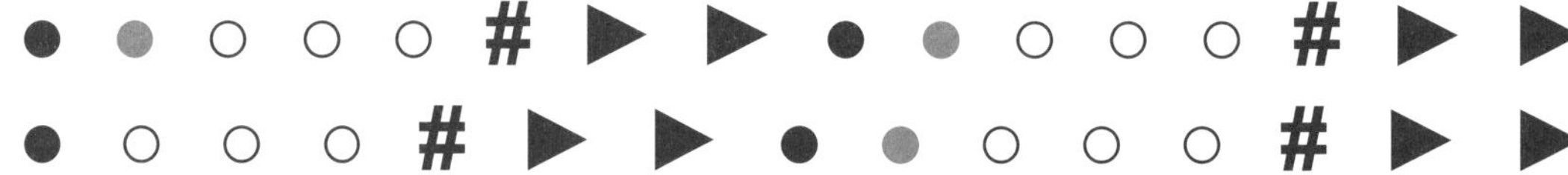

Which is the missing symbol?

#	○	●	▶	▲
A	**B**	**C**	**D**	**E**

10.

→ $ ♫ ↓ ¶ § & → $ ♫ ↓ ¶ §
& → $ ¶ § & → $ ♫ ↓ ¶ § &

Which two symbols are missing?

¶ §	& →	→ $	$ ♫	♫ ↓
A	**B**	**C**	**D**	**E**

More Challenging

11.

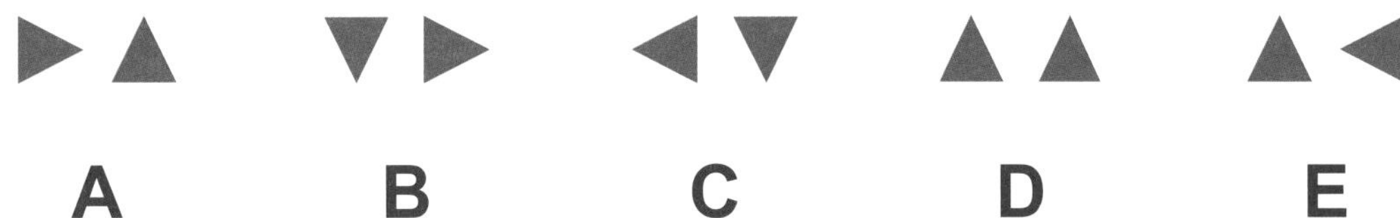

Which two symbols are missing?

A B C D E

12.

Which is the missing symbol?

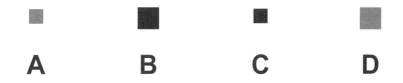

A B C D

More Challenging

13.

§ ♫ # ☺ ♀ ◀ — ♫ § ♫
# ☺ ◀ — ♫ § ♫ # ☺ ♀
◀ — ♫ § ♫ # ☺ ♀ ◀ — ♫

Which is the missing symbol?

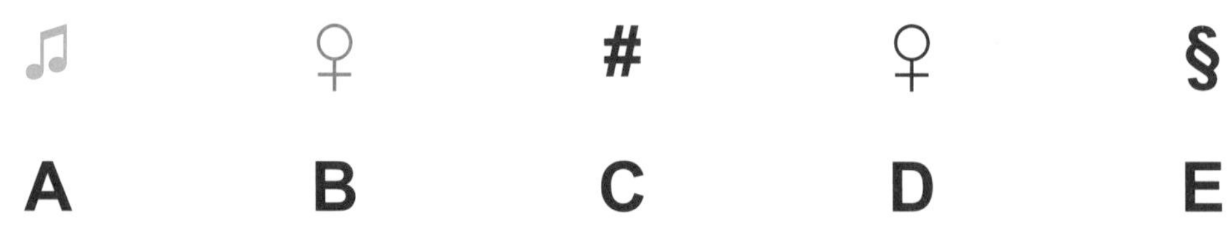

14.

¥ ☺ ∑ — ╬ ♫ ▲ ¥ ☺ £ ≠ ∑ — ╬ ♫ ▲ ¥
☺ £ ≠ ∑ — ╬ ♫ ▲ ¥ ☺ £ ≠ ∑ — ╬ ♫ ▲

Which two symbols are missing?

≠ ∑	╬ ¥	☺ £	£ ≠	╬ ♫
A	**B**	**C**	**D**	**E**

Difficult

15.

∑♫§■◀♠£╬▲∑♫§■◀♠£╬▲∑♫§■◀♠£╬
▲∑♫§■£╬▲∑♫§■◀♠£╬▲∑♫§■◀♠£╬▲

Which two symbols are missing?

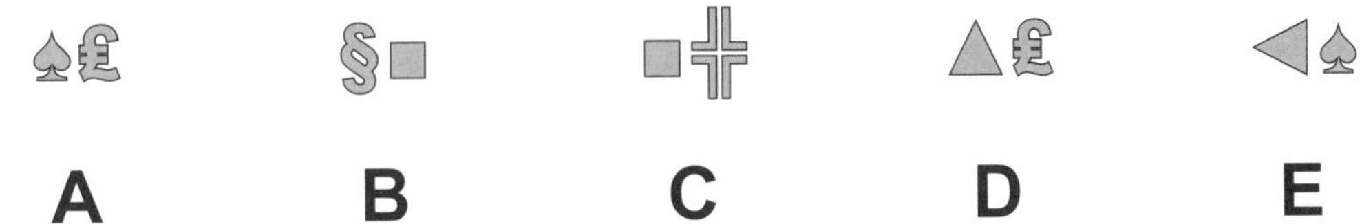

16.

& $ + ¶ ¥ © ☺ Θ Ψ $ + ¶ ¥ © ☺ Θ Ψ ● ♥ & $
+ ¶ ¥ © ☺ Θ Ψ ● ♥ & $ + ¶ ¥ © ☺ Θ Ψ ● ♥

Which three symbols are missing?

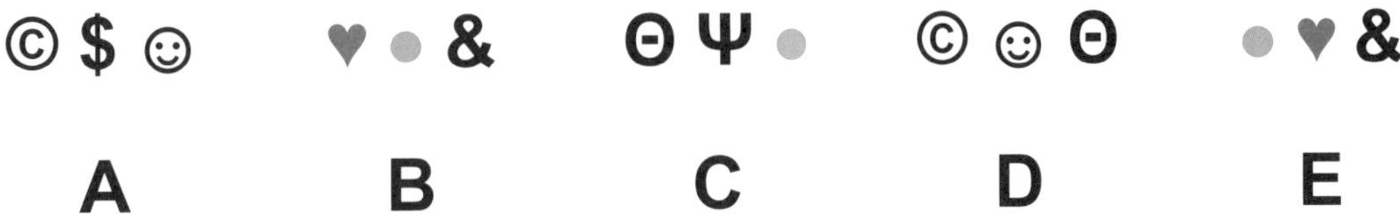

Difficult

17.

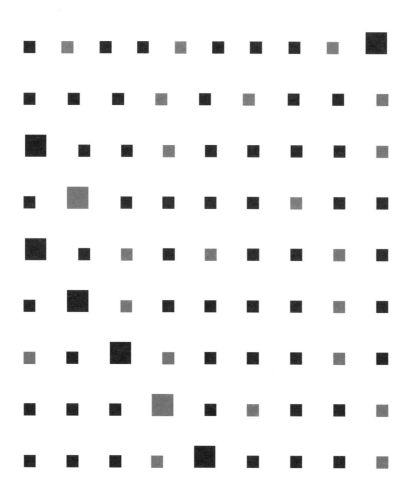

Which are the two missing symbols?

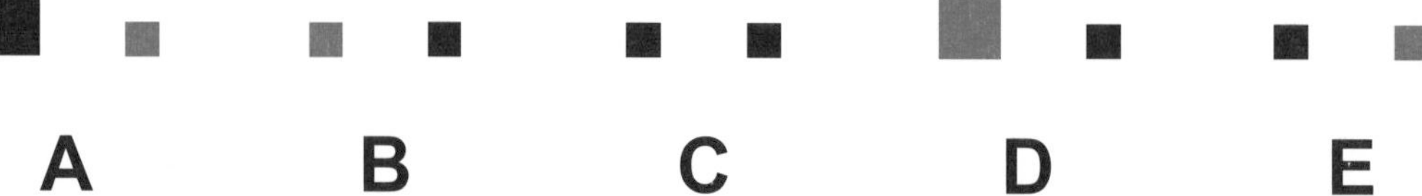

Difficult

18.

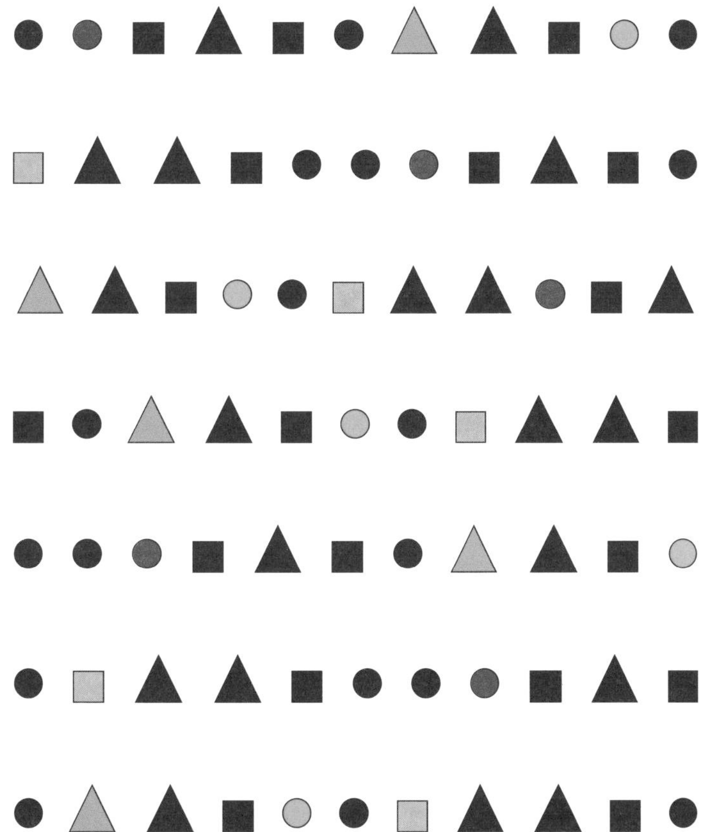

Which are the three missing symbols?

Difficult

19.

▲ ▶ ▼ ▶ ▲ ◀ ▶ ▲ ▼ ▼ ▼ ▶ ◀

▲ ▲ ▼ ▲ ▶ ▼ ▶ ▲ ◀ ▶ ▲ ▼ ▼

▼ ▶ ◀ ▲ ▲ ▼ ▲ ▶ ▼ ▶ ▲ ◀ ▶

▲ ▼ ▼ ▼ ▶ ◀ ▲ ▲ ▼ ▲ ▶ ▼ ▶

▲ ◀ ▶ ▲ ▼ ▼ ▼ ▶ ◀ ▲ ▲ ▼ ▲

▶ ▼ ▶ ▲ ◀ ▶ ▲ ▼ ▼ ▼ ▶ ▲ ▼

Which are the two missing symbols?

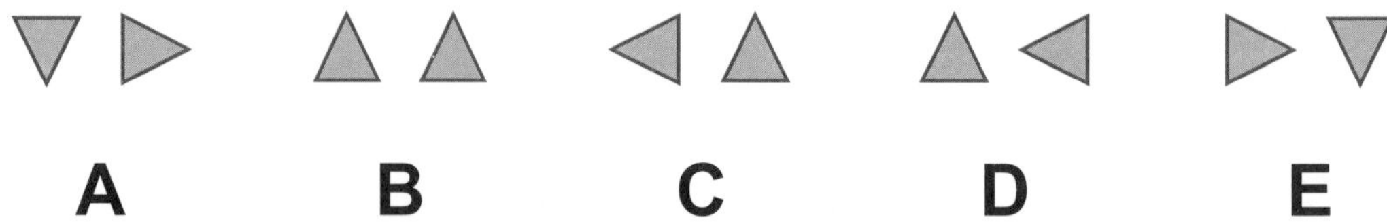

Difficult

20.

Which is the missing symbol?

A

B

C

D

E

Solutions – Quick Fire

1. D.

2. A.

3. C.

4. A.

5. D.

6. C.

7. B.

More Challenging

8. C.

9. C.

10. E.

11. B.

12. A.

13. D.

14. D.

Solutions – Difficult

15. E.

16. E.

17. B.

18. A.

19. C.

20. D.

Performance Rating

Score 1 point for each correct answer

Total Score	Rating	Percentage of Population
19 / 20	Genius level	Top 5%
17 / 18	High Expert	Top 10%
15 / 16	Expert	Top 30%
13 /14	High Average	Top 40%
11 / 12	Middle Average	Top 60%
9 / 10	Low Average	Bottom 40%
7 / 8	Borderline Low	Bottom 30%
5 / 6	Low	Bottom 10%
0 / 4	Very Low	Bottom 5%

Transfer your score to the chart in the Assessment Section on page 302.

Brain Fact

Neurons are the oldest and longest cells in the body and we have many of the same neurons for our whole life. Although other cells die and are replaced, many neurons are never replaced when they die. Therefore, we have fewer neurons when we are old compared to when we are young. On the other hand, data published in the late 1990s shows that in at least one area, the hippocampus, new neurons can grow in adult humans.

Memory

Every part of our life relies to some extent on memory. It is what enables us to walk, study, relax, communicate and enjoy our leisure time. Whatever function we perform, some sort of memory process is at work. Memory can be broadly divided into three types: sensory (immediate) memory, working (short-term) memory and long-term memory.

Sensory, or immediate, memory is of all present occurrences, such as noises and sights. It filters the different stimuli received at a given instant and only passes to short-term memory what is of interest.

Working, or short-term, memory enables the brain to evaluate the mass of incoming stimuli, or information, and select what is to be retained and memorized and what is to be rejected. This part of the memory enables us to temporarily recall any information currently under process; for example, if someone is speaking to you, it is only possible to understand them if you can recall what they said when they started speaking.

Because working memory decays rapidly it only has a limited capacity. There are ways in which short-term memory can be improved. One of these techniques is known as 'chunking'; for example, a hyphenated telephone number is easier to memorize than a single long number. This technique can lead to an increase, albeit temporarily, in short-term memory capacity.

A hindrance to short-term memory, which all of us will have experienced many times, is interference. This is when your train of thought is interrupted thus causing a disturbance in short-term memory retention. It is, therefore, desirable to complete tasks involving short-term memory as quickly as possible and without interruption.

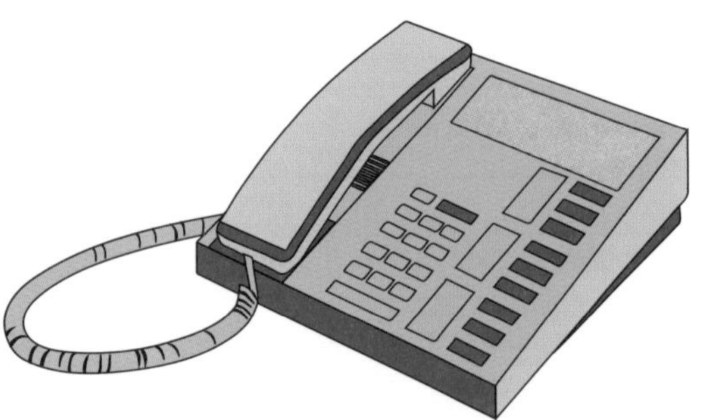

Long-term memory is intended for the storage of information over a long period and involves things like telephone numbers, holiday plans, names and addresses, and memories evoked from the past.

Information from the working memory is transferred to long-term memory after a few seconds and, unlike working memory, there is little decay.

While very little is yet known about the mechanics of memory it is accepted that the more you use it the better it becomes. It is also accepted that while it is impossible to improve on past memories, it is possible to improve one's memory for the present and future by practising active recall during learning, by periodic reviews of the material, and by over learning the material beyond the point of mastery. In addition there is the technique of mnemonics, which involve the use of association, imagination and location to remember particular facts.

The puzzles and tests in this section are designed to test your powers of memory and to assist you in improving your memory by developing your powers of concentration and disciplining yourself to focus your mind on the subject being studied.

Brain Fact

Communication in the brain takes the form of electrical impulses which run along pathways connecting the various sectors. These connections are formed by a group of dendroids which are threadlike extensions that grow out of neurons, the specialized cells of the nervous system. As well as dendroids, neurons have extensions called axons. Dendrites bring information to the cell body and axons take information away from the cell body.

Quick Fire

1. Study this picture for five seconds then turn to page 236.

2. Study this set of figures and numbers below for 30 seconds, then wait for five minutes and turn to page 237.

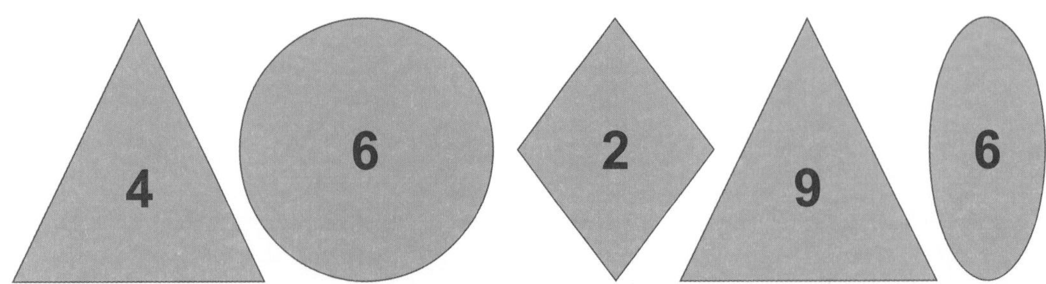

Quick Fire

3. Study the picture below for five seconds, then wait for five minutes and turn to page 237.

4.

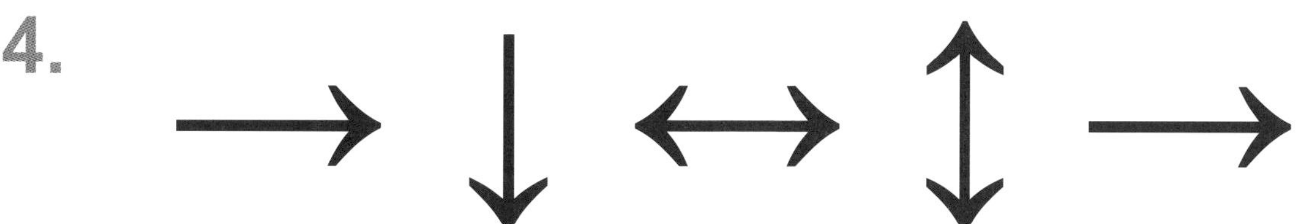

Study the above for 15 seconds and then turn straight to page 238.

More Challenging

5. Study the picture below for one minute then turn straight to page 239.

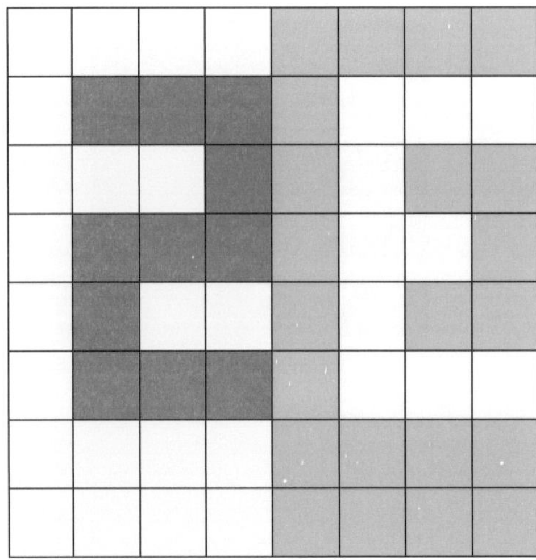

6. This exercise tests your ability to remember pairs of words and form associations.

CAMERA
RAFT

CHAIN
MOUSE

CHURCH
BEACH

VASE
YACHT

RABBIT
CLOCK

WHEEL
HAYSTACK

TOWEL
WALLPAPER

CHIMNEY
HOTEL

HAND
ELEPHANT

TRAMPOLINE
RICKSHAW

TELEPHONE
ALSATIAN

NEWSPAPER
RIVER

Study the 12 pairs of words for 10 minutes and use your imagination to link each pair of words, as shown above, in as many ways as possible.

Now turn to page 239.

More Challenging

7. Study the picture below for 30 seconds then turn straight to page 239.

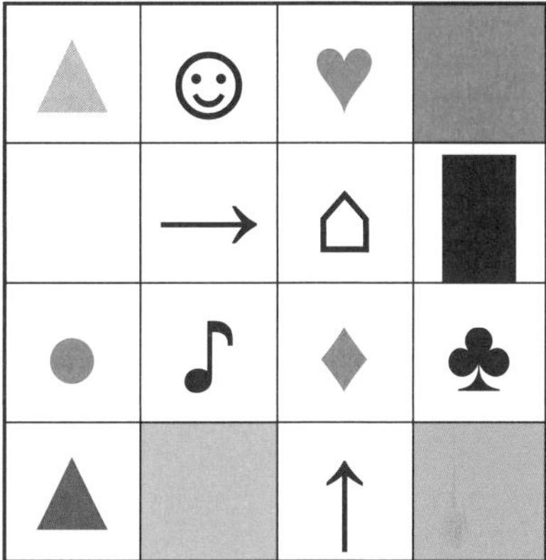

8. Ask a friend or family member to read aloud each row of numbers digit by digit at a steady rate. After each line has been read out, see if you can then repeat the line of numbers in the correct order from memory. The number of digits in each row of numbers increases by one each time, thus the task gets progressively more difficult.

Repeat the test as many times as you wish with your own selection of numbers. The more you practise the more proficient at remembering the numbers you will become.

3 8 1

4 9 8 6

7 2 9 4 6

9 2 7 6 9 1

3 7 5 0 2 4 8

0 4 7 1 8 4 7 2

8 5 7 3 0 1 8 6 4

6 9 3 0 4 4 7 2 8 5

7 1 8 9 5 7 0 4 6 2 7

More Challenging

9. This exercise tests your ability to remember people's names and form associations.

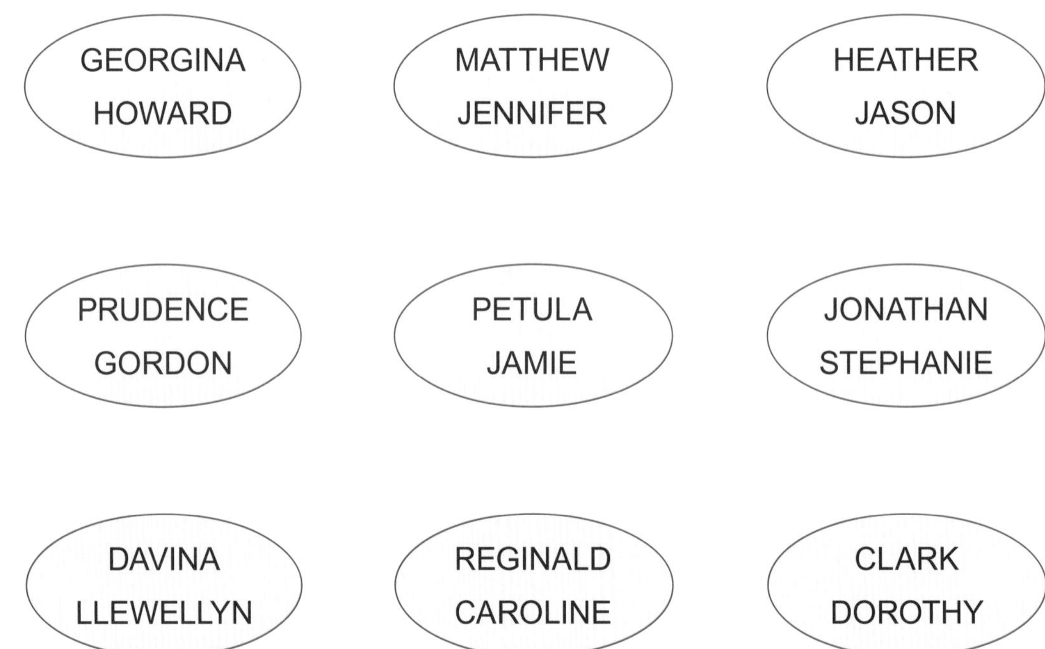

Study the nine pairs of names for three minutes and use your imagination to link each pair of names, as shown above.

Now turn to page 240.

10. ♫ § ♦ ↓ ® ¤ & ▲ ♦

Study the above set of figures for two minutes then turn straight to page 240.

Difficult

11. ≠ ▼ ¶ § $ Ŋ Ω Ξ Д ∏ & ≈ ℓ β

Study the above set of characters for one minute then turn immediately to page 241.

12. Memorize the directions below for five minutes then turn immediately to page 241.

Start at 2

Go from 2 to 7

Go right

Then down

Then left

Then up

Then go to 3

Then left

Then back to 7

Difficult

13. Try to memorize the rows of figures in five minutes then turn straight to page 242.

6 4 2 7 9 3 1

7 9 6 1 8 5 2

5 6 3 8 2 9 6

3 7 9 1 5 4 2

6 5 3 9 4 7 1

14. Study these names and professions for five minutes then turn straight to page 242.

John Finch	Farmer
Alfred Driver	Cook
Harold Field	Chauffeur
Tom Kitchen	Baker
Ellen Taylor	Carpenter
Kenneth Wood	Tailor
Emily Cook	Ornithologist

Difficult

15. Study the grid below for five minutes. Try to memorize the numbers and their position in the grid, then turn straight to page 243.

	3			5	6		8
2			1			3	6
			2				
2							9
9						5	
	7			5			1
5			3			0	
6			4				7

16.

Study the above for five minutes then turn straight to page 243.

Questions

1. Which of the following have you just looked at?

Questions

2. a. Which geometric figure appears twice in the set?

b. Which number appears twice in the set?

3. Which one of the following did you look at five minutes ago?

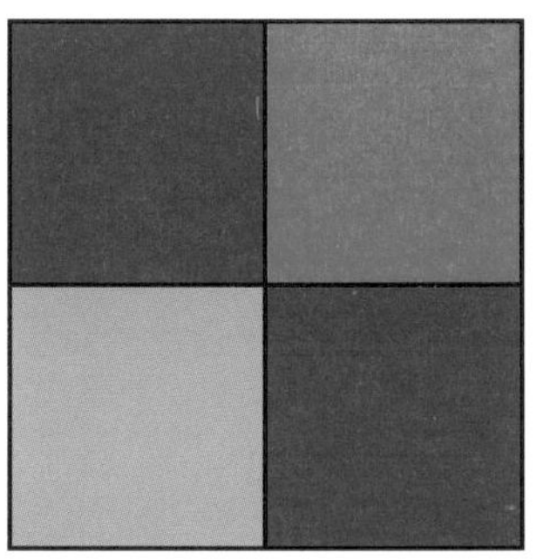

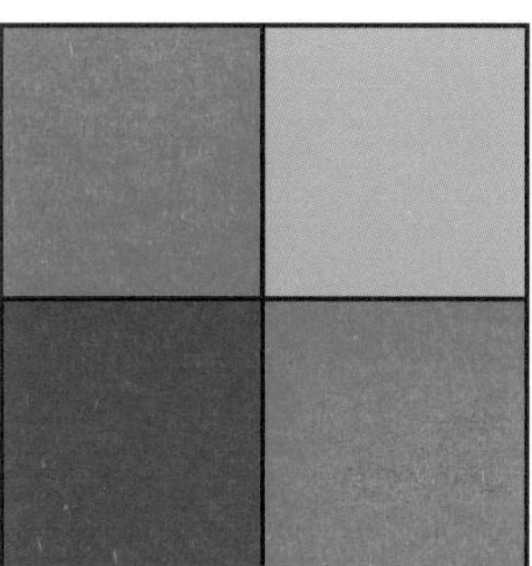

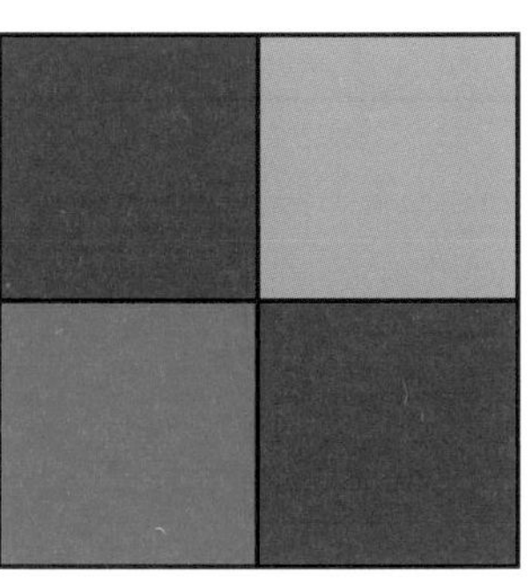

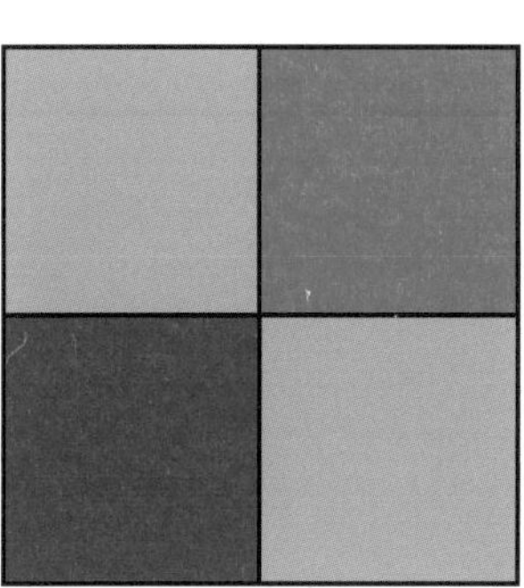

Questions

4. Which of the following have you just looked at?

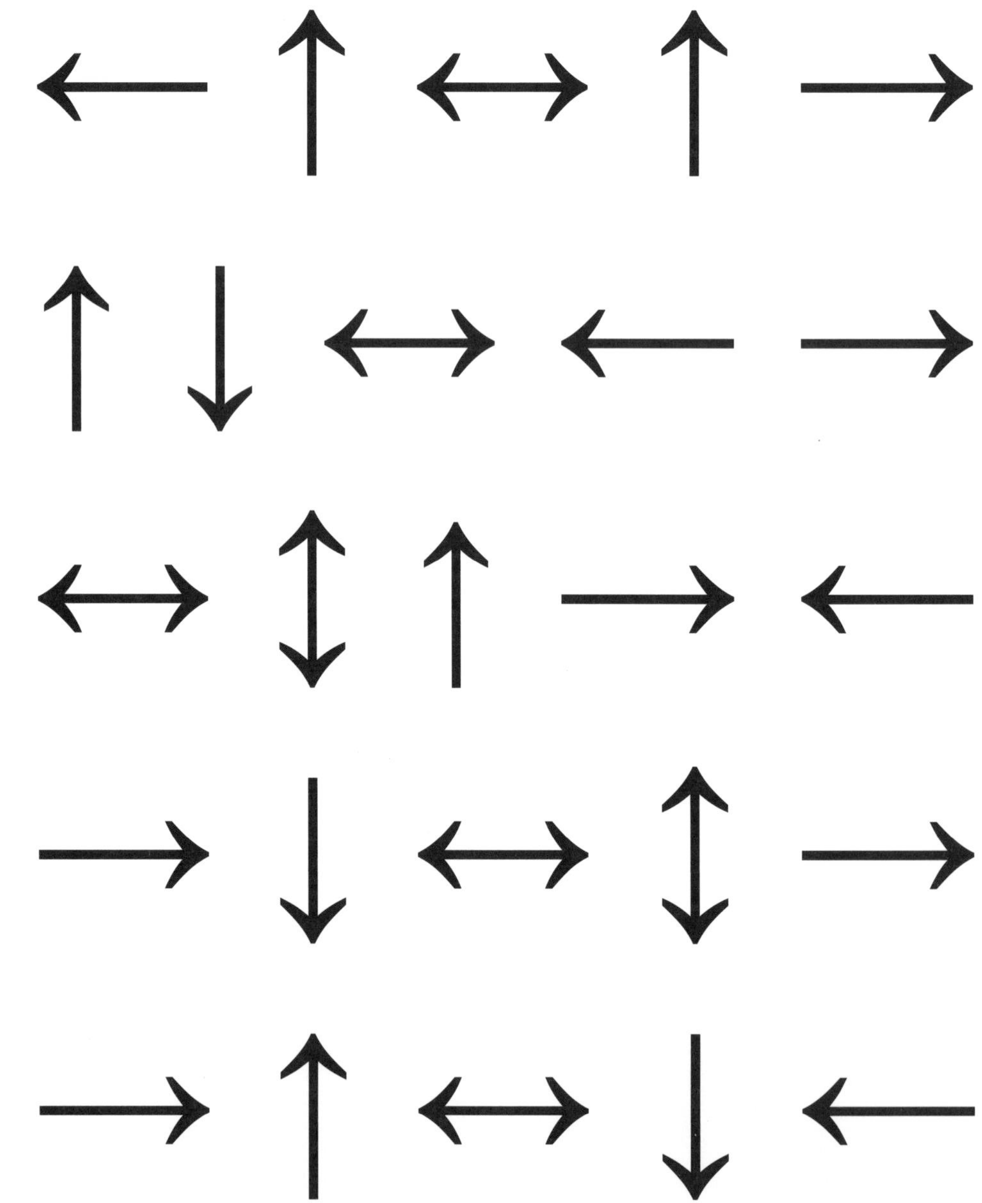

Questions

5. List the three ways in which the figure below has changed from the original.

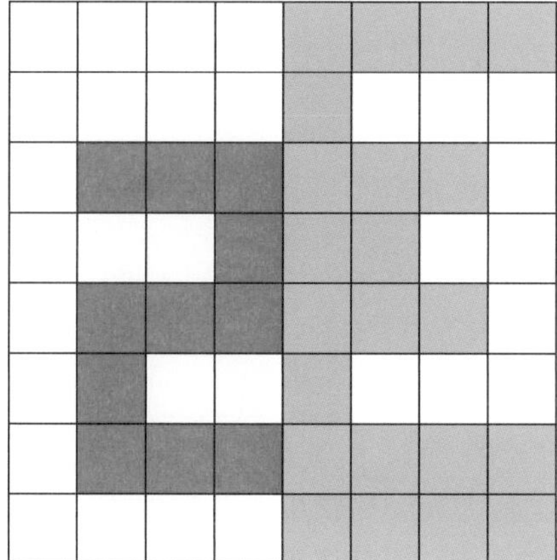

6. Put a letter A against one pair, the letter B against a second pair, etc, through to the letter L until you have matched what you think are the original 12 pairs of words.

RICKSHAW	CHURCH
TOWEL	RIVER
CAMERA	CHAIN
BEACH	CHIMNEY
NEWSPAPER	YACHT
VASE	HAYSTACK
MOUSE	TRAMPOLINE
ELEPHANT	CLOCK
RAFT	WHEEL
HAND	HOTEL
TELEPHONE	ALSATIAN
RABBIT	WALLPAPER

7.

a. Which two coloured squares have changed places?

b. Which two symbols have changed places?

Questions

9. Put a letter A against one pair, the letter B against a second pair, etc, through to the letter I until you have matched what you think are the original nine pairs of names.

LLEWELLYN	DAVINA	PRUDENCE
JASON	CAROLINE	MATTHEW
PETULA	DOROTHY	STEPHANIE
JONATHAN	JAMIE	REGINALD
GEORGINA	HOWARD	HEATHER
GORDON	CLARK	JENNIFER

10.

a. Which symbol appears immediately to the right of the symbol ®?

b. Which set of three symbols appears in the order shown below:

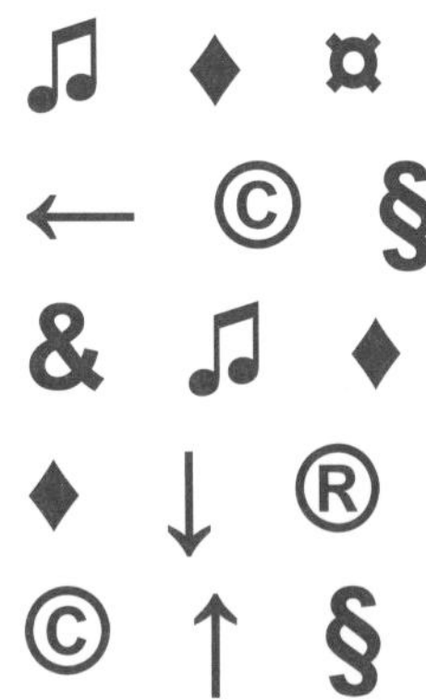

c. Which symbol appears between the & and the ♦?

Questions

11. ≠ ▼ ¶ § $ ŋ Ω = Ξ ∏ Д & ≈ ℓ β

a. Which new symbol has been introduced?

b. Which symbol has changed colour?

c. Which two symbols have changed places?

12. Which set of instructions below have you just followed?

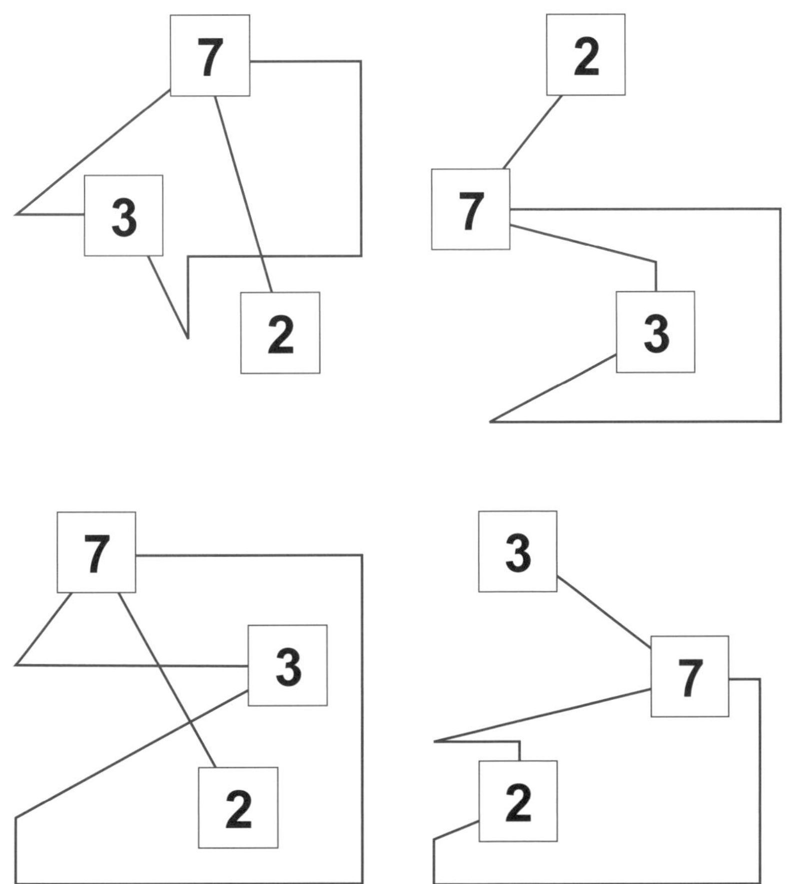

Questions

13. a. List the top row of figures in the correct order.

b. Which is the only number that appears in every row of figures?

c. Which is the only number to appear twice on the same row?

d. List the middle numbers in each row from top to bottom.

14. Complete the table with the surnames and professions correctly inserted:

A. Cook, Driver, Kitchen, Wood, Finch, Field, Taylor

B. Baker, Cook, Carpenter, Ornithologist, Tailor, Farmer, Chauffeur

	Surname (A)	Profession (B)
John		
Alfred		
Harold		
Tom		
Ellen		
Kenneth		
Emily		

Questions

15.

a. Which is the only number to appear on the third line across?

b. What is the total of the numbers that appear in the corner squares?

c. How many times does zero appear in the grid?

d. Which number appears in the grid the most number of times?

e. Which five numbers appear in the right-hand column reading downwards?

f. Which four consecutive numbers appear reading down the fourth column?

16.

a. Which suit follows the two spades on the second line?

b. Which three symbols below appear on the third line?

c. Which suit appears three times on the first line?

d. Which suit appears at the extreme right on two of the lines?

e. Which suit appears only twice on the third line?

Tests

Part 2 consists of five separate memory tests which are all timed and assessed. A total of 50 points are available in this test section.

In all the tests you should follow carefully each set of instructions. Study and memorize the details in each test for the allotted period of time, then turn to the page indicated and answer the question/s you will find there.

In addition to the memory puzzles and tests contained in this section, there are several other things that can be done to improve memory performance. It is very desirable, for example, to allow the brain to have enough sleep and rest in order for our memory to function efficiently. Also, the intake of alcohol is one of the main causes of memory loss as alcohol interferes with short-term memory in particular, which impairs the retention of new information.

It is important to continually stimulate the memory by using it to the utmost, by accepting different challenges and learning new skills. In addition to the enriching of our lives this could also stimulate our brain's neural circuits to grow and strengthen.

Brain Fact

The area of the cortex concerned with hearing is the auditory area, which is in the upper part of the temporal lobe; the area for seeing, the visual cortex, is in the back portion, or occipital lobe; and the area governing our sense of smell, the olfactory area, is in the front portion of the temporal lobe.

The area for language and speech, known as Broca's Area, is responsible for the muscle movements of the throat and mouth used in speaking. Distinct from this is the area responsible for our understanding of speech and reading, which is between the auditory and visual areas.

Memory Test

1. Study the diagram below for five minutes then turn straight to page 247.

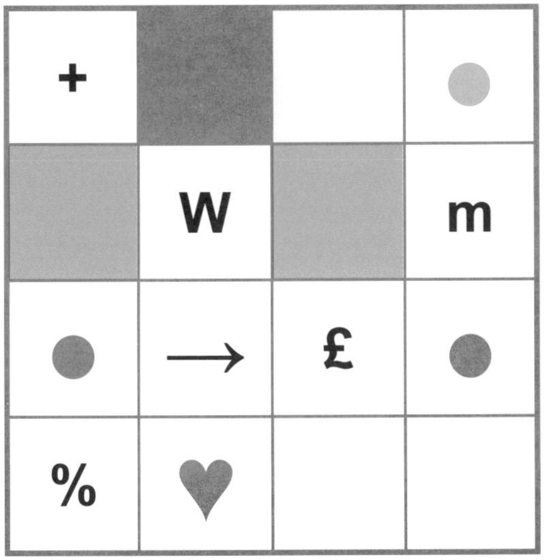

+			●
	W		m
●	→	£	●
%	♥		

2.

MICROSCOPE
PAINTBRUSH

MONKEY
BUNGALOW

PUDDLE
BUTTER

COMPASS
SNOW

GREENHOUSE
THERMOMETER

APPLE
BALL

PAPERWEIGHT
DOOR

CHEESE
PYRAMID

HORSE
CAKE

PRINTER
SCISSORS

This exercise tests your ability to remember pairs of words and form associations.

Study the 10 pairs of words for eight minutes and use your imagination to link each pair of words, as shown above, in as many ways as possible.

Now turn to page 247.

Memory Test

3. Study the address below for 10 minutes then turn immediately to page 248.

Chris Monteverde-Smythe,

The Willows,

7th Floor,

649 Fairfax Street,

Welbeck Estate,

Ty Newydd,

Hurstpierpoint,

HP3 9DJ

4. Study the diagram below for five minutes then turn straight to page 248.

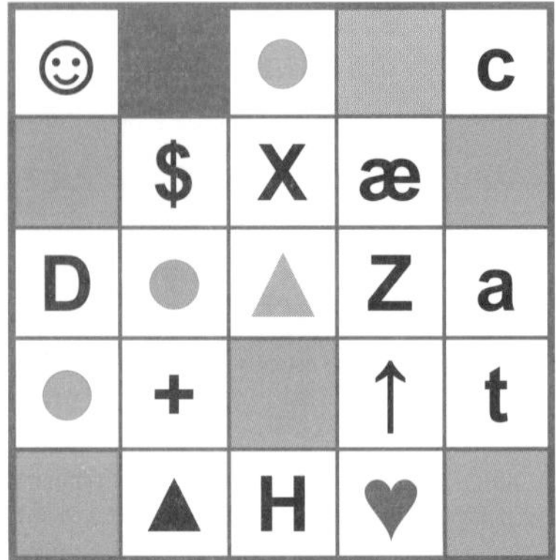

5. Memorize this shopping list for five minutes then turn straight to page 248.

You must try to remember the full details of each item.

Pack of 12 frozen fishfingers	A tube of English mustard
A dozen eggs	Packet of digestive biscuits
Box of cornflakes	Wholemeal loaf
2 lb pack of carrots	Cheshire cheese
A jar of coffee	Butter

Questions

1.

a. How many yellow squares does the grid contain?

b. The arrow is pointing to which symbol?

c. What letter appears immediately under the red square?

d. What symbol is in the top right-hand square?

e. What symbol is in the bottom left-hand square?

f. The letter m is immediately to the right of which coloured square?

g. What symbol appears immediately below the arrow?

h. How many red dots are in the grid?

i. What letter is immediately below the blue dot?

j. Which is the only line across; in the grid, that does not contain a coloured square?

Now check back with the original and score 1 point for each correct answer.

2.

Put a letter A against one pair, the letter B against a second pair, etc, through to the letter J until you have matched what you think are the original 10 pairs of words. Score 1 point for each correct pair of answers.

THERMOMETER	PAINTBRUSH	CAKE	MICROSCOPE
DOOR	CHEESE	SNOW	MONKEY
PUDDLE	BUTTER	BALL	GREENHOUSE
SCISSORS	APPLE	PRINTER	HORSE
PYRAMID	BUNGALOW	COMPASS	PAPERWEIGHT

Questions

3. Complete the address by filling in the blanks. Score 1 point for each correct answer.

Chris _ _ _ _ _ _ _ _ _ _ _ – Smythe

The _ _ _ _ _ _ _ _,

_ th Floor,

_ _ _ _ _ _ _ _ _ _ _ Street

_ _ _ _ _ _ _ _ Estate,

Ty _ _ _ _ _ _ _

Hurst_ _ _ _ _ _ _ _ _ _

_ _ 3 _ DJ

5. Write out the ten items on the shopping list. The order is not important, but the details of each item are.

Score 1 point for each *completely* correct answer.

4.

a. What symbol is in the top left-hand corner square?

b. What word is spelled out by the letters down the extreme right-hand column?

c. How many blue circles appear in the grid?

d. What mathematical symbol appears immediately below the green circle?

e. Which four letters appear in the grid in capitals?

f. What colour is the left-hand bottom corner square?

g. Which two letters appear joined together on the second row?

h. What symbol appears immediately below the letter X ?

i. What symbol is immediately below the arrow?

j. How many green squares appear in the grid?

Now check back with the original and score 1 point for each correct answer.

Assessment

In total, 50 points are available in the five tests:

Total Score	Rating	Percentage of Population
40 / 50	Genius level	Top 5%
35 / 39	High Expert	Top 10%
30 / 34	Expert	Top 30%
26 / 29	High Average	Top 40%
22 / 25	Middle Average	Top 60%
18 / 21	Low Average	Bottom 40%
14 / 17	Borderline Low	Bottom 30%
9 / 13	Low	Bottom 10%
0 / 8	Very Low	Bottom 5%

Transfer your score to the chart in the Assessment Section on page 302.

Brain Fact

The temporal lobe, which is located under the temporal bone above the ears is thought to be particularly important for the storage of past events and includes the temporal neocortex which is thought to be potentially the region involved in long-term memory. This region also contains a group of interconnected structures that appear to perform the declarative memory function. Studies suggest that one of these circuits through the hippocampus and thalamus may be involved in spatial memories, whereas another circuit through the amygdala and thalamus may be responsible for our emotional memories.

Tests

In general the term personality refers to the patterns of thought, feelings and behaviour that are unique to each one of us. These characteristics are what distinguish us from other people.

The concept of Emotional Intelligence (EQ) – the ability to be aware of, control and manage one's emotions – contends that IQ is too narrow and simplistic a measure of intelligence and that behavioural and character traits, for example, are as important as determiners of how successful we are.

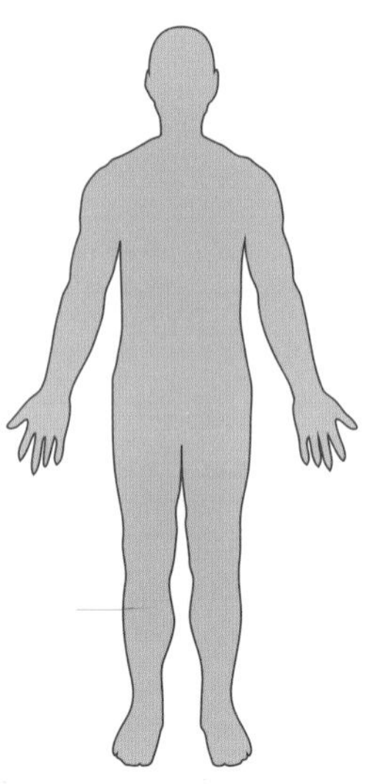

The tests in this section measure two aspects of understanding your own personality traits – self-confidence and attitude. The procedure for answering the questions is to be true to yourself and answer each question as truthfully and realistically as possible.

There is no need to read through the tests first before attempting them; just answer intuitively and without too much consideration. There are no right or wrong answers and, although you should work as quickly as possible, there is no set time limit.

Brain Fact

The brain is not inactive during sleep. The brain waves of a sleeping person with rapid-eye movement (REM), which takes place when that person is dreaming, are similar in frequency and amplitude to when that person is awake and alert. In non-REM sleep, the brain waves have a higher amplitude and lower frequency which indicates that the neurons in the brain are firing more slowly and in a coordinated fashion.

Test 1 – Self-confidence

Answer each question or statement by choosing which one of the three alternative responses given is most applicable to you.

1. How important is it to conform to be accepted?

a. It is necessary to conform in many respects
b. Very important
c. Not at all important

2. Does being alone in a strange place worry you?

a. Perhaps so, until I find my bearings
b. Yes, I like to be on familiar territory with people I know
c. No, I like exploring and finding out more about new places

3. Do you believe in the power of positive thinking?

a. Not sure
b. Not really as for the most part what will be will be
c. Yes, think positively and you are more likely to make good things happen

4. Do long journeys make you feel nervous?

a. Sometimes
b. Yes
c. No

5. How often do you feel sad or depressed?

a. Occasionally
b. More than occasionally
c. Rarely or never

Test 1 – Self-confidence

6. Do you ever express your support for the underdog in an argument?

a. Occasionally
b. Not really, as I usually try to keep out of strong arguments
c. I have done so on several occasions, and I always will support the underdog when I think they are correct

7. Are you confident that you will achieve most of the things that are important to you?

a. More hopeful than confident
b. Not really
c. Yes, quite confident

8. Do you like flirting with members of the opposite sex?

a. Occasionally perhaps
b. Not at all
c. Yes

9. Do you value your own opinions more than those of others?

a. Usually, but not always
b. I do like to run my opinions past others
c. Yes

10. You have made a purchase at a local store and on leaving realize that the assistant has slightly short-changed you. What is most likely to be your reaction?

a. Not sure, it would probably depend on a number of factors such as how many people were in the shop or how I was feeling at the time
b. I would probably let it go as such a small amount of money isn't worth the fuss
c. I would go back and point out the mistake to the assistant

Test 1 – Self-confidence

11. You are on a committee and the position of chair becomes vacant. Which of the following is most likely to apply?

a. I would think about who might make a good chairperson
b. I would decline if someone approached me to be chairperson
c. I would aspire to being nominated as the new chairperson

12. If you were asked to make a speech at a function attended by a large number of people, would you accept?

a. I probably would but would be quite nervous at the prospect
b. No, I don't do speeches
c. Yes, I would accept

13. Does the thought of meeting very powerful and important people make you feel nervous?

a. Slightly perhaps
b. Yes, very nervous
c. Not at all

14. At social gatherings which of the following best describes your actions?

a. I usually keep within my own circle of acquaintances
b. I dislike social gatherings and tend to keep myself to myself, and am relieved when it's all over
c. I enjoy circulating, meeting people and making small talk

15. You are invited to a Christmas Karaoke party at your next door neighbour's house. Which of the following is most likely to be your reaction?

a. Accept the invitation but hope very much that you won't be asked to perform a number
b. Politely decline as the thought of performing a Karaoke number in front of a large number of guests terrifies you
c. Accept the invitation and start rehearsing your party piece

Test 1 – Self-confidence

16. Do you feel good about yourself?

a. Generally although there are a number of things I wouldn't mind altering
b. When I have the approval of others I do tend to feel good about myself
c. Yes

17. I am happy to accept myself for what I am.

a. I would like to be better in some respects
b. I would like to be better in many respects
c. True

18. Would you like to take part in a live television debate?

a. Not sure, I might consider it
b. No way, the thought alone would terrify me
c. Yes, I would relish the idea

19. What would your likely feelings be if you were told there was to be a major reorganisation at your place of work?

a. I would be quite apprehensive especially if I was satisfied with things as they are now
b. It would worry me as it could mean disruption or at the worst redundancies
c. I would hope to be involved in the reorganisation process as it might provide me with better career opportunities

20. Do you ever feel self-conscious in public places?

a. Occasionally
b. More than occasionally
c. Never

Test 1 – Self-confidence

21. I believe it is essential to set high but realistic goals.

a. It is essential for some people, but I'm not really one of those people
b. There is no point setting myself targets that I feel I will not be able to achieve
c. Agree

22. When you take part in a sport or game do you expect to win?

a. Not necessarily but I try my best
b. I'm not really bothered whether I win or lose
c. Yes, I always play to win

23. I am very good at selling myself.

a. Not as good as perhaps I could be
b. I don't believe in being too pushy
c. Yes

24. If I do not agree with someone I say so.

a. Sometimes – it depends upon the importance or relevance of the subject
b. Not usually as it is more prudent sometimes to maintain a discreet silence
c. Yes, always

25. I set my own personal standards.

a. Generally yes
b. Not always as it is often best to set the standards necessary to obtain the approval of others
c. Yes, always

Analysis

People with a high degree of self-confidence are likely to be assured and self-reliant in their own abilities. Such people, although needing to be wary of over-confidence, will very rarely feel unsure of themselves or be preoccupied with negative self-thoughts. Nor are they ever likely to put themselves down, or feel sad, depressed or lonely.

As self-confident people do not feel the need to conform in order to be accepted they are not dependant on others to feel good about themselves, indeed they are willing to risk the disapproval of others because of the confidence they have in themselves and their ability to accept themselves for what they are. Because self-confidence also means the ability to take a realistic view of oneself, self-confidence need not necessarily apply to all aspects of a person's life, and some individuals will have total confidence in certain aspects of their life, such as sporting prowess or negotiating skills, but have other aspects of their life in which they do not feel so confident, such as practical skills.

As a result self-confident people (Keywords: secure, positive, sensible) are usually able to develop an attitude in which they can, to a great extent, take control of their own lives and stand up for their own rights and aspirations, while at the same time keeping these aspirations realistic.

For people who have not scored as highly as they might have wished on this test, there are a number of strategies that can be adopted for developing a greater degree of self-confidence. These may be summarized as follows:

- Evaluate your talents and play to your strengths.
- Even if you do not meet your aspirations give yourself credit for everything you try to achieve.
- View every disappointment as a learning experience and as a way of achieving personal growth.
- Do not be afraid of taking calculated risks. View such risk taking as a possible opportunity rather than a risky venture which is likely to result in disappointment.
- Never be afraid of change.
- Accept that perfection does not exist.
- Balance the need for continual improvement with the ability to accept yourself for what you are.
- Never try to please everyone at the same time.
- Carry out a continual process of self-evaluation.
- Take control of your own life.
- Focus on how you feel about yourself, your own lifestyle and your own aspirations rather than the aspirations others, such as parents, may have for you.
- Beware of over-confidence as this may result in disappointment and loss of confidence.

Assessment

Award yourself:

2 points for every 'c' answer, 1 point for every 'a' answer, and 0 points for every 'b' answer.

Total Score	Rating
40-50	Exceptionally high self-confidence factor
35-39	High self-confidence factor
30 – 34	Above average self-confidence
25 – 29	Average self-confidence
20 -24	Below average self-confidence
15 – 19	Low self-confidence factor
10 - 14	Very low self-confidence factor
Below 10	Extremely low self-confidence factor

Divide the score obtained by two, round up to the nearest whole number and transfer the figure to the chart in the Assessment Section on page 302.

Brain Fact

When it comes to human brain size bigger is not necessarily better. In fact, scientists believe bigger could be worse, because increased size may impede rapid communication between nerve cells within the brain.

Test 2 – Attitude

Answer each question or statement by choosing which one of the three alternative responses given is most applicable to you.

1. Change is:

a. Not always for the better
b. A whole new challenge
c. Inevitable, like death and taxes

2. How often do you worry about climate change?

a. Rarely or never as I believe it is an overrated problem
b. Quite a lot
c. Occasionally, especially when it is in the news

3. How often do you think about how people perceive you?

a. Rarely or never
b. More than occasionally
c. Occasionally

4. How much time each day do you spend purely watching television and not doing anything else at the same time?

a. More than five hours
b. Less than two hours
c. Between two and five hours

Test 2 – Attitude

5. How often do you find yourself feeling bored because you have too little to do?

a. More than occasionally
b. Never
c. Occasionally

6. What is your attitude to new technology?

a. I'm not sure some of it is necessary, in fact much new technology seems very gimmicky, and not for me
b. It is an exciting new challenge
c. I have to accept it but worry sometimes whether I am able to keep pace with it, let alone master it

7. Why do you work?

a. In order to maintain my standard of living and pay the bills
b. For job satisfaction and money
c. For money and something to do

8. Imagine it is your sixtieth birthday, what are your feelings?

a. The best years of my life are behind me, but hopefully I will keep active for many years yet
b. Sixty is the new forty
c. I'm getting older but I will make the best of my life despite this

Test 2 – Attitude

9. Which of the following is most appropriate when dealing with customers?

a. Serve them
b. Please them
c. Assist them

10. How proud are you of your nationality?

a. I think proud may be putting it too strongly
b. Very proud
c. It is not something I think about a great deal

11. How much do you have to motivate yourself to do very mundane tasks?

a. A great deal
b. A little, but if they have to be done they have to be done
c. Quite a lot but I will probably get round to doing them when I am in the right frame of mind

12. How often do you vote at General and Local elections?

a. Occasionally or never
b. Always
c. I usually vote at General elections but not always at Local elections

Test 2 – Attitude

13. At the end of the normal working day you have a half-finished job which will take you about 30 minutes to complete. What would you usually do under those circumstances?

a. Complete the job the morning after
b. Complete the job either by staying behind or taking the work home
c. Complete the job but claim overtime payments

14. It is the responsibility of all parents to teach their children the difference between right and wrong at a very early age.

a. I agree in principle, but things are not always that simple
b. Very strongly agree
c. Agree

15. What is your attitude to taking chances?

a. Taking chances gives me a buzz
b. It is necessary to take chances from time to time
c. I wouldn't take a chance if there was an alternative

16. Do you continually look forward to, and plan for the future?

a. Live for today is a much better philosophy
b. Yes
c. Generally, but there comes a time in life when this philosophy is not so important

Test 2 – Attitude

17. I am very concerned about the level of crime and anti-social behaviour in our society today.

a. It doesn't concern me that much as I believe people are basically decent, and in the area where I live I do not see many such instances
b. Yes, it does concern me
c. It is something that concerns me from time to time

18. I am happy when others like and respect me.

a. It doesn't bother me as people need to take me for what I am
b. True
c. More pleased than happy

19. I always try to see the other person's point of view.

a. Sometimes, but not when I know that the other person is wrong to hold an opposing viewpoint to mine
b. Yes, as it is essential in every argument or dispute to do so
c. Usually

20. Do you tend to complain a lot?

a. I suppose I do; in fact there is unfortunately much to complain about in today's world
b. Not particularly
c. Perhaps not a lot; however, I will certainly complain if I feel there is something to complain about

Test 2 – Attitude

21. Which of these best describes your attitude to work?

a. It is something that has to be done to make a living
b. It should be fun
c. I wish I could earn enough money to retire early

22. It angers me when people or groups of people become stereotyped.

a. Not particularly
b. Yes
c. Not anger, but perhaps we could be more tolerant of certain groups of people in our society

23. It is unusual for me to stand or walk with my hands in my pockets.

a. Not sure – it's not something I have previously ever thought about
b. Yes
c. Maybe I do stand or walk with my hands in my pockets occasionally

24. It is important that I keep myself in good shape physically.

a. It is not something I go out of my way to achieve
b. Yes, I agree emphatically
c. I do like to keep myself active

25. I think it is possible to judge people on first appearances.

a. Agree
b. No, you have to get to know them before you can even start to make judgments about them
c. Sometimes this is true

Analysis

Having the right attitude is increasingly important in modern life. When we buy goods, for example, we expect the person serving us to be enthusiastic and knowledgeable about the products they are selling, and at the same time eager to help and anxious to please. This type of enthusiasm is conveyed to others in all kinds of different situations.

Attitudes are not born with us, but formed in a variety of ways – for example, through our experiences with people – especially our parents, whose beliefs often inform our own – and of events.

Our attitudes can change, hence the phrase 'developing an attitude'. These changes may be positive, in which case the individual develops a better attitude; or negative, in which case the attitude is worse.

Sometimes an attempt to change the attitude of an individual can result in the opposite of what was intended. As our attitudes are often formed by external influences, individuals whose results in this test are less than encouraging may find it worth looking at themselves and considering whether the influences present in their lives can be changed in order to reverse any negativity that might be holding them back.

The greater our understanding of our own attitudes and beliefs, the greater the chance we have of identifying and changing our negative attitudes to positive ones.

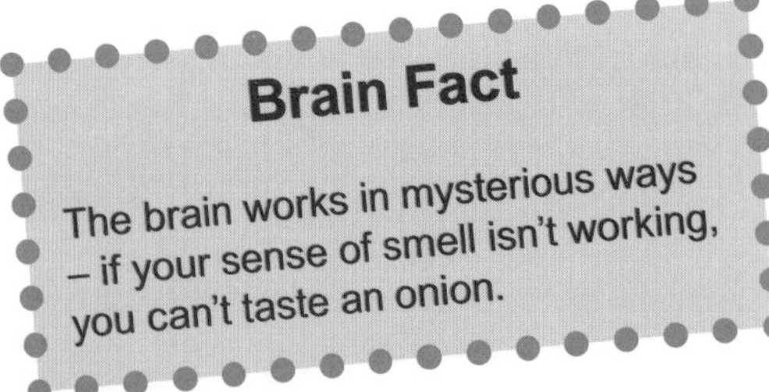

Brain Fact
The brain works in mysterious ways – if your sense of smell isn't working, you can't taste an onion.

Assessment

Award yourself:

2 points for every 'b' answer, 1 point for every 'c' answer, and 0 points for every 'a' answer

Total Score	Rating
40-50	Exceptionally high positive attitude factor
35-39	High positive attitude factor
30 – 34	Above average attitude factor
25 – 29	Average attitude factor
20 -24	Below average attitude factor
15 – 19	Negative attitude factor
10 - 14	Very negative attitude factor
Below 10	Extremely negative attitude factor

Divide the score obtained by two, round up to the nearest whole number and transfer the figure to the chart in the Assessment Section on page 302.

Brain Fact

The brain comprises three distinct but connected parts; the cerebrum, the cerebellum and the brain stem.

Tests

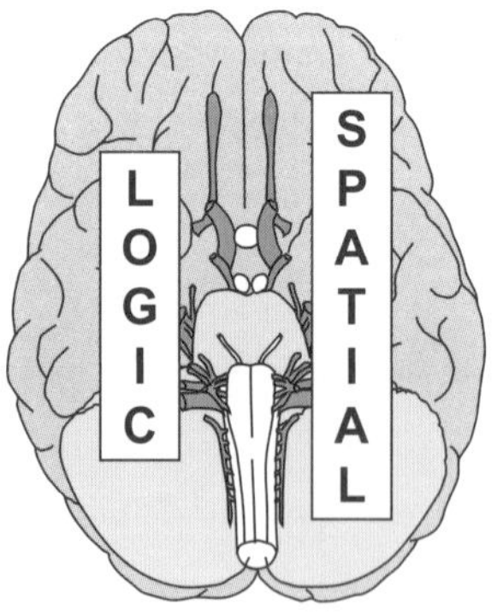

The two tests presented here are designed to encourage you to develop whole brain thinking, by challenging both your logic (a left-brain function) and your spatial awareness (a right-brain function). If you are to achieve a high score, both sides of the brain must work together.

In common with almost all the puzzles and tests in this book, no specialized knowledge is required in order to solve the questions that follow. What is required is the ability to think clearly and analytically and follow a commonsense reasoning process step by step to its conclusion.

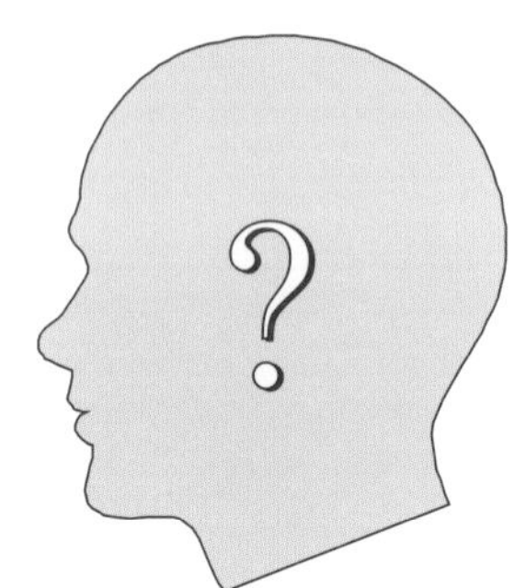

In both tests it is recommended that you study the examples provided before attempting the tests, which should be completed within the set time limit.

Brain Fact

The human tongue contains approximately 10,000 taste buds which work in conjunction with the brain to provide us with our sense of taste.

When chemicals from the food we eat are dissolved in the moisture of the mouth, they enter the taste buds through pores in the surface of the tongue where they come into contact with sensory cells, which send nerve impulses to the brain. The frequency of repetition of these impulses tells the brain the type and strength of the flavour we are experiencing.

Test 1 – Light Switch Test

This test consists of 20 questions which gradually increase in difficulty. A time limit of 90 minutes is allowed in which to complete the 20 questions.

Instructions

An electrical circuit wiring a set of four lights depends on a system of switches A, B, C and D. Each switch when working has the following effect on the lights:

Switch A turns lights 1 and 2 on/off or off/on
Switch B turns lights 2 and 4 on/off or off/on
Switch C turns lights 1 and 3 on/off or off/on
Switch D turns lights 3 and 4 on/off or off/on

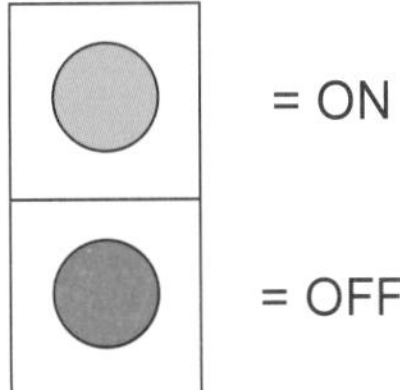

= ON

= OFF

In the following example, switches D, A and C are thrown in turn, with the result that Figure 1 is transformed into Figure 2. Therefore, one of the switches is not working and has had no effect on the numbered lights. Identify which switch is not working:

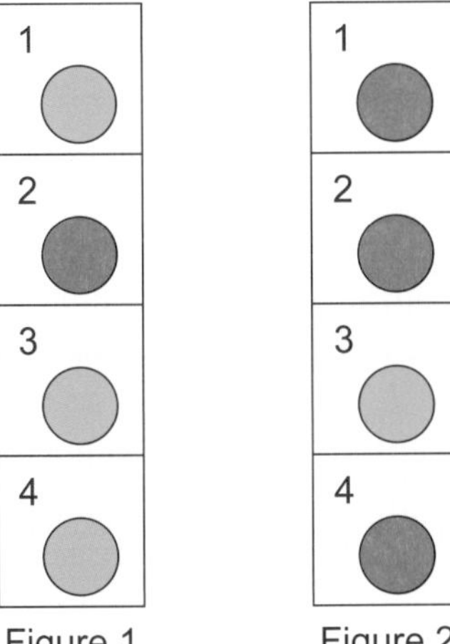

Figure 1 Figure 2

Test 1 – Light Switch Test

Answer: Switch A is faulty.

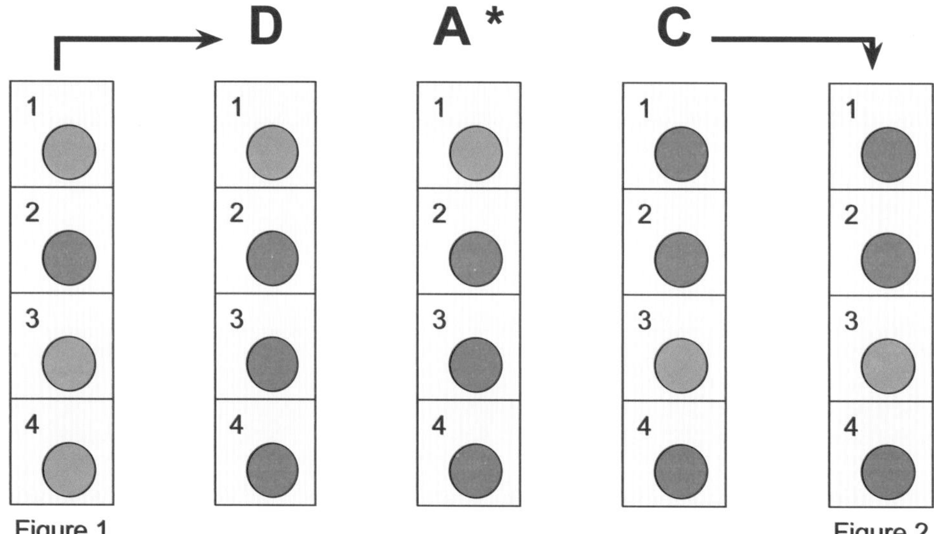

Explanation:
When Switch D is thrown it has the desired effect on lights 3 and 4.
When Switch A is thrown it has no effect on any of the lights and, therefore, is faulty.
When Switch C is thrown it has the desired effect on lights 1 and 3.

Quick Fire

1. In the following, switches C, D and B are thrown in turn, with the result that Figure 1 is transformed into Figure 2. One of the switches is not, therefore, working and has had no effect on the numbered lights. Identify which one of the switches is not working:

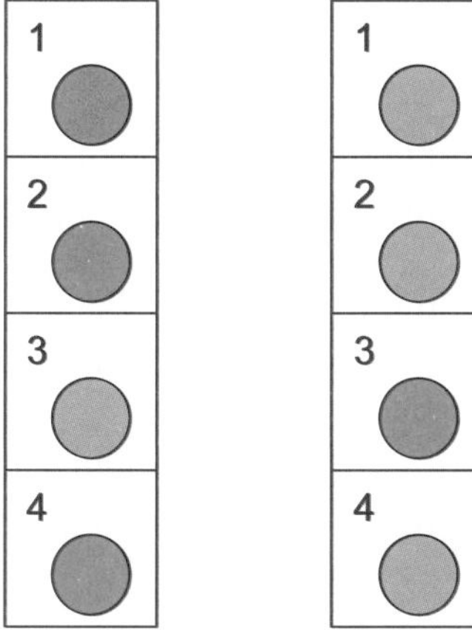

Figure 1 Figure 2

2. In the following, switches B, C and A are thrown in turn, with the result that Figure 1 is transformed into Figure 2. Therefore, one of the switches is not working and has had no effect on the numbered lights. Identify which switch is not working:

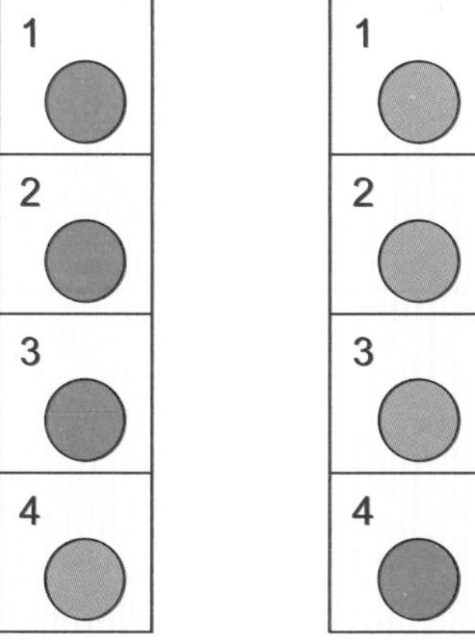

Figure 1 Figure 2

Quick Fire

3. In the following, switches B, C and D are thrown in turn, with the result that Figure 1 is transformed into Figure 2. Therefore, one of the switches is not working and has had no effect on the numbered lights. Identify which switch is not working:

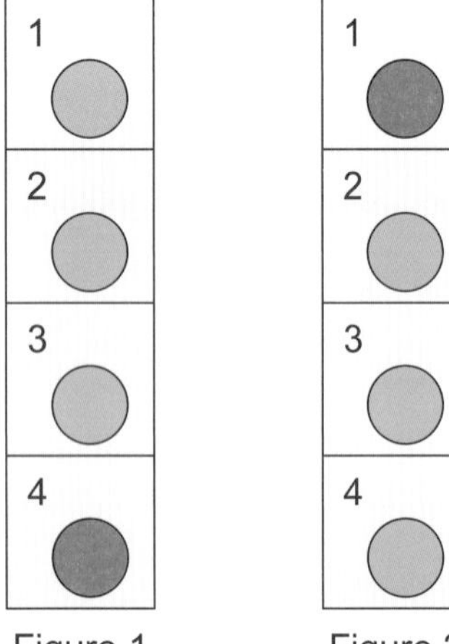

Figure 1 Figure 2

4. In the following, switches C, A and D are thrown in turn, with the result that Figure 1 is transformed into Figure 2. Therefore, one of the switches is not working and has had no effect on the numbered lights. Identify which switch is not working:

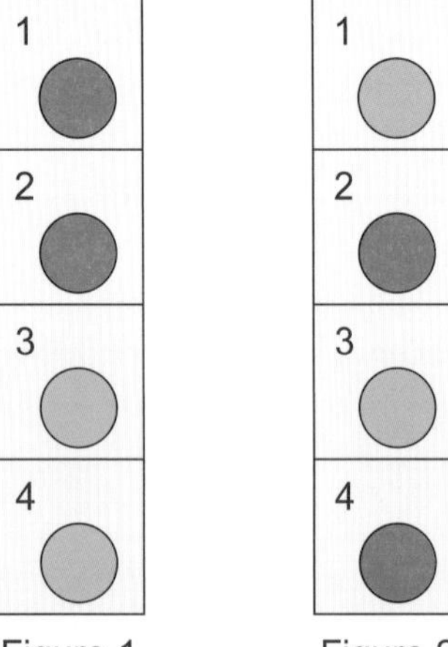

Figure 1 Figure 2

Quick Fire

5. In the following, switches D, A and C are thrown in turn, with the result that Figure 1 is transformed into Figure 2. Therefore, one of the switches is not working and has had no effect on the numbered lights. Identify which switch is not working:

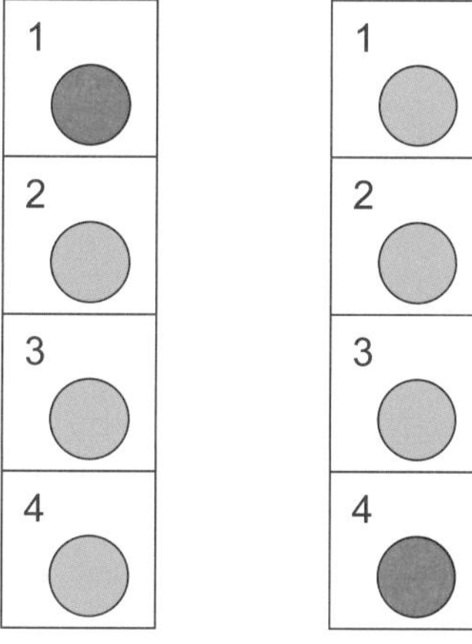

Figure 1 Figure 2

6. In the following, switches B, C and A are thrown in turn, with the result that Figure 1 is transformed into Figure 2. Therefore, one of the switches is not working and has had no effect on the numbered lights. Identify which switch is not working:

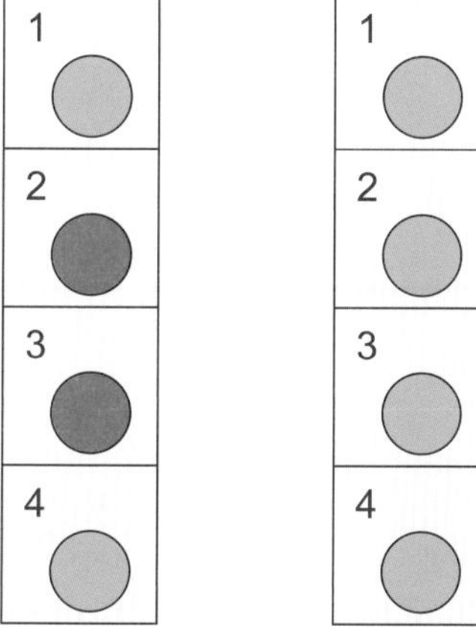

Figure 1 Figure 2

More Challenging

7. In the following, switches C, B, D and A are thrown in turn, with the result that Figure 1 is transformed into Figure 2. Therefore, one of the switches is not working and has had no effect on the numbered lights. Identify which switch is not working:

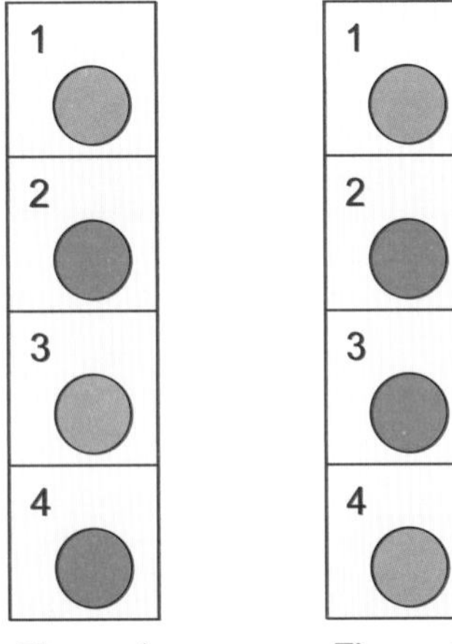

Figure 1 Figure 2

8. In the following, switches C, B, A and D are thrown in turn, with the result that Figure 1 is transformed into Figure 2. Therefore, one of the switches is not working and has had no effect on the numbered lights. Identify which switch is not working:

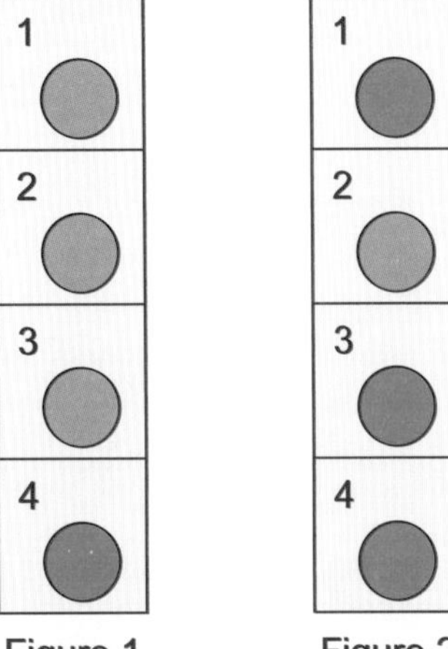

Figure 1 Figure 2

More Challenging

9. In the following, switches B, A, C and B are thrown in turn, with the result that Figure 1 is transformed into Figure 2. Therefore, one of the switches is not working and has had no effect on the numbered lights. Identify which switch is not working:

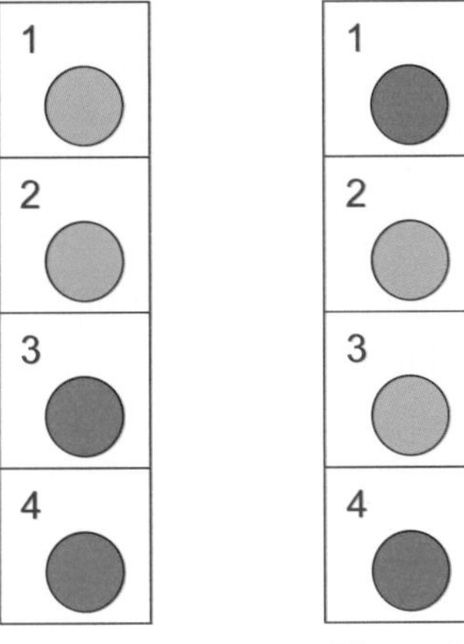

10. In the following, switches C, B, A and D are thrown in turn, with the result that Figure 1 is transformed into Figure 2. Therefore, one of the switches is not working and has had no effect on the numbered lights. Identify which switch is not working:

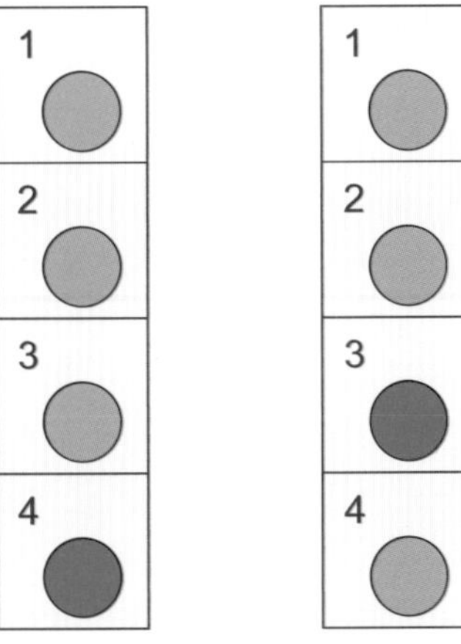

More Challenging

11. In the following, switches C, B, A and D are thrown in turn, with the result that Figure 1 is transformed into Figure 2. Therefore, one of the switches is not working and has had no effect on the numbered lights. Identify which switch is not working:

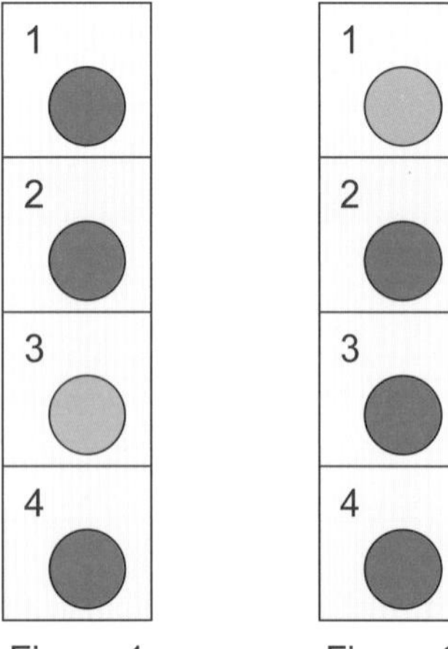

Figure 1 Figure 2

12. In the following, switches B, D, A and C are thrown in turn, with the result that Figure 1 is transformed into Figure 2. Therefore, one of the switches is not working and has had no effect on the numbered lights. Identify which switch is not working:

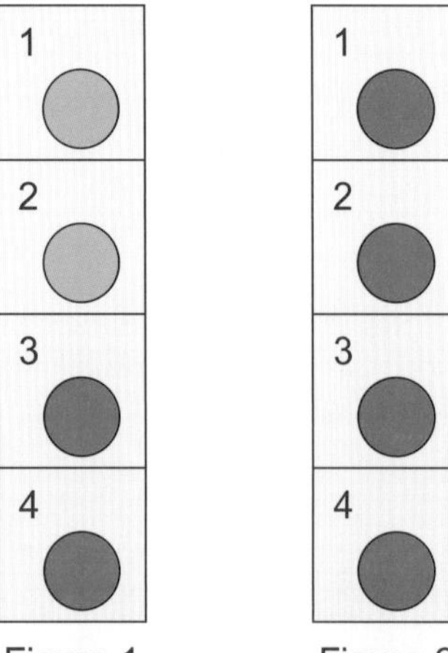

Figure 1 Figure 2

More Challenging

13. In the following, switches D, C, B and A are thrown in turn, with the result that Figure 1 is transformed into Figure 2. Therefore, one of the switches is not working and has had no effect on the numbered lights. Identify which switch is not working:

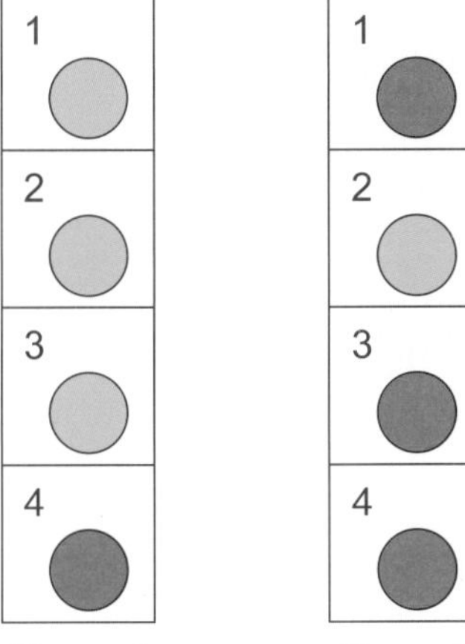

Figure 1 Figure 2

14. In the following, switches A, B, C and D are thrown in turn, with the result that Figure 1 is transformed into Figure 2. Therefore, one of the switches is not working and has had no effect on the numbered lights. Identify which switch is not working:

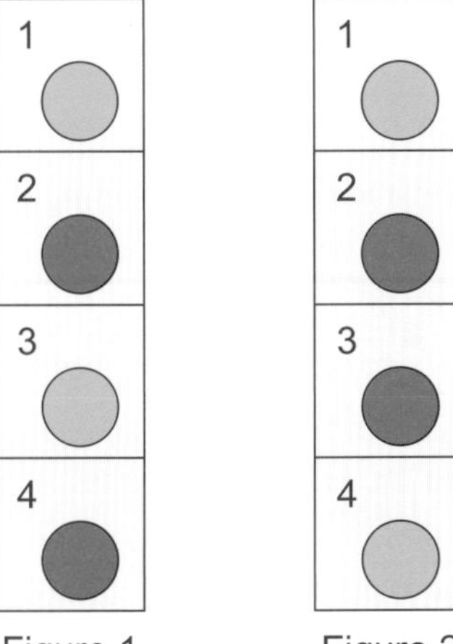

Figure 1 Figure 2

More Challenging

15. In the following, switches B, C, A and D are thrown in turn, with the result that Figure 1 is transformed into Figure 2. Therefore, one of the switches is not working and has had no effect on the numbered lights. Identify which switch is not working:

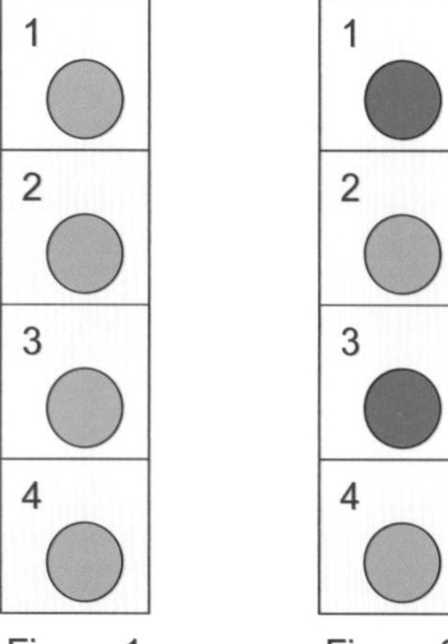

Figure 1 Figure 2

Brain Fact

The actual process of seeing is performed by the brain rather than the eye. The eye is our light sensitive organ of vision that translates electromagnetic vibrations of light into patterns of nerve impulses which are instantaneously transmitted to the brain for conversion into what appears in our sight.

Difficult

16. In the following, switches C, D, A, B and D are thrown in turn, with the result that Figure 1 is transformed into Figure 2. Therefore, one of the switches is not working and has had no effect on the numbered lights. Identify which switch is not working:

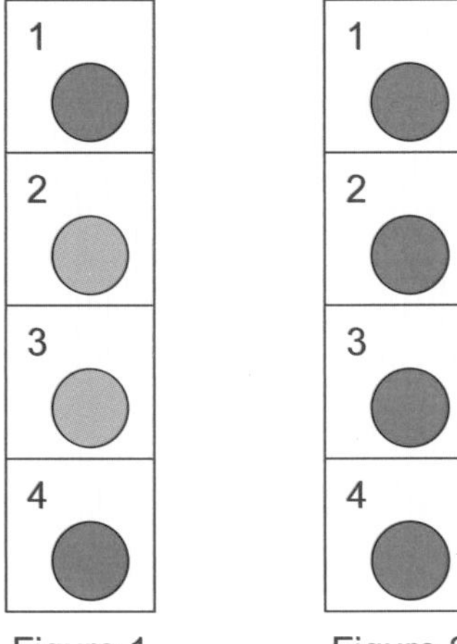

Figure 1 Figure 2

17. In the following, switches C, B, A, D and C are thrown in turn, with the result that Figure 1 is transformed into Figure 2. Therefore, one of the switches is not working and has had no effect on the numbered lights. Identify which switch is not working:

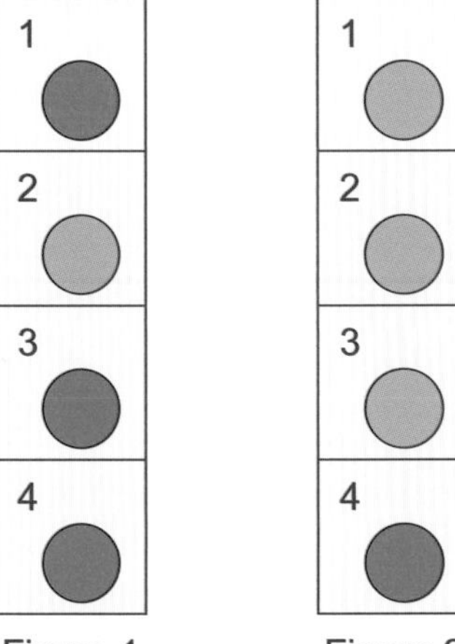

Figure 1 Figure 2

Difficult

18. In the following, switches A, D, C, A and B are thrown in turn, with the result that Figure 1 is transformed into Figure 2. Therefore, one of the switches is not working and has had no effect on the numbered lights. Identify which switch is not working:

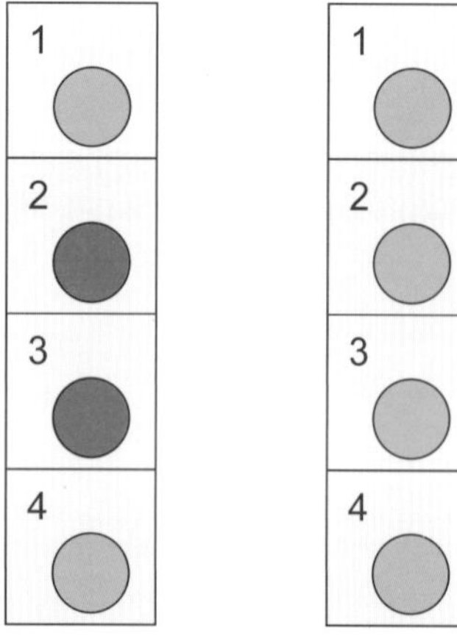

Figure 1 Figure 2

19. In the following, switches C, B, D, A and B are thrown in turn, with the result that Figure 1 is transformed into Figure 2. Therefore, one of the switches is not working and has had no effect on the numbered lights. Identify which switch is not working:

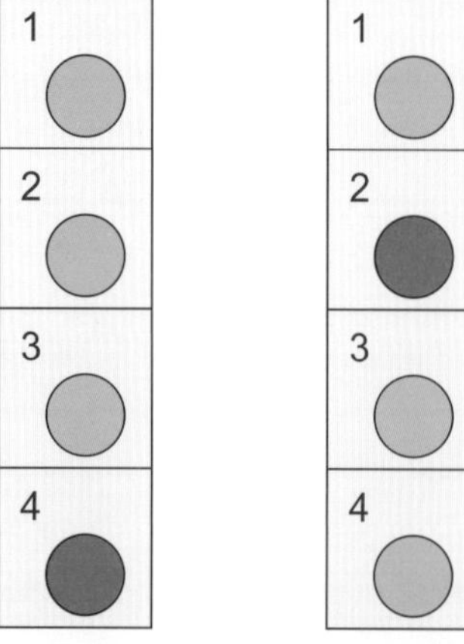

Figure 1 Figure 2

Difficult

20. In the following, switches D, C, A, B and C are thrown in turn, with the result that Figure 1 is transformed into Figure 2. Therefore, one of the switches is not working and has had no effect on the numbered lights. Identify which switch is not working:

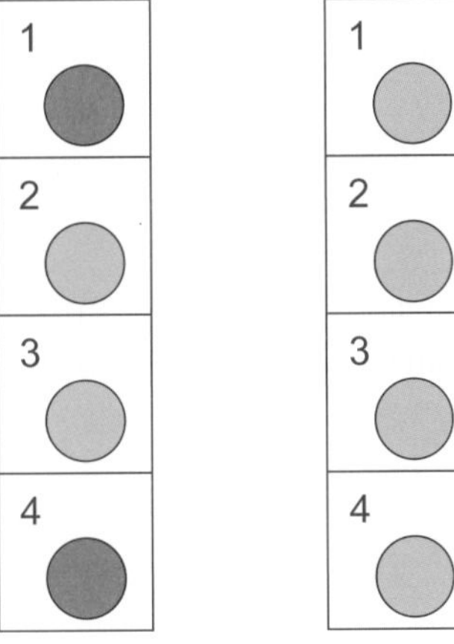

Figure 1 Figure 2

Brain Fact

The brain is the control centre for virtually every vital activity necessary for survival including movement, sleep, hunger and thirst. In addition, all human emotions including love, hate, anger, elation and sadness are controlled by the brain. It also receives and processes signals that are sent to it from other parts of the body and from sources external to the body.

Test 2 – Progressive Matrices Test

This test is designed to test and exercise your appreciation of pattern and design, your ability to think logically, but at the same time use your creative powers to explore with an open mind the various possibilities that might lead to a correct solution.

In tests of this nature, a matrix is an array of squares in which usually one or more squares has been omitted and you must choose the missing square or squares from a number of options.

It is, therefore, necessary to study the matrix to decide what pattern is occurring, either by looking across each row and down each column, looking at the array as a whole, or studying the relationship between different squares within the array.

This test consists of 20 questions which gradually increase in difficulty. A time limit of 90 minutes is allowed in which to complete the 20 questions.

Examples

1.

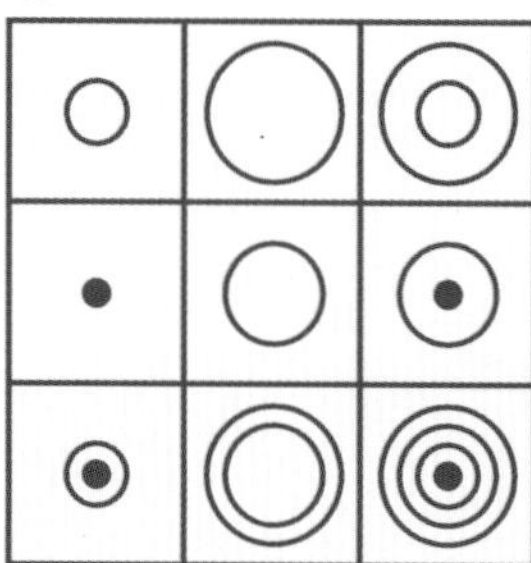

2.

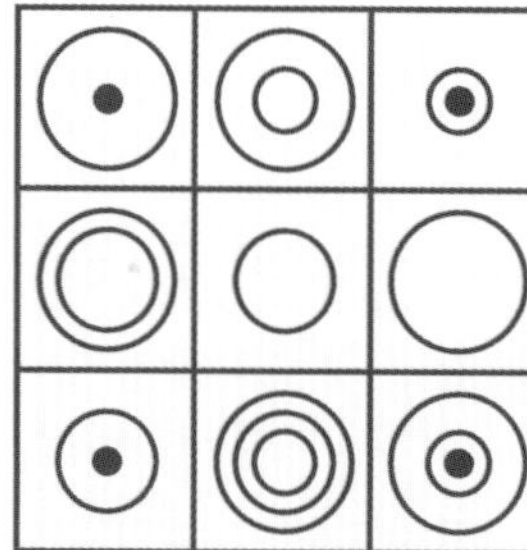

Example 1
Looking across each line and down each column the contents of the first two tiles are combined to arrive at the contents in the third tile.

Example 2
Looking across each line and down each column the contents of the first two tiles are combined to arrive at the contents in the third tile, with the exception that when the same line or symbol appears in the same position in the first two tiles it is then cancelled out.

Quick Fire

1. Which is the missing tile?

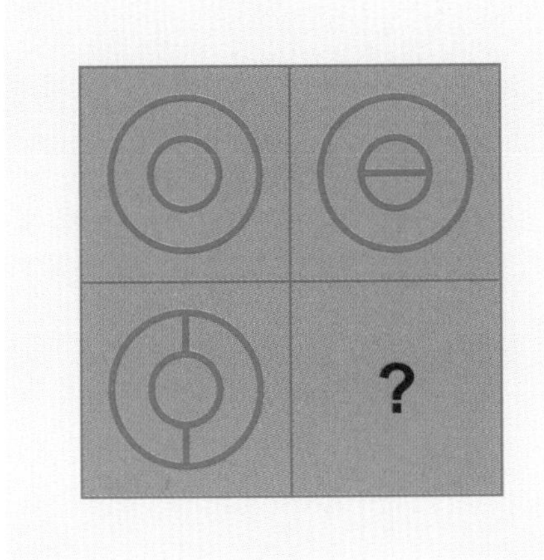

A

B

C

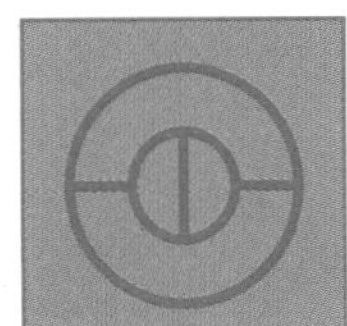

D

2. Which is the missing tile?

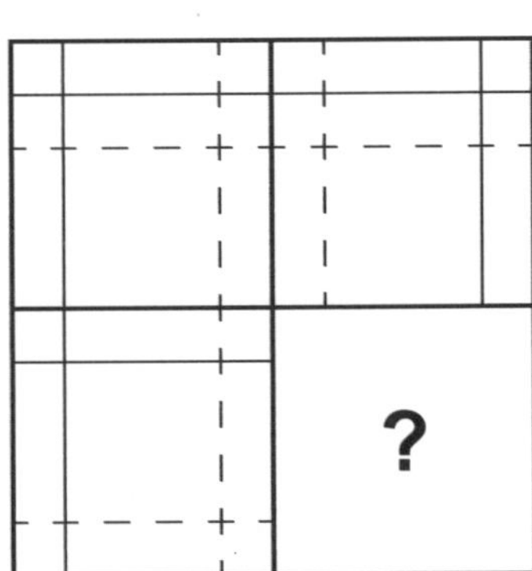

A

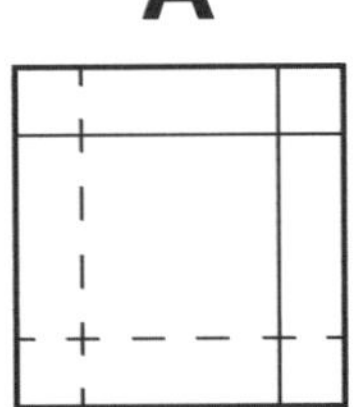

B

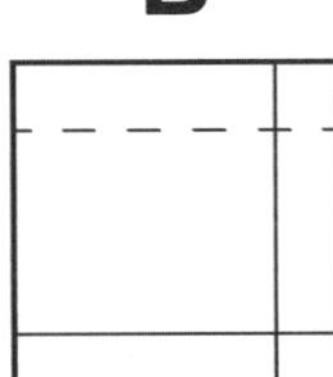

C

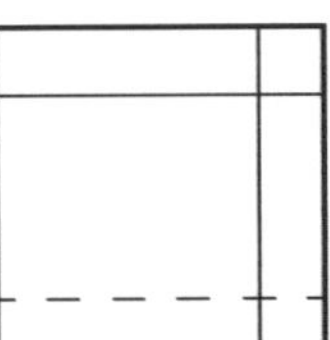

D

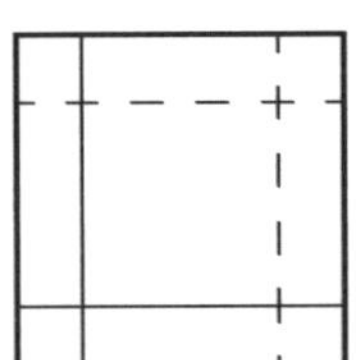

Quick Fire

3. Which is the missing tile?

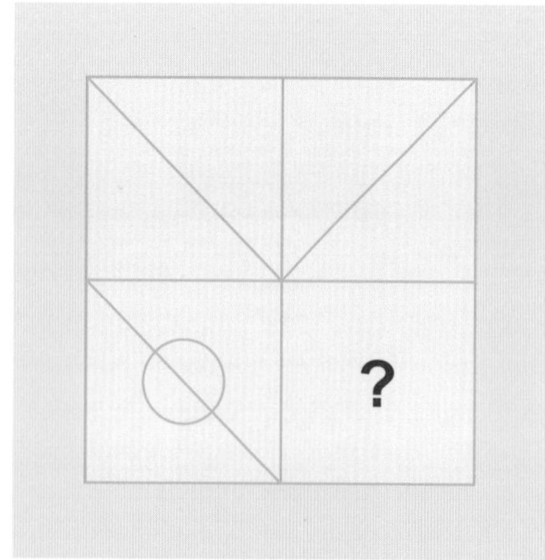

A

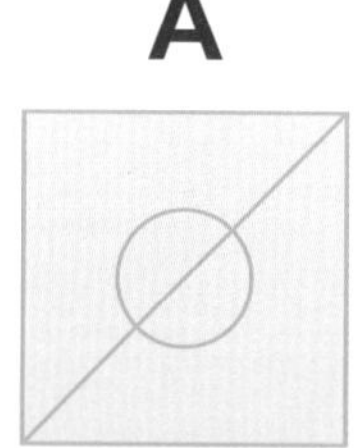

B

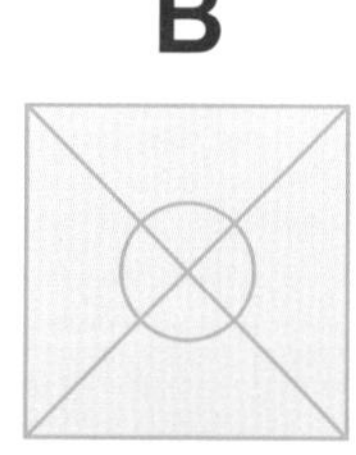

C

D

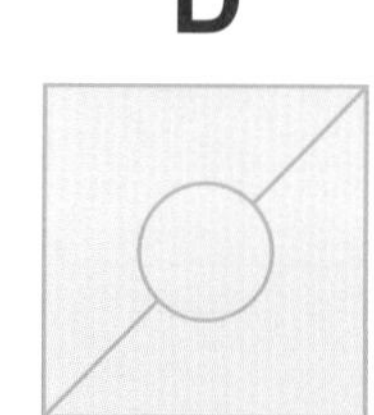

4. Which is the missing tile?

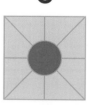

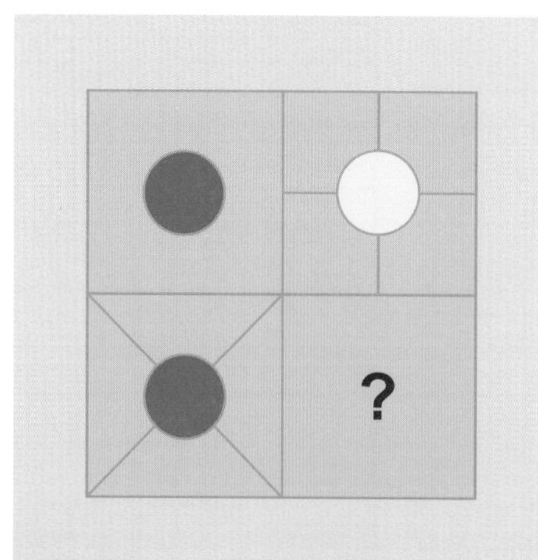

A

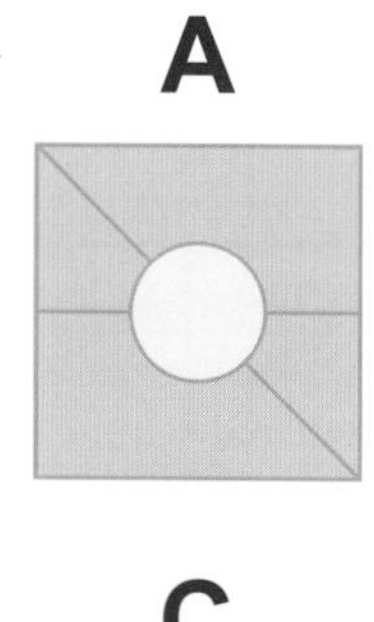

B

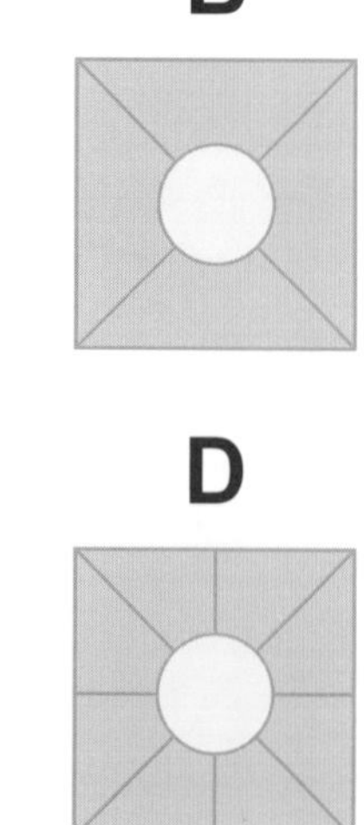

C

D

Quick Fire

5. Which is the missing tile?

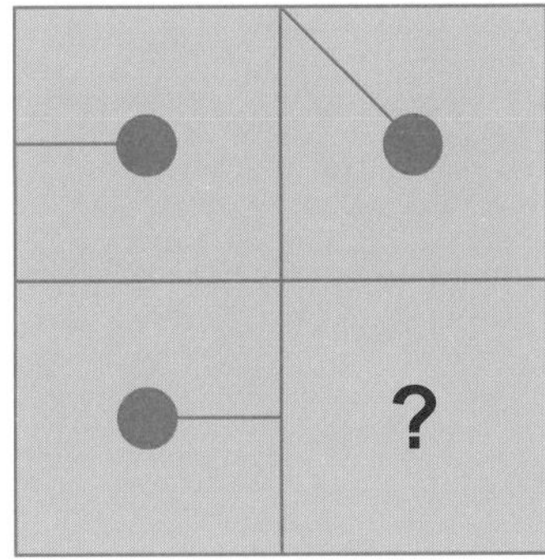

A

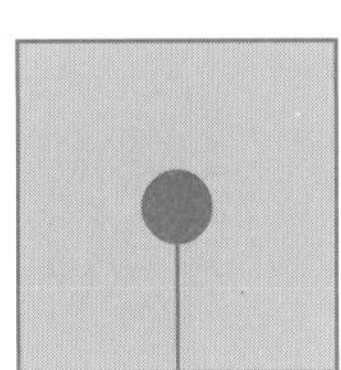

B

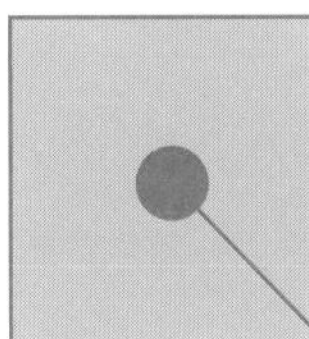

C

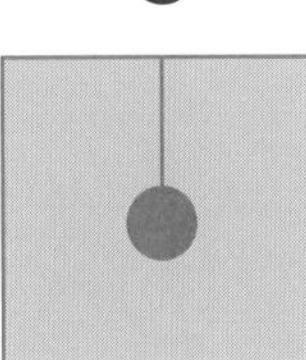

D

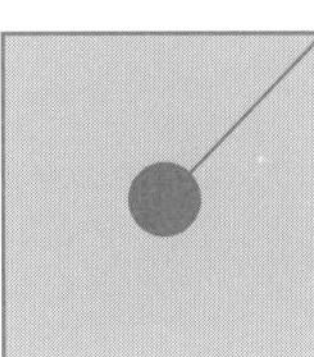

6. Which is the missing tile?

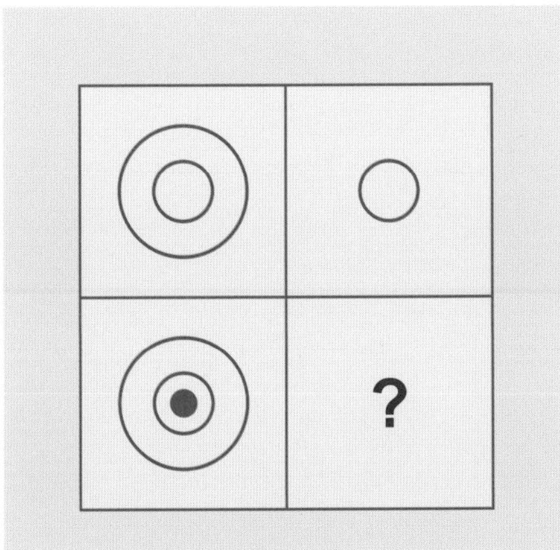

A

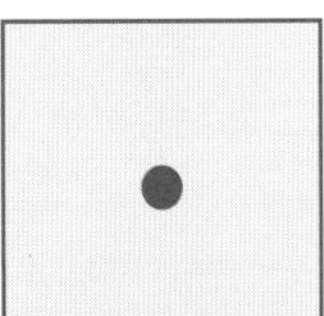

B

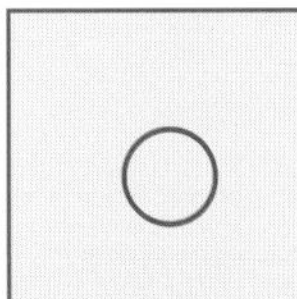

C

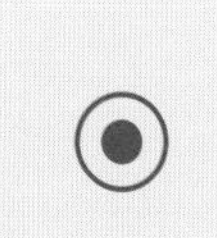

D

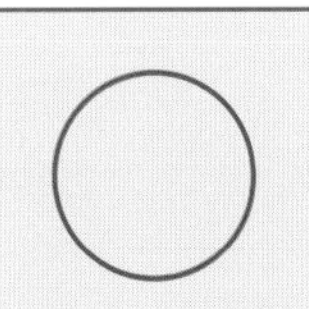

Quick Fire

7. Which is the missing tile?

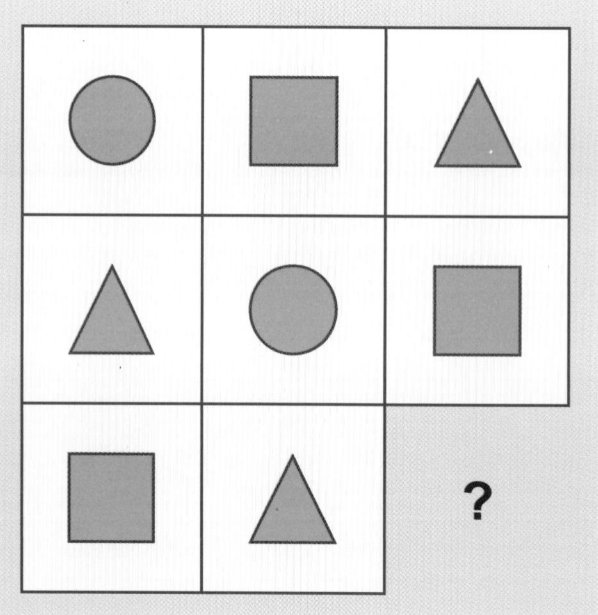

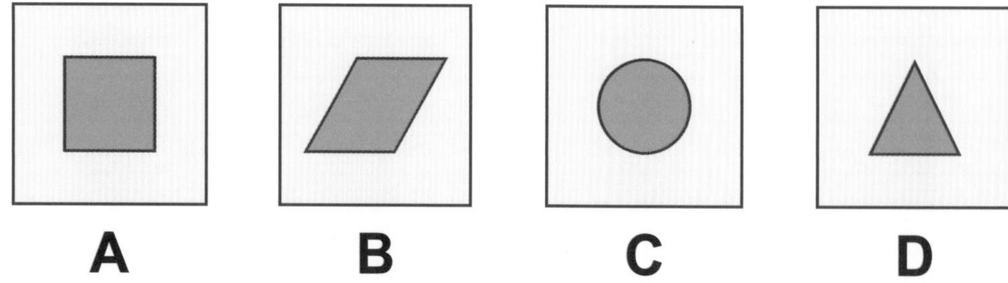

Quick Fire

8.

Which is the missing tile?

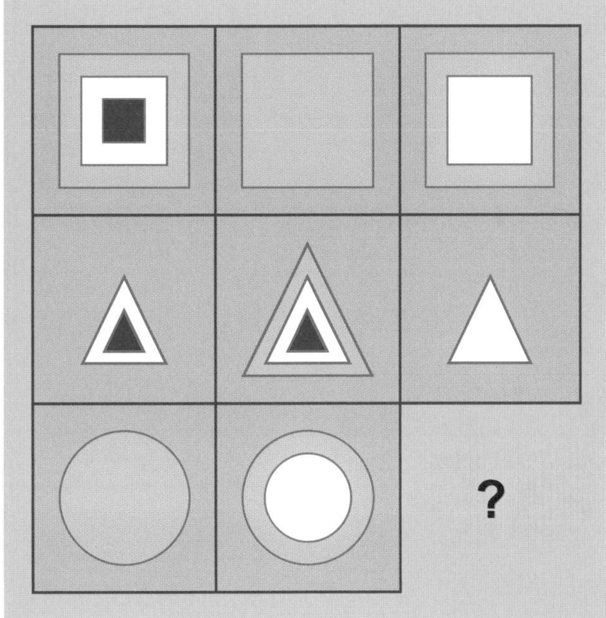

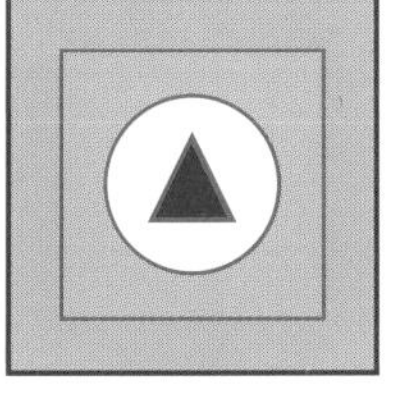

A

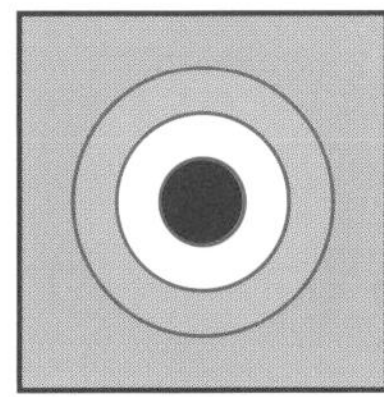

B

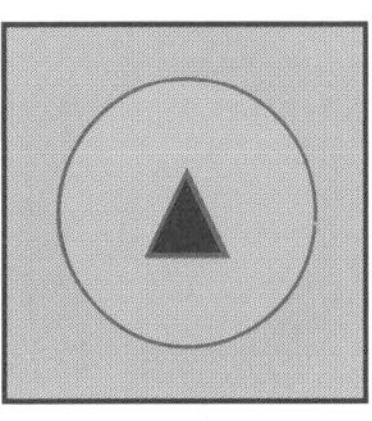

C

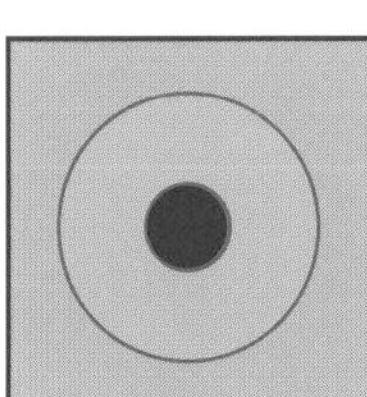

D

Quick Fire

9.

Which is the missing tile?

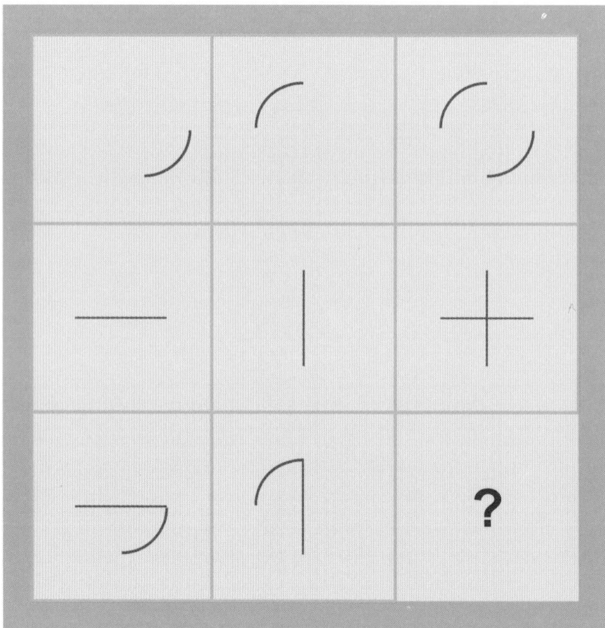

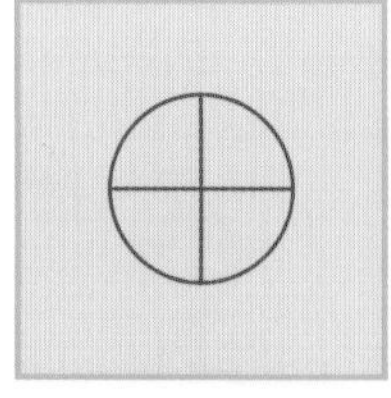

A

B

C

D

More Challenging

10. Which is the missing tile?

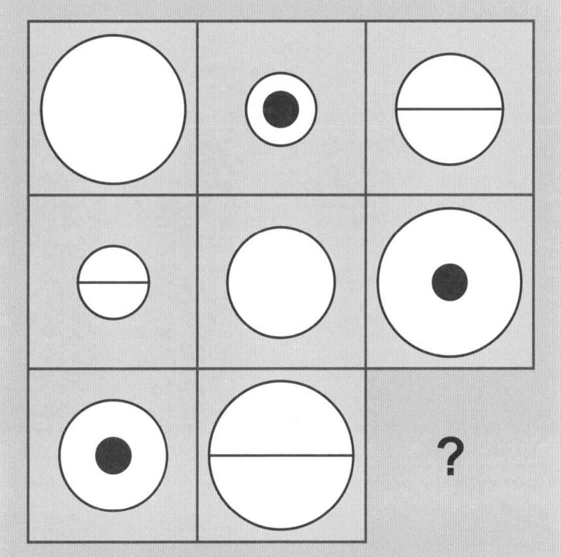

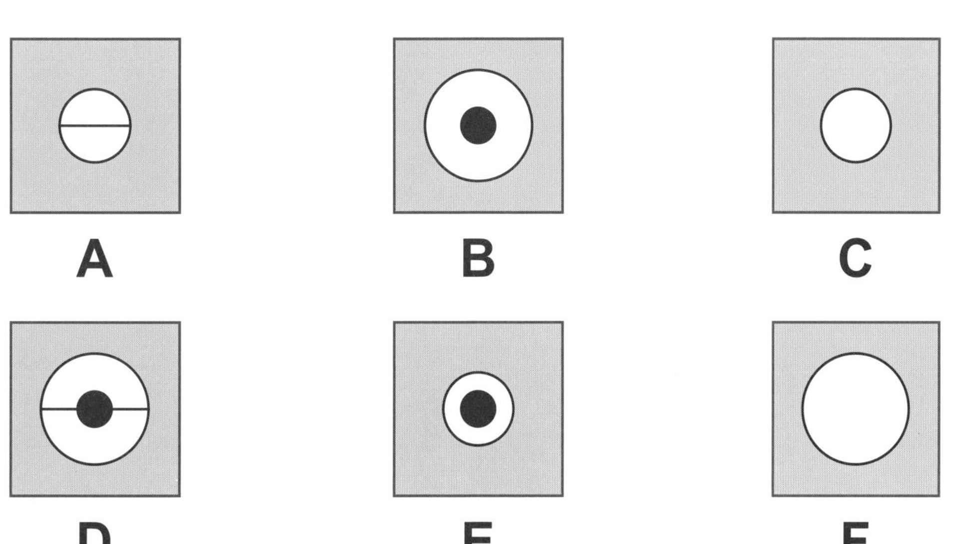

More Challenging

11. Which is the missing tile?

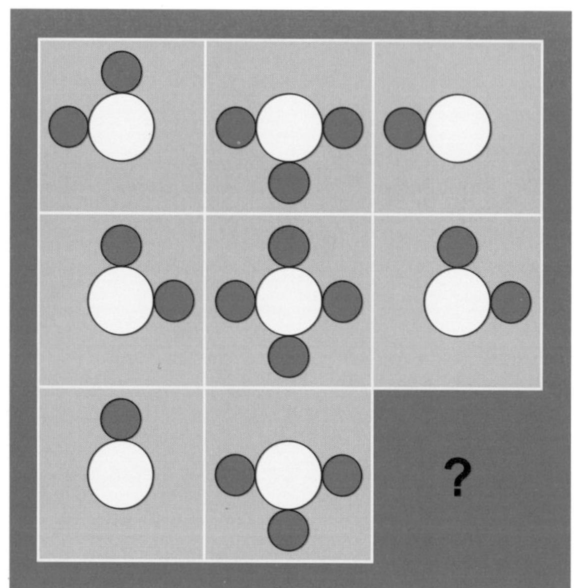

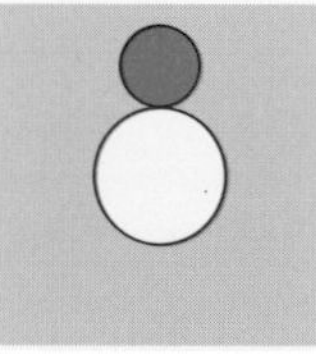

A

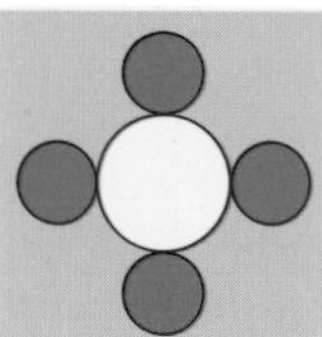

B

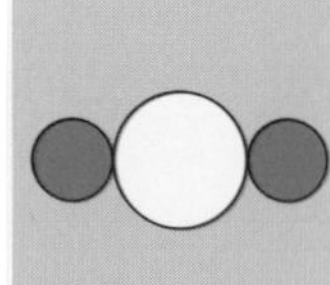

C

D

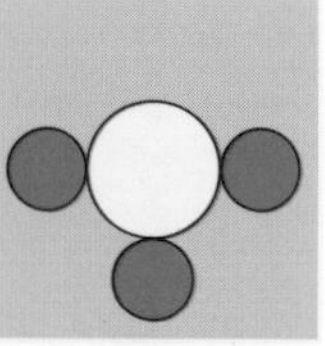

E

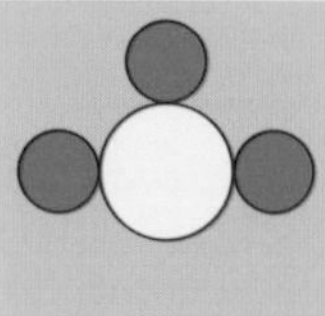

F

More Challenging

12. Which is the missing tile?

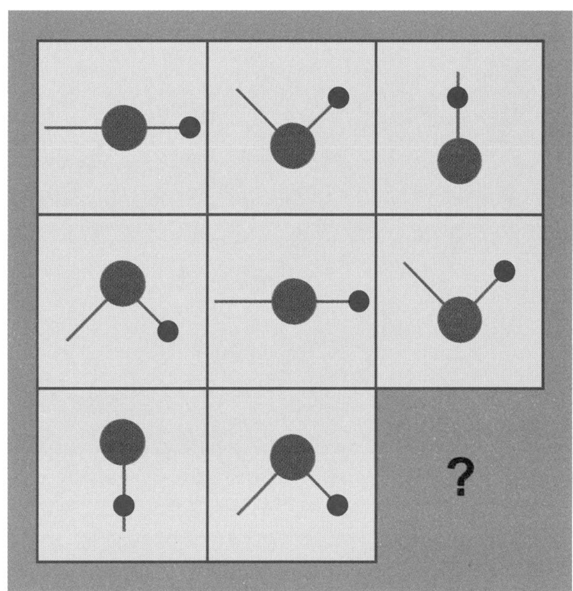

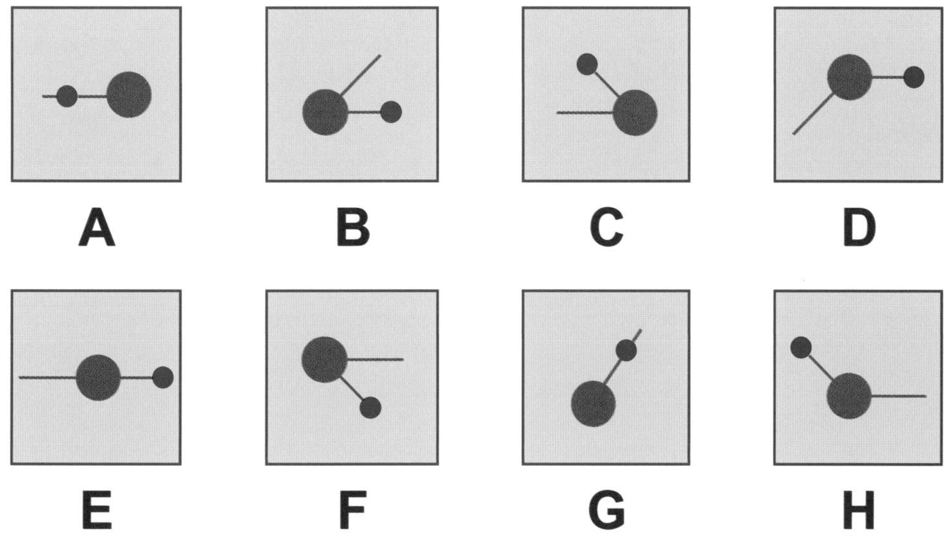

More Challenging

13.

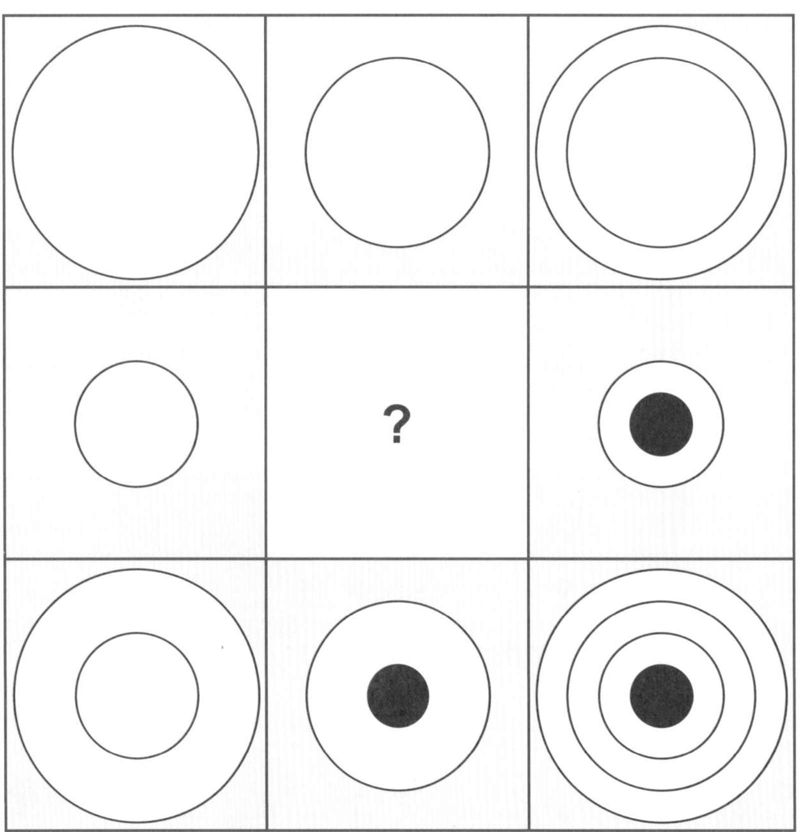

Draw the contents of the middle tile in accordance with the rules of logic already established.

More Challenging

14.

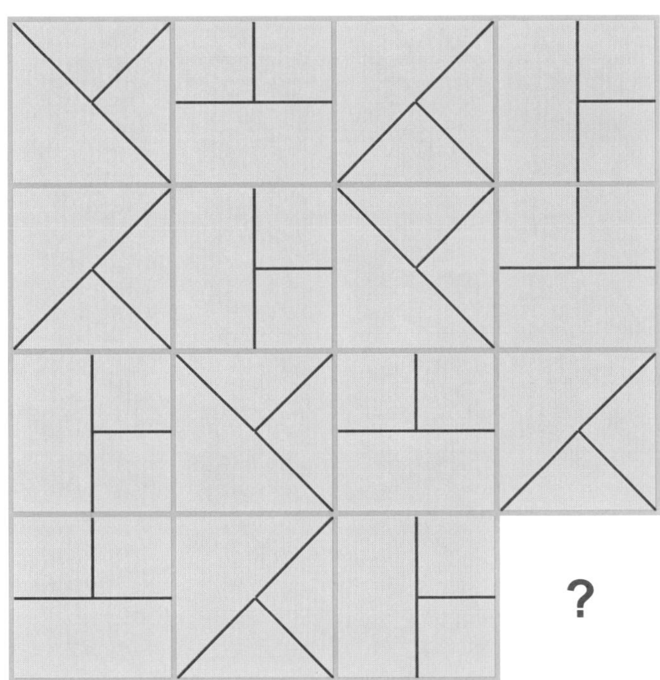

?

Which is the missing tile?

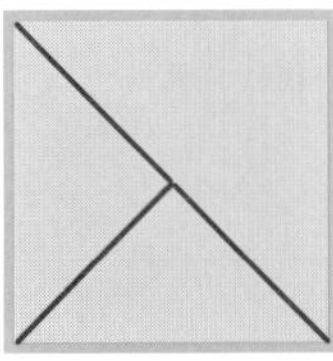

A

B

C

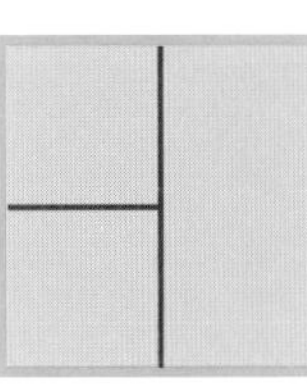

D

E

More Challenging

15.

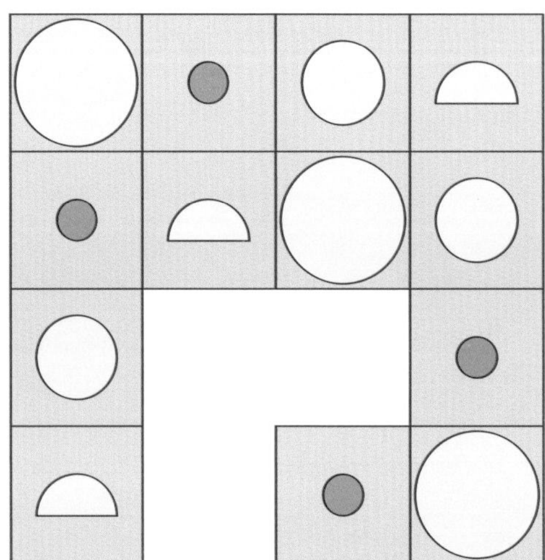

Which section is missing?

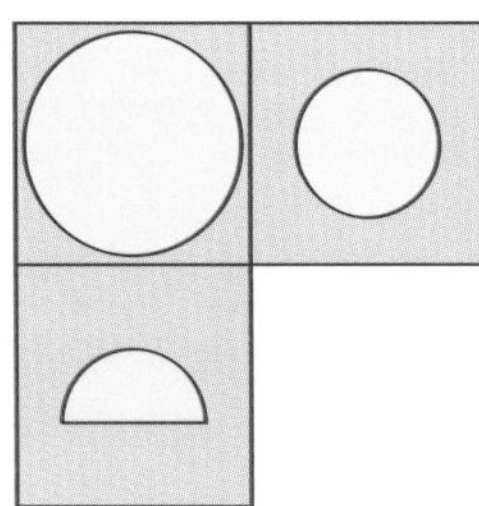

A

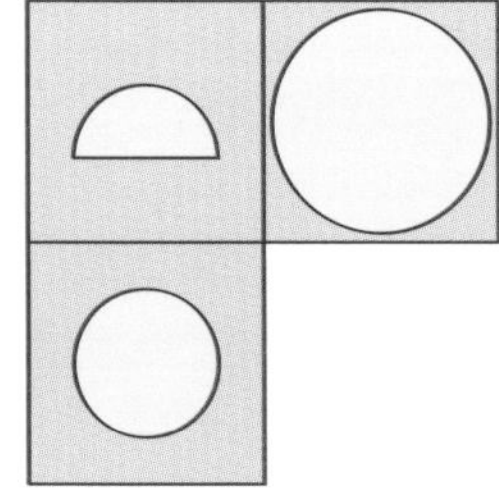

B

C

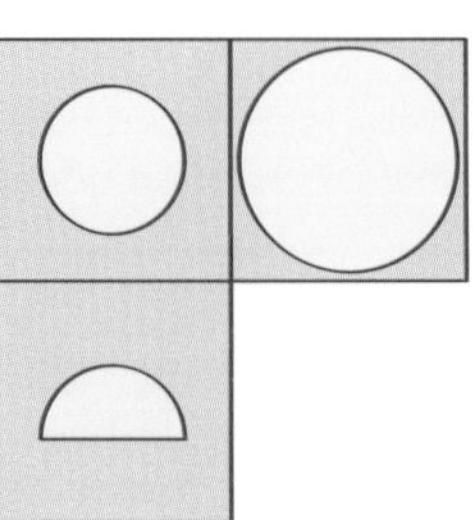

D

Difficult

16.

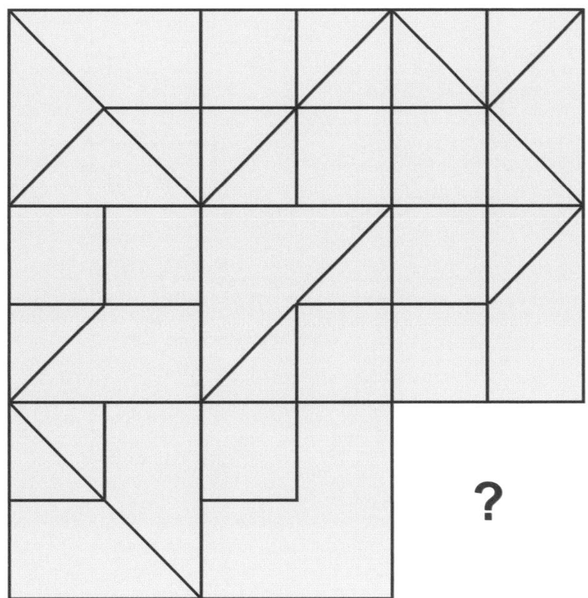

Which is the missing tile?

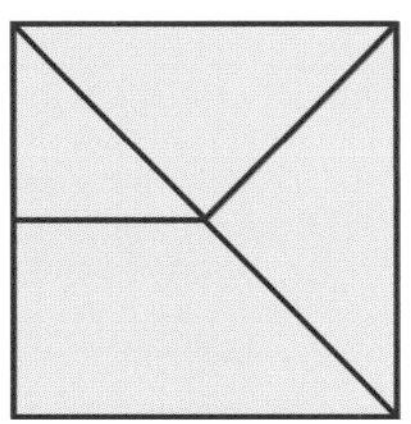

A

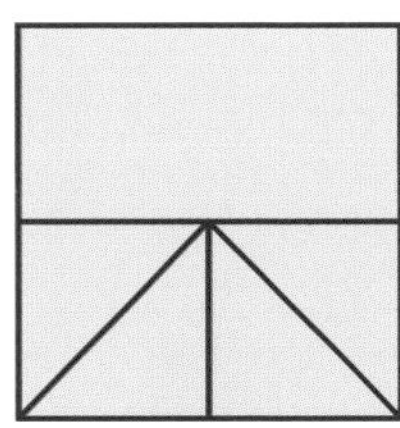

B

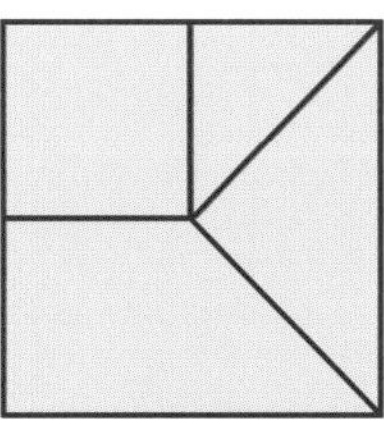

C

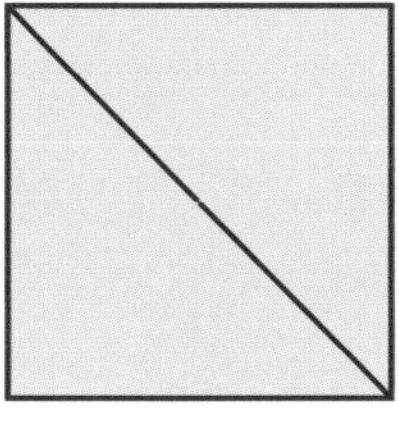

D

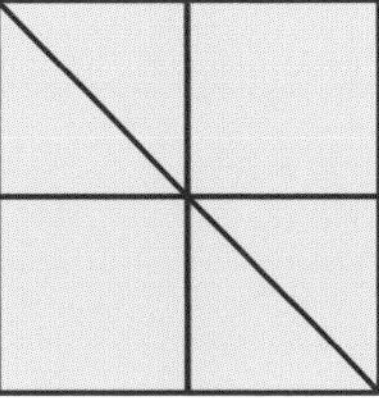

E

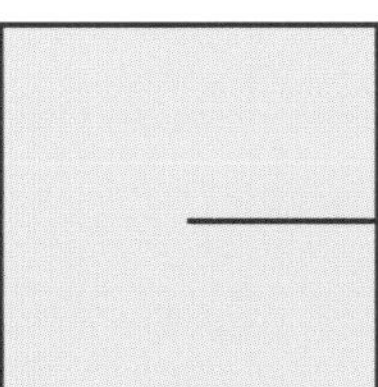

F

Difficult

17.

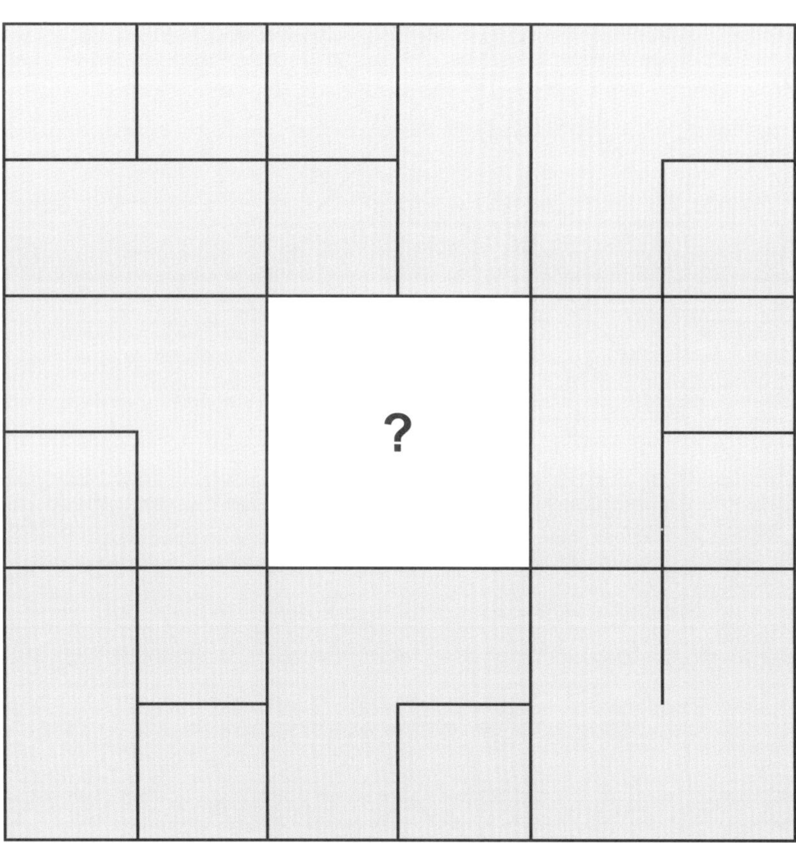

Draw the contents of the middle tile in accordance with the rules of logic already established.

Difficult

18.

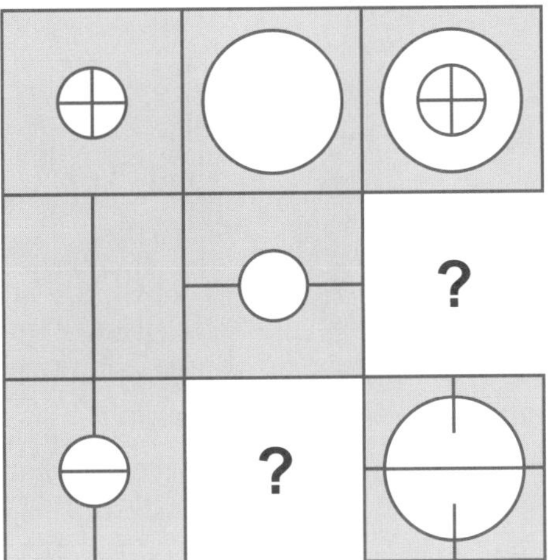

Which two tiles are missing?

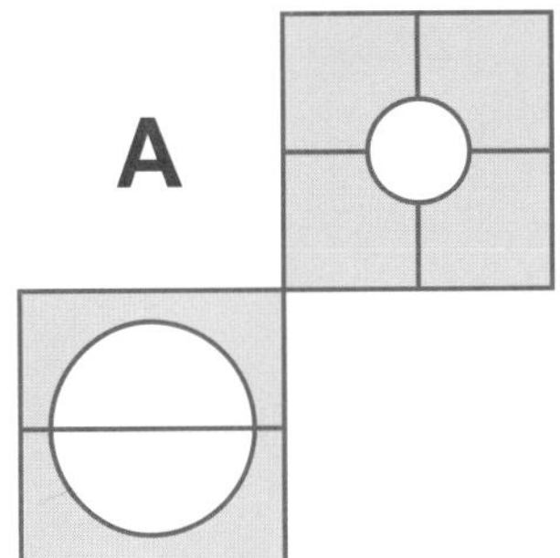

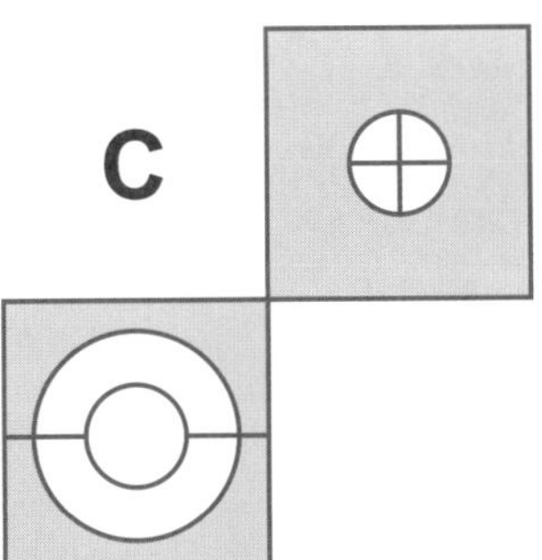

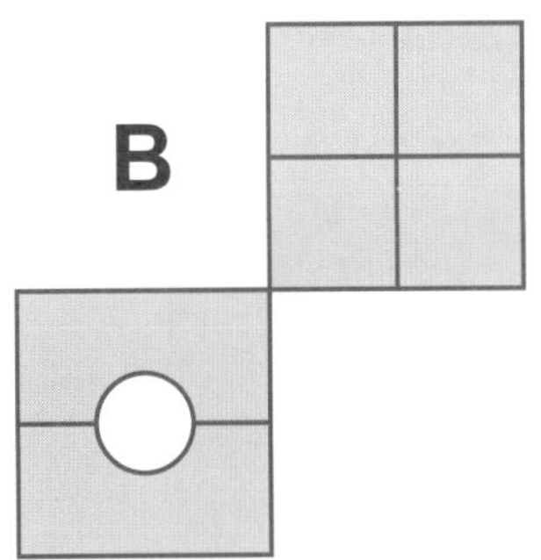

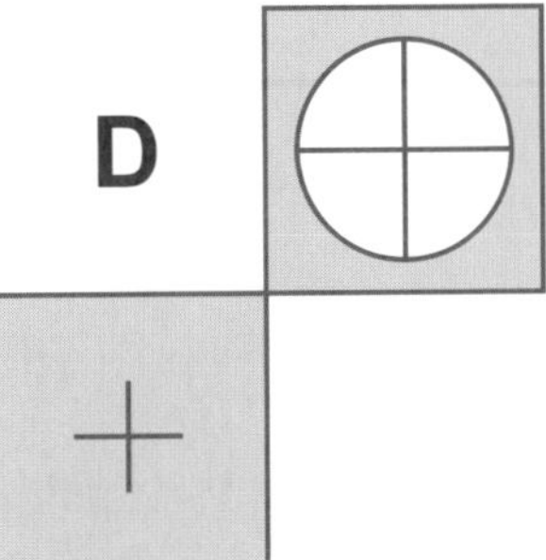

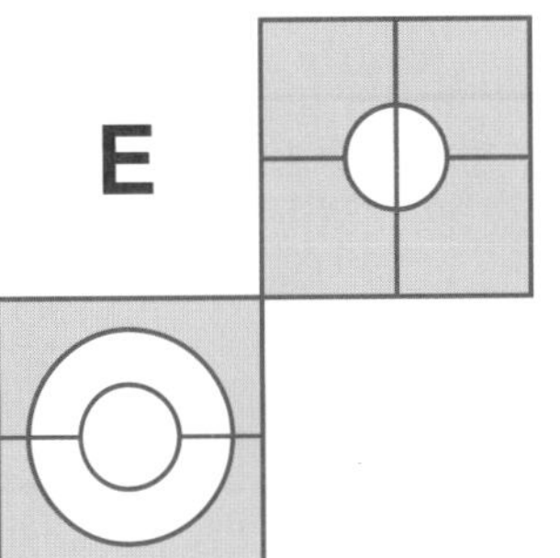

Difficult

19.

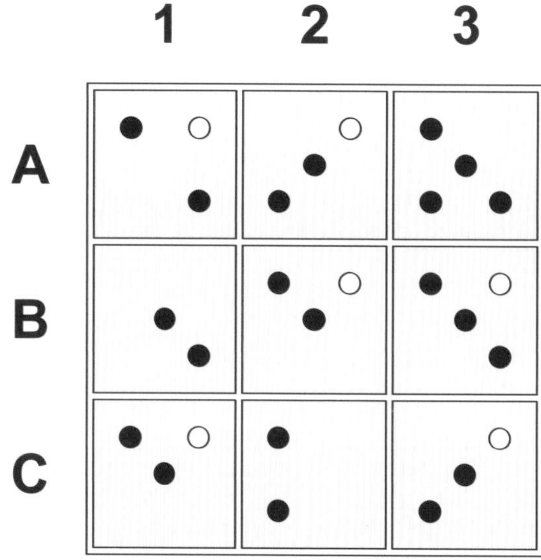

Looking at lines across and down, if the contents of the first two tiles are combined to produce the third tile, with the exception that identical circles are cancelled out, which of the above tiles is incorrect, and with which of the tiles below should it be replaced?

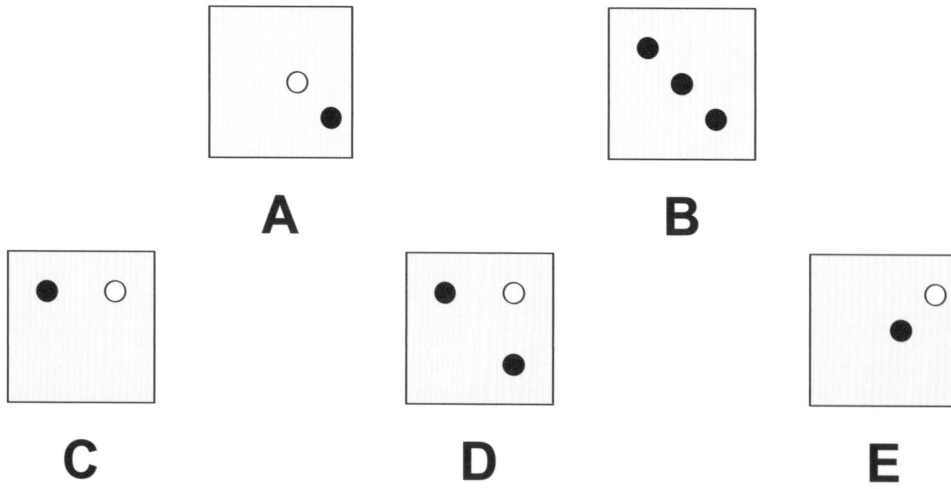

Difficult

20.

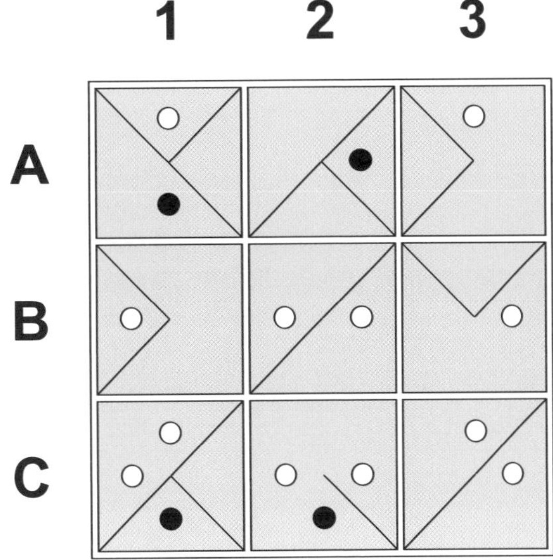

Looking at lines across and down, if the contents of the first two tiles are combined to produce the third tile, with the exception that identical lines and circles are cancelled out, which of the above tiles is incorrect, and with which of the tiles below should it be replaced?

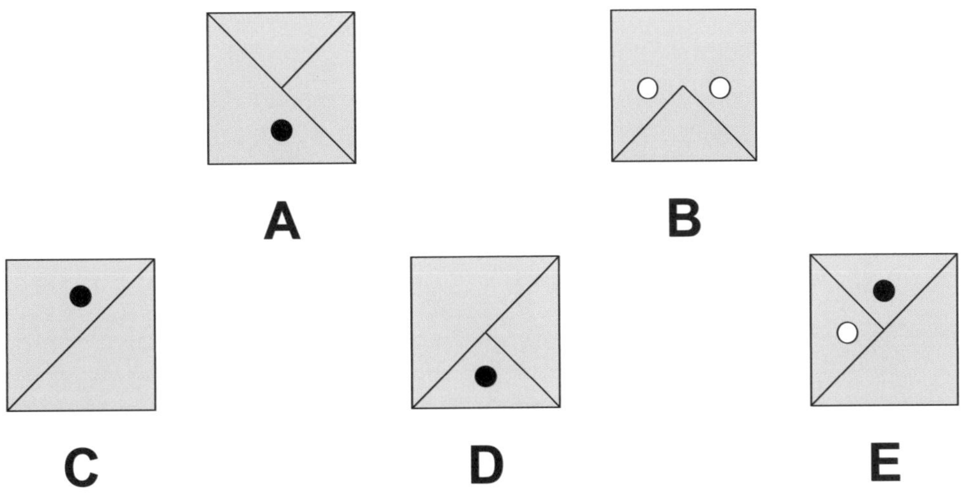

Solutions – Test 1

1. Switch D is faulty.
2. Switch A is faulty.
3. Switch B is faulty.
4. Switch A is faulty.
5. Switch A is faulty.
6. Switch B is faulty.
7. Switch D is faulty.
8. Switch C is faulty.
9. Switch A is faulty.
10. Switch D is faulty.
11. Switch C is faulty.
12. Switch A is faulty.
13. Switch C is faulty.
14. Switch D is faulty.
15. Switch C is faulty.
16. Switch B is faulty.
17. Switch C is faulty.
18. Switch C is faulty.
19. Switch B is faulty.
20. Switch D is faulty.

Performance Rating

Score 1 point for each correct answer

Total Score	Rating	Percentage of Population
19 / 20	Genius level	Top 5%
17 / 18	High Expert	Top 10%
15 / 16	Expert	Top 30%
13 / 14	High Average	Top 40%
11 / 12	Middle Average	Top 60%
9 / 10	Low Average	Bottom 40%
7 / 8	Borderline Low	Bottom 30%
5 / 6	Low	Bottom 10%
0 / 4	Very Low	Bottom 5%

Apply a multiplication factor of 1.25 to the score you have obtained, round up to the nearest whole number and transfer your score to the chart in the Assessment Section on page 302.

Solutions – Test 2

1. D – Looking across, a horizontal line is added to the middle circle only. Looking down a vertical line is added to the large circle only.
2. A – All lines are carried on from one tile to the next, either broken or unbroken.
3. A – Looking across, the line rotates 90 degrees. Looking down a circle is added.
4. D – Looking across, the circle changes from red to yellow and a St Andrew's cross is added. Looking down a Greek cross is added.
5. B – Looking across, the line moves 45 degrees clockwise. Looking down, it moves 180 degrees.
6. C – Looking across, the large circle is removed. Looking down, a dot is added to the middle circle.
7. C – Each line across and down contains a circle, square and triangle.
8. B – Looking across, the lines contain squares, triangles, circles in turn, and each line across and down contains a tile with one, two and three symbols.
9. C – Looking across and down, the contents of the first two tiles are combined to produce the contents of the third tile.
10. C – Looking across and down, each line contains a large white circle, medium white circle, small white circle and a smaller black circle, and one white circle has a line through the centre.
11. D – Looking across and down, only symbols that are common to the first two tiles are carried forward to the third tile.
12. E – Looking across, the long line moves 45 degrees clockwise, and looking down, it moves 45 degrees anti-clockwise. Looking across, the short line with the circle moves 45 degrees anti-clockwise, and looking down, it moves 45 degrees clockwise.
13. 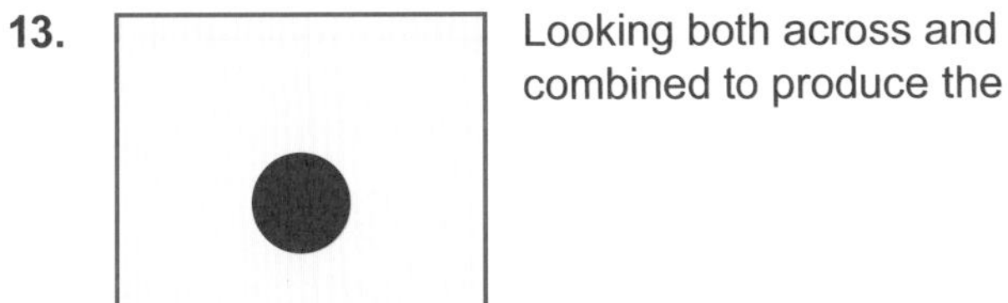 Looking both across and down, the contents of the first two tiles are combined to produce the contents of the third tile.
14. D – Each line across and down contains one of the four different internal patterns.

Solutions – Test 2

15. C – The fourth line is a repeat of the symbols in line one, but in reverse. The third line is a repeat of the symbols in line two in reverse.

16. D – Looking across and down, the contents of the first two tiles are carried forward to produce the contents of the third tile; however, when two lines appear in the same position in the first two tiles they are cancelled out.

17. 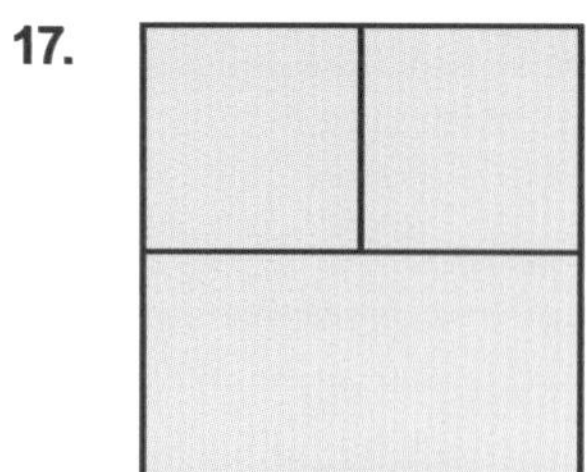 Looking across and down, the contents of the first two tiles are carried forward to produce the contents of the third tile; however, when two lines appear in the same position in the first two tiles they are cancelled out.

18. E – Looking across and down, the contents of the first two tiles are combined to produce the contents of the third tile; however, like lines and symbols are cancelled out.

19. Tile 3B is incorrect and should be replaced by Tile D.

20. Tile 2A is incorrect and should be replaced by Tile D.

Brain Fact

The French mathematicians Poincaré and Hadamard defined the following four stages of creativity:

Preparation – the attempt to solve a problem by normal means.
Incubation – when you feel frustrated that the above methods have not worked and as a result you then move away to other things.
Illumination – the answer suddenly comes to you in a flash via your subconscious.
Verification – your reasoning powers take over as you analyse the answer which has come to you, and you assess its feasibility.

Performance Rating

Score 1 point for each correct answer

Total Score	Rating	Percentage of Population
19 / 20	Genius level	Top 5%
17 / 18	High Expert	Top 10%
15 / 16	Expert	Top 30%
13 / 14	High Average	Top 40%
11 / 12	Middle Average	Top 60%
9 / 10	Low Average	Bottom 40%
7 / 8	Borderline Low	Bottom 30%
5 / 6	Low	Bottom 10%
0 / 4	Very Low	Bottom 5%

Apply a multiplication factor of 1.25 to the score you have obtained, round up to the nearest whole number and transfer your score to the chart in the Assessment Section on page 302.

Brain Fact

Scientists believe the storage capacity of the brain is sufficient to record a thousand new bits of information every second from birth to old age and still have room to spare.

Assessment

Enter your transferable scores, obtained for each of the tests in the previous six sections, into the table below in order to obtain your overall performance rating. A total of 300 points are available (50 points for each section).

Apart from giving the brain a workout, one of the objects of this book has been to identify different types of intelligence and provide an objective assessment of abilities in a number of different disciplines.

Section	Test (Points Available)	Score (transferable)
1. Word Power	Word Power Test 1 (25) Word Power Test 2 (25)	
2. Thinking Numerically	Complete the Equation (20) Mental Arithmetic (20) Number Sequence (10)	
3. Visual	Symbolic Odd One Out (20) Symbolic Sequence (20) Symbolic Complete the Sequence (10)	
4. Memory	Tests 1 – 5 (50)	
5. Personality	Self-confidence (25) Attitude (25)	
6. Advanced Logic	Light Switch Test (25) Progressive Matrices Tests (25)	
	Total Score	

The above table, apart from revealing an overall Brain Quotient (©Philip Carter) as indicated in the following table, gives readers the opportunity to identify their own strengths and weaknesses.

Overall Brain Quotient (BQ) Assessment

Maximum points available: 300

Total Score	Rating	Percentage of Population
260 / 300	Genius level	Top 5%
240 / 259	High Expert	Top 10%
201 / 239	Expert	Top 30%
170 / 200	High Average	Top 40%
135 / 169	Middle Average	Top 60%
111 / 134	Low Average	Bottom 40%
85 / 110	Borderline Low	Bottom 30%
51 / 84	Low	Bottom 10%
0 / 50	Very Low	Bottom 5%

Analysis

In addition to the above Performance Rating, it is recommended you analyse your performance for each of the six sections. An analysis of individual scores in each of these sub-sections will enable you to build and capitalize on your strengths, and work on improving performance in areas of weakness.

While the puzzles and exercises contained in this book may not turn you into a genius, or even more of a genius, overnight, hopefully your strengths will be something on which you can build. If after reading this book you are convinced that it is possible to increase and maximize your brainpower, then there is a need to constantly work out your brain in order to strengthen its performance even more.

By continually exploiting the enormous potential of the brain, each of us has the ability to expand our brainpower whatever our age or lifestyle, with the result that not only our mental but also our physical wellbeing will improve.

Notes